The Profession of Eighteenth-Century Literature

The Profession of Eighteenth-Century Literature

Reflections on an Institution

Edited by

Leo Damrosch

THE UNIVERSITY OF WISCONSIN PRESS

The University of Wisconsin Press
114 North Murray Street
Madison, Wisconsin 53715

3 Henrietta Street
London WC2E 8LU, England

5 4 3 2 1

Printed in the United States of America

Library of Congress Cataloging-in-Publication Data
The Profession of eighteenth-century literature: reflections on an
    institution / edited by Leo Damrosch.
    240 pp.   cm.
    Includes bibliographical references and index.
    ISBN 0-299-13300-1   ISBN 0-299-13304-4 (pbk.)
    1. English literature—18th century—History and criticism—
Theory, etc.   2. English literature—18th century—Study and
teaching—History.   3. Great Britain—Civilization—18th century—
Historiography.   4. Eighteenth century—Study and teaching—
History.   I. Damrosch, Leopold.
PR442.P69   1993
820.9' 005–dc20   92-1076

Contents

The Profession of Eighteenth-Century Literature

Introduction

In recent years the consensus in which literary studies once reposed—some would say slumbered—has broken down spectacularly, with two important consequences: critics now recognize the need to identify and defend their fundamental assumptions, and the academic profession has become interested in the ways in which institutional pressures shape the questions its members ask. Until quite recently, specialists in eighteenth-century literature have been markedly less receptive to novel ideas than those in the contiguous areas of Renaissance and Romanticism. But the orthodoxies of the 1950s and 1960s are at last dwindling away, and here too proliferating approaches are beginning to dominate the scene.

We are in the midst of a time of change, then, that from one point of view is a leave-taking and from another a flowering. It would be deeply discouraging if every "approach" were to be uncritically assimilated by an academic machine that can run on any fuel, following the process described by Gerald Graff in *Professing Literature* in which "the innovators are appeased, having become insiders with their own positions or programs, while the university gets to congratulate itself for its up-to-dateness and tolerance."[1] As against this kind of self-serving omnitolerance, it might seem best to promote one or another approach with the explicit claim that it is superior to its competitors and ought to replace them. This is the message of an influential recent collection called *The New Eighteenth Century*,

3

whose premise is that "the most important work . . . always insists on the relations between ideology, gender, race, and class, and on the functions of the oppressed and excluded in texts and cultural formations."[2] But such a formulation, even while it seeks to expose the implicit ideology of the older scholarship, has its own reductiveness. Assailing the complacent abstractions that used to elide profound differences in individual and cultural experience, the new critique privileges its own abstractions (gender, race, class, power) and at times adopts a tone of moral superiority that rivals that of F. R. Leavis.

Bertrand Russell once remarked, "The belief that I am sitting in a chair, or that 2 + 2 = 4, can be doubted by few except those who have had a long training in philosophy."[3] The joke has a double edge: most people never question common sense, but once they do the unraveling never stops, and truth for a philosophical pragmatist is nothing more than a cultural consensus that works so long as people agree that it does. The New Critics spoke for such a consensus, or acted as if they did; our problem now is that no consensus seems possible, uncomfortable though most people find life without it. The current umbrella terms "poststructuralism" and "postmodernism" are particularly revealing, defining contemporary theory by what it is not (similarly, "anticommunism" is not a coherent philosophy).

Not surprisingly, therefore, even intellectual movements that exalt indeterminacy and contestation have their own mechanisms of group solidarity. A notable strength of Marxism, or feminism, or Lacanian analysis is the opportunity it gives to work within a shared structure of explanation. The besetting temptation of such methodologies, conversely, is to rest content with the approval of an in-group and to ignore or denounce people who hold different assumptions. The demise of the old novitiate has not dispelled the need to belong.

Marc Bloch, one of the founders of the *Annales* school of historiography, rightly observed that "the very progress of our studies is founded upon the inevitable opposition between generations of scholars."[4] Or as Pope put it long ago in *The Temple of Fame,*

> Critics I saw, that other names deface,
> And fix their own with labor in their place.

Today, however, one sees an encouraging willingness to debate constructively between generations as well as within them. The present volume is neither an institutional history nor a manifesto for particular modes of "newness" (a category that has repeatedly failed to take root in eighteenth-century studies, as is evidenced by the many conferences at which the title "New Approaches" has been a euphemism for "whatever the participants are currently working on"). Rather, it represents an occasion for currently active scholars to consider their relationship to the academic past.

It has been said that one can judge an argument by the quality of its straw men; in this book the aim is to take the straw out and to try to think about the past in a less polemical way. Our discipline has had a long and complex history, and we modify or repudiate what preceded us only after it has brought us to the place where we now stand. The original invitation to contributors was as follows:

The volume proposes to consider the institutional history and assumptions of modern eighteenth-century studies. The aim will not be to look back in scorn at past scholarship and criticism, but rather to understand how they have shaped present preoccupations, both positively and negatively. In part this will mean reassessing the seminal work of major scholars and schools of criticism; in part it will mean pondering the relation of current approaches to what went before, both in general and in personal terms.

The resulting essays reflect a wide variety of experiences, interests, and expectations. It may well be that later generations will see our time as a coming together of ideas whose coherence will be apparent in retrospect, so that critics' local fascination with Wittgenstein or Lacan or Althusser will have been part of a larger shift that looked fragmentary only because we were still inside it. But it is also possible that that kind of coherence will seem apparent because retrospective vision can afford to be selective; as C. S. Lewis memorably wrote in an attack on generalizations about the past, "The 'canals' on Mars vanished when we got stronger lenses."[5]

In the present moment of self-consciously incomplete transition, at any rate, a highly structured conclusion may be neither desirable nor possible, and would not necessarily be greater than the sum of its parts. The study of the eighteenth century has been built upon shared texts and overlapping intellectual interests, pursued within an academic framework that endows "the Restoration" or "the Age of Sensibility" with familiarity if not with actual being. The profession is like a sea in which its inhabitants swim (or sink), not like an organism whose parts carry out interdependent functions. Or if it is in some sense organic, the model should be a colony of discrete organisms like the Portuguese man-of-war, which carries some members for digestion, some for locomotion, and some for stinging. So also this book is a group endeavor, adding up to a mosaic picture whose shifting viewpoints may give a wider range than any single perspective could.

Notes

1 Gerald Graff, *Professing Literature: An Institutional History* (Chicago: University of Chicago Press, 1987), 250.
2 "Revising Critical Practices: An Introductory Essay," in *The New Eighteenth Century*, ed. Felicity Nussbaum and Laura Brown (New York: Methuen, 1987), 20.
3 Bertrand Russell, "William James's Conception of Truth," orig. in Russell's *Philosophical Essays* (1910), rpt. in *Pragmatic Philosophy*, ed. Amélie Rorty (New York: Doubleday Anchor Books, 1966), 312.
4 Marc Bloch, *The Historian's Craft*, trans. Peter Putnam (New York: Vintage Books, 1953), 4.
5 C. S. Lewis, *English Literature in the Sixteenth Century* (Oxford: Clarendon, 1954), 64.

1 *Lawrence Lipking*

Inventing the Eighteenth Centuries: A Long View

The eighteenth century is plural. Any long view of the development of eighteenth-century studies must come to terms with the way that scholars partly invent the periods and subjects that they study. Every age makes its own past, projecting its own preoccupations back into time. The modern discipline of "English Literature" is a notorious example: it depends on formulating two categories, "English" (including, perhaps, Anglo-Saxon, Scottish, and Irish, but not American or colonial) and "Literature" (as opposed to "lower" sorts of writing), that would have been recognized by few of the writers who are now held to constitute the field. There is nothing illegitimate about this process. Every profession defines itself by drawing lines that take in some concerns and eliminate others. But problems arise when such distinctions, like lines on a map, are assumed to be natural rather than conventional—for instance, when two eighteenth-century scholars quarrel about the "nature" of the period, each believing himself or herself to be in possession of *the* eighteenth century. Very likely they are offering singular definitions of something that makes sense only in the plural. There are enough eighteenth centuries to satisfy everyone.

Most scholars know this in theory. In practice, however, the temptation to write the history of eighteenth-century studies in terms of a single theme or timeworn opposition (like Whig versus Tory) often proves irresistible. Such histories reduce the many to the few. Consider, for example, the introduction to a recent collection of essays, *The New Eighteenth Century*. The old eighteenth century, according to the editors, was characterized by its resistance to theory. Yet their own choice of four major critics from whom "contemporary eighteenth-century studies received its definition"[1]—R. S. Crane, W. K. Wimsatt, Earl Wasserman, and Reuben Brower—sufficiently refutes the generalization, since each of the four spelled out explicit theoretical assumptions. In fact the introduction caricatures all four, not least by lumping them together as "formalists" who were thus "in no position to propose or to challenge a particular historical narrative of the age." Crane and Wimsatt were enemies, in part because the historical narratives they proposed differed so much.[2] Wasserman and Brower, who are said to have "confined themselves more narrowly to the eighteenth century," did most of their work outside the period; and they too wrote original narratives of literary history. But these four critics belonged to different schools. It is only from the perspective of another age, which might notice some points (none of the four was a feminist) and overlook others (though Wimsatt, Wasserman, and Brower were all "New Critics," New Criticism meant something different to each of them), that they can be joined in a single party. Nor would many eighteenth-century scholars of the time have acknowledged such wide-ranging intellectuals as representative of the field. *The New Eighteenth Century* invents an old one for its own purposes. I do not object to that, but only to the definite article. "A" is not "the."[3]

What perspective can do more justice to the pluralism of eighteenth-century studies? Perhaps a long view might help; a view that regarded the various inventions of an eighteenth century not as distortions of an original, unitary truth but as reflections of a double complexity, the knots tied between a ragged past and a ragged present. If scholars do not agree about what eighteenth-century studies have been or should be, the reason is likely to be that they differ about both the field of study and the instruments with which to study it. But these differences also have a history. They respond to more than a century of professional arguments and accommodations, a century in which the character of eighteenth-century studies has been forged out of conditional answers to intractable problems. The plural eighteenth century embodies a series of modern quandaries, each with a potential for breaking the field apart. Four questions, in particular, seem crucial to me: When does the period begin and end? What purpose has been served by the development of eighteenth-century studies? What sort of scholarly approach is best suited to the eighteenth century? Who have eighteenth-century scholars been, and where have they come from? These questions are far from simple; any answer to them will be involved in conflicts from the start. That is why they need to be asked. This essay will consider them in turn.

I

The eighteenth century began in 1660 and ended in 1798. So, at least, one might conclude from the authorities on the field, its bibliographies, anthologies, literary histories, and professional organizations. A chronology that stretches from the Restoration of Charles II to the publication of *Lyrical Ballads* has been so well established that scholars tend to accept it as inevitable or sanctioned by the nature of things. Of course it is nothing of the kind. Like other examples of belated periodization (such as The Middle Ages), the elastic eighteenth century has been shaped by the interests of a later time. To a large extent it seems a nineteenth-century invention, ratified by twentieth-century scholars who found it convenient (when annual bibliographies of eighteenth-century studies began, in 1926, in *Philological Quarterly*, their inclusion of the Restoration both confirmed the identity of the period 1660–1798 and insured its perpetuation). Other chronologies might easily be imagined. Why not begin the eighteenth century in 1701, or 1641, or 1689, and end it in 1789, or 1800, or 1820? All these demarcations, and many others, would have their uses, indicating a different set of priorities and continuities. But 1660–1798 has the weight of tradition behind it. It lends a specious unity to the field, and helps to define its character and contradictions.

A period does not live by dates alone, however. In selecting the authors whose work embodies it, we regularly fall into anomalies and anachronisms. Thus *Paradise Lost*, though published in 1667 (the year of Dryden's *Annus Mirabilis*), is always grouped among works of an earlier age—a Restoration Milton seems unthinkable—while Hobbes's *Leviathan*, conceived in civil war and published in 1651, somehow helps initiate the eighteenth century. Similar inconsistencies occur at the end of the period, where Burns and Blake, for instance, are often promoted to Romantics, while Frances Burney and sometimes Jane Austen are sent back. The power of period stereotypes is strong. A writer who comfortably spans two ages without fitting the mold of either, like Edmund Waller or George Crabbe, may be in danger of dropping out of literary history. Chronology exerts its tyranny; those poets were born and died at inconvenient times. Fortunately the second generation of English Romantic poets died young, without intruding on the Victorian Age and messing it up. Of accidents like these a period is formed.

The anomalies of periodization may matter less, though, than the seeming unity a label can confer. Such an appearance of harmony probably accounts for the dates assigned to "the eighteenth century," which happened *after* the civil wars and *before* the poetic "revolution." The invention of that eighteenth century suggests a stable settlement in England (consider, for instance, how unsettled a century would seem that began when Charles I left London in 1642 and ended with the fall of Walpole in 1742). Objectively, the period 1660–1798 might be described as an era of cataclysmic change, the building of a colonial empire, growing class conflicts, and the relentless undermining of old certainties by modern philosophy and science. One might emphasize, that is to say, the *distance* between 1660 and 1798. But scholars who work on the 1660s and the 1790s belong to the same associations and subscribe to the same journals. In that respect the profession of eighteenth-century studies creates the sense of stability that some of its members attribute to the period itself.

It also creates some tension. Among the standard periods of English literature, the eighteenth century stands out for its length, a span of 140 years that resists or outlasts any attempt to define its coherence. Scholars within the field may see no coherence or common interest at all. Only "The Middle Ages" is longer; and here too, many scholars resent the facile assumption of homogeneity, as if people kept repeating the same few slogans for many centuries. Specialists know better. Moreover, some eighteenth-century scholars look back to the Renaissance for continuities, while others look forward to the Romantics or beyond for new directions. The time frame is very expansive. Hence, even when scholars seem to be working on the same problem, they may be relying on incommensurable frames of reference and period assumptions. Michael McKeon's *The Origins of the English Novel*, for instance, directly addresses the issues of Ian Watt's *The Rise of the Novel* and offers a persuasive alternative account. Yet the two books are separated not only by theoretical divergences but by the length of a century. Watt draws his model from the social and economic conditions of the mid-eighteenth century, and McKeon from the crises of the mid-seventeenth. It is no wonder, then, that Defoe, Richardson, and Fielding should look, from one point of view, like the cutting edge of the contemporary scene, and from another like the culmination of more than a hundred years of experiment and conflict. The disparity is typical of many exchanges in eighteenth-century studies. A period so generously conceived, or so spread out, admits an abundance of ways of carving up the territory. Scholars are free to stake out calendars of their own.

In many cases, moreover, the 1740s function as a hinge or turning point. This decade (as I have argued elsewhere)[4] might well be nominated the most innovative in English literature, with striking departures not only in fiction and poetry but in history, philosophy, and other sorts of intellectual prose. The relative neglect of this spirit of innovation suggests that historians do not like to change their hobbyhorses in mid-century. But the ferment of the 1740s helps separate two wings of eighteenth-century studies. To scholars who concentrate on the earlier period, the decade often serves as a terminus ad quem, the era when fiction at last arrived at the novel, the dominance of the heroic couplet died with Pope, and religious and epistemological faith visibly yielded to skeptical challenges. To scholars who concentrate on the later period, the decade serves as a terminus a quo, the source of those stirrings (once called preromantic) that would eventually flower in an age of political and artistic revolutions. This division indicates only one among several ways of partitioning the extended eighteenth century into smaller and more manageable units. Another common scheme would draw a line at 1700, which Dryden himself proclaimed the end and beginning not only of a century but of an age. All such subdivisions of the field have at once the virtue of leaguing scholars in practical communities of interest and the defect of dispersing eighteenth-century studies into pockets and fiefdoms. Scriblerians and Blakeans do not always talk the same language. But no one can be a specialist in all aspects of a period so interminable and diverse. The traditional chronology of the eighteenth century insures that it will be plural.

II

If the length of the period partly determines its character, however, the mission of eighteenth-century scholars to refute misconceptions about the period may be still more decisive. Most scholars in the field link arms against a hostile world. Indeed, eighteenth-century studies were born defensive. At the time when literary scholarship became professionalized, in the late nineteenth century, dismissive attitudes toward eighteenth-century literature were common. "Dryden and Pope are not classics of our poetry, they are classics of our prose," according to Matthew Arnold,[5] and Johnson (as every schoolboy knew) was interesting not as a writer but as a collection of quirks and prejudices. Such attitudes prevailed especially in the United States, whose sense of nationhood depended on rebellion against the eighteenth-century British establishment and all its repressive, aristocratic, and antirepublican values. Earlier periods had less to answer for—to some extent Chaucer, Shakespeare, and Milton could be considered honorary Americans—and later periods, from the Romantics onward, were progressive and populist enough to suit American tastes. But the eighteenth century was not so easy to redeem.

Hence right from the start scholars of eighteenth-century literature found themselves warding off the fallacies and anachronisms, the mere blind fixing of labels like Neoclassicism or the Age of Reason, that kept the public from reading authors of the period with understanding, or from reading them at all. The defense deserves much credit. In 1950, when Louis A. Landa looked back at the growth of scholarship represented by twenty-five years of *Philological Quarterly* bibliographies, he took some pride in "the corrective process" through which the twentieth century had repaired the nineteenth century's abuse of the eighteenth.[6] At last the prejudices were being overcome. Yet even then, and even now, the eighteenth-century scholar tends to sound defensive. The imperative of the field has always been to set the record straight.

"The corrective process" still continues today. Much of the development of eighteenth-century studies seems motivated by reactions against false or oversimplified images of the past. All scholars oppose reductionism, of course, but eighteenth-century scholars have been unusually sensitive to the way that generalizations about history omit or distort any facts that they find inconvenient. Short views predominate. This distaste for abstractions may be identified with hostility toward one critical school or another. But in fact a version of the same antagonism has been in place for nearly a century. Eighteenth-century scholarship began by rejecting the ideas of Arnold, the leading critic of the day, and it has rejected most popular theories of literature ever since. Indeed, a refusal to accept long views and period labels, an antipathy for the sort of prescriptive definition that might exclude Pope from the rank of poets or Defoe from the masters of fiction, might be thought the major theoretical (or antitheoretical) contribution of eighteenth-century scholars. Many take considerable satisfaction at being permanently out of fashion.

Yet defining the period remains an important concern. If prejudices against the eighteenth century were not to prosper, a better sense of its accomplishments would need to be formulated. Eighteenth-century scholars have responded to this need, during the past century, by inventing a whole new scholarly field: the history of ideas. The project is international. In Germany, it goes back at least to Hegel. In France, a history of the history of ideas could be organized around the single figure of Rousseau. Coming to terms with his thought, whether as an integral system or as a dynamic struggle against the thought of Voltaire, Diderot, and other giants, has stimulated new ways of writing intellectual history from Lanson to Derrida and de Man. But it was an American scholar, A. O. Lovejoy, who originated "the history of ideas" as a discipline in its own right. In his influential essays of the 1920s on such topics as "nature" and "progress" and "romanticism," in *The Great Chain of Being* (1936), and not least in founding and editing the *Journal of the History of Ideas* (1940), Lovejoy set the example of a model of inquiry that still retains its power—above all in eighteenth-century studies.

Many scholars rely on Lovejoy's method, whether or not they know his work firsthand. To trace the origins and changing fortunes of a term such as "wit," "probability," "the sublime," "authority," "sentiment," "Augustan," or "culture" over the course of a century or more is one of the approved programs for the eighteenth-century scholar, and one that continues to bear fruit. In this respect the field seems intensely alive to ideas, or at least to their history. One way to refute the bias implicit in the label "Neoclassicism" is to examine its genealogy. From a historical perspective, such terms are likely to be exposed as counters in some long-dead argument, now fit to be retired. That tactic has proved a favorite of eighteenth-century scholars. Perhaps no other period has had its ideas, and the words that express them, examined so closely.

The relation between the history of ideas and other sorts of scholarship can be uneasy, however. Lovejoy did take long views. Significantly, when the founder of the *Philological Quarterly* bibliographies reviewed the founder of the *Journal of the History of Ideas*, he warned that "unit-ideas," when divorced from the specific contexts that lend them meaning, quickly deteriorate into "floating commonplaces or themes," as indeterminate as Beauty in the abstract.[7] R. S. Crane, like Lovejoy, might have been described as a historian of ideas, but he always insisted that the value of ideas in literature depends on their function in particular works; and similarly, that no hypothesis about history can be better than the details that embody and validate it. Lovejoy, he thought, did not always remember this. Many eighteenth-century scholars have tended to agree with Crane. They take their stand as particularists, not generalists, and identify truth less with the quality of ideas than with the quantity of evidence. In other scholarly fields, such distinctions might seem artificial, if not out of date. In eighteenth-century studies they still draw blood.

Consider, for instance, the incompatibility of Donald J. Greene and W. J. Bate—distinguished, influential, and much-honored Johnsonians of the same generation. One might expect two such scholars, whose interests so often agree, to have something in common. But in 1972, when Greene reviewed Bate's *The Burden of the Past and the English Poet*, he accused it of mongering mere "isms" and "essences," the "reified abstractions" of "an unreconstructed compartmentalizer and labeller."[8] Not only does Greene disapprove of Bate's work; as their later exchange makes plain, he considers it utterly useless at best, and often positively *dangerous*. The incompatibility is defined by the anecdote with which the review begins. "Late in his life, the venerable Coleridge was introduced to Harriet Martineau, then young and (as always) brash. After some discussion, at cross-purposes, of social and economic topics, Coleridge exclaimed in surprise, 'You appear to consider that society is an aggregate of individuals!' 'I certainly do,' the undaunted Harriet replied to the astonished sage."[9]

Greene has doctored the story (from Martineau's *Autobiography*). Coleridge's remark did not, in fact, follow a discussion; it was a comment on

Martineau's fiction. She herself never said that he was surprised or astonished, though she mentions her *own* surprise that such a metaphysician
had read her. Like many of Coleridge's visitors, Martineau listened pas-
sively to a monologue. But Greene wants to give her the initiative, because
he takes her side. A "dyed-in-the-wool Coleridgean" like Bate may think
that the "essence" of a period somehow transcends the aggregate of its
"individual intellectual and artistic events." Undaunted individualists like
Greene and Martineau will not let the wool be pulled over their eyes. They
know that truth consists of particular cases, of fixities and definites, and
that history of ideas ("whatever *that* is," Greene comments) deals only
with pseudoproblems—"paradox, and word-play and cloud-painting, and
cocoon-spinning out of one's own interior." [10] What Martineau was to
Coleridge, so Greene is to Bate: the witness who notices that the emperor
is not wearing any clothes.

There is less to this exposure, I think, than meets the eye. Is society *really*
an aggregate of individuals? Surely the answer to such a question depends
entirely on definition and point of view. Not even Martineau was unaware
of "the many-sided fact of an organised human society, subject to natural
laws in virtue of its aggregate character and organisation together." [11] To
a soldier an army may be a collection of soldiers, to a general it may be
a single body obeying principles that no one soldier comprehends. Both
points of view are justified, in their own sphere. And so with history. The
historian (such as Sir Lewis Namier) who concentrates on individuals and
their interests, and the historian (such as Fernand Braudel) who surveys the
vast landscapes that reduce the individual to insignificance, can be equally
useful to those who pursue their lines of thought. Particularists and generalists may want to bridle each other, but a well-balanced field cannot
do without either. Both Greene and Bate have inspired many disciples to
follow their ways.

Nevertheless, the argument between them continues. Short and long
views of the eighteenth century are not easy to reconcile. Should a modern
biography of Johnson, for instance, place him insistently within the context
of his times, the specific occasions that formed such a singular person, year
by year and day by day? Or should it rather portray him as a representative
man, interpreting each of his peculiarities as one way of coping with the
universal predicaments of life? These modes might each claim Johnsonian
sanction; and each has led in practice to fine biographies. A disinterested
reader might well want both kinds. But eighteenth-century scholars like
to choose. Cumulatively, such choices have led to two different ways of
reading the eighteenth century.

III

Perhaps they also represent a debate within the century itself. When English literary history first began to be written, two competing models of scholarship divided the field: the short views of "antiquarianism," the long views of "philosophic history." Both were significant innovations. Arnaldo Momigliano, who has described the eighteenth century as the Age of the Antiquaries (especially in England), thinks that "it meant a revolution in historical method," [12] a new preoccupation with original sources and material remains. The history of antiquarianism remains largely unwritten. Antiquarians themselves have no ambition to write it. They tend to collect information about a single subject matter or locality, and may be quite uninterested in information about the neighboring shire; they do not insist that the facts they gather contribute to solving some problem or answering some question; and they are often amateurs, unconcerned with professional organizations or rewards. Yet the evidence they cull and classify, without attending to any grand synthesis, helps make history possible.

The philosophic historian, on the other hand, cares less about collecting facts than arranging them into a chronological pattern of cause and effect. Montesquieu, Voltaire, and Gibbon do not dig for themselves; their task is explanation. Each piece of relevant information serves to answer a question about how something originated, why it rose, declined, and fell, how it elucidates the present or has contributed to the advance of civilization. The local does not detain them. Philosophic historians like to travel through time and space. They compete with each other to construct longer views and better syntheses, and they require access to secondary sources as well as national and international associations. The eighteenth century laid the ground for such communities of scholars. It is the first Age of the Philosophic Historians.

The legacy of these two movements still survives. Without the antiquarians, modern scholarship would be inconceivable; the original sources preserved by the eighteenth century support our research now. A major part of twentieth-century scholarship has consisted of opening and publishing such records. The eighteenth, one might say, is a very *collectible* century. It offers the troves of journals and letters whose uncovering provided so much material for the Boswell and Walpole and Burney industries, the country houses that perpetuate the life and art of the time, the periodicals that register each seasonal fashion, the churchyards and archives that inscribe whatever passes. These reserves are far from exhausted; new discoveries wait to be made. Hence many scholars, both amateur and professional, have been drawn to the eighteenth century by the pleasures of antiquarianism.

To be sure, those pleasures are not always innocent. The poor do not leave many monuments, nor houses where their papers may be stored, and the passing of time only exaggerates the inequalities of the class system. Moreover, collectors tend to be men of means and members of clubs. For a long while after its founding, eighteenth-century scholarship itself might have been regarded as a sort of gentlemen's club, where those who belonged to the wrong race or class or gender or religion need not apply. Even in twentieth-century America, antiquarianism has promised a retreat from threatening social changes, a refuge not unlike those imaginary pastoral sanctuaries so popular among seventeenth- and eighteenth-century writers and readers. But an antiquarian cannot live for long in fantasy land; too many facts demand attention. The pursuit of a missing document or a correct date enforces a solid respect for evidence, the more particular and irreducible the better. In this regard antiquarianism seems essentially democratic. It prefers the literal to the symbolic, and nothing at all to the truth. Much of the best antiquarian research of recent years has been devoted, in fact, to women and the poor. There is no hierarchy among diggers. Hence alliances continue to be built between those who keep the records and those who turn them to new purposes.

The heritage of the philosophic historians has been quite different. If the eighteenth century offers a refuge, it also represents a world in change, a competition of ideas for the future. The revolutions at the end of the century, viewed by some scholars as a rejection of its conservative values, are viewed by others as a fulfillment of its enlightened spirit. Thus the period has always attracted intellectuals in search of the moment when the modern world came into being, when the force of skeptical philosophy, or capitalism, or political justice, or the common reader could no longer be resisted. Romanticists may perceive the age of revolution as a sudden dawn, but those who believe in continuities will turn inevitably to the preceding age—to Adam Smith, Sir William Jones, or Condorcet. A number of the most influential works of modern scholarship, *The Great Chain of Being* and *The Mirror and the Lamp* among them, pause in the antechamber of the eighteenth century so long that the Romantic movement, when it finally arrives, may seem less a breakthrough than an afterthought. It is no accident that such works should have to think their way through the cogitations of eighteenth-century minds. Their very projects, their fascination with the way that ideas are modified, over the course of centuries, not only by individual thinkers but by something like a collective mind, derive from the philosophic historians who first began to grasp that ideas can have a history.

The eighteenth century also gave rise to the idea of progress. For most philosophic historians, an interest in history could hardly be separated from an analysis of the betterment of mankind, the gradual triumph of enlightenment over superstition and civilized values over barbarity. Eventually a version of this forward-looking, melioristic doctrine—the "Whig interpretation of history"—came to be used against the eighteenth century itself. Many of the best English authors, it was argued, had warred with the ancients against the moderns and set themselves against enlightenment. Yet even those authors (and not only Whigs) were fascinated by the long new vista of historical progress, whether or not they found it to their liking. To many it seemed that Locke as well as Newton had initiated a new science, and that the laws of human society, like those of nature, would be increasingly discovered and refined. The idea of progress also spread among ordinary people. Even a formal term such as "the novel" reveals a positive attitude toward change; readers were attracted to a form that brought the news, to something new.

Modern scholars have voted for progress as well. Many books on the novelty of the novel, for example, agree on one main point: what is most important about eighteenth-century fiction, what most needs to be explained, is how it produced the one form that would last. A scholar of antiquarian leanings might object that this focus on one sort of fiction to the exclusion of others—not only "the romance" but the allegory, imaginary voyage, oriental tale, Menippean satire, etc.—imposes the expectations and definitions of a later age on an age that hardly cared whether its fictions were "novels" or not. An obsession with the novel is Whiggish. Yet eighteenth-century critics themselves believed that literary forms progress. Thomas Warton, who wrote the first considerable *History of English Poetry*, was certainly an antiquarian, and rebuked his contemporaries for condescending to early works or holding them to inappropriate standards of taste, but he never doubted the superior sense and sensibility of his own times.[13] His affection for "Gothic" extravagance and "fine fabling" implies a conscious retrogression, as an adult might envy childish joys. Twentieth-century literary historians seldom express their wistfulness, or the pride of their sophistication, so openly. Yet many of their assumptions still resemble Warton's. Even "the corrective process" of scholarship seems inherently progressive; it implies that nineteenth-century scholars did not understand the eighteenth century, and that modern scholars do.

The progressive attitudes of the philosophic historians and their modern counterparts have often collided, however, with antiquarian affinities for whatever is venerable and dated. To be sure, not many scholars now would align themselves with either camp. The professionalizing of eighteenth-century studies has changed the terms. Traditionally antiquarians, no matter how learned, have been amateurs, and the decline of the amateur scholar in relation to the professional, who is certified by degrees and institutions, has tended to discredit the pursuit of knowledge for its own sake, without portfolio or publications.[14] Few professors would admit to being antiquarians. But many do share their spirit, if we define it in part as resistance to the idea of progress. Insofar as professionalism implies the acceptance of current standards and idioms, or a willingness to keep changing as the field changes, quite a few scholars might identify themselves as antiprofessional—loyalists to the past. At any rate, the friction between those who strive to preserve and replicate eighteenth-century works, and those who believe that the century must be reshaped, every decade or so, according to the best modern lights, still makes scholars hot. The war of ancients and moderns has never ended.

Perhaps a more subtle strain in eighteenth-century studies also descends from the old idea of progress. If a proud commitment to enlightened values is one great legacy of the century, so is a deep disappointment with the failure of that enlightenment to live up to its promise. Not even the philosophes were sure that the future would follow their lead. And what they left remains a contested issue: democracy and totalitarianism can both be traced to them. Their enemies have argued that enlightenment failed; their friends, that it has yet to be tried. But enemies and friends alike judge the accomplishments of eighteenth-century thinkers by criteria those thinkers themselves devised. Liberty, human rights, freedom of inquiry and belief, government by the people, equality before the law, and arguments based on reason and experience rather than authority are living ideals. Did the eighteenth century live up to them? As long ago as 1876, in his *History of English Thought in the Eighteenth Century*, Leslie Stephen phrased that question again and again, and was not contented with his own answers. Too often the century had compromised its ideals. Like a child unhappy because its parents have not been faithful to their own best principles, Stephen criticizes the common sense and materialism of English thought for begging the ultimate questions that the best minds in Europe had posed. The Enlightenment had not been enlightened enough.

A similar critique continues to inform eighteenth-century studies. There is certainly no lack of issues. So many modern problems first surfaced in the period that it offers a remarkable laboratory in which to investigate the generation of every movement from consumerism to animal rights. Nor have those issues become obsolete. A scholar who studies eighteenth-century justifications of colonialism, or the rigidities of gender codes, or the ways that authors made a living, or the treatment of old people, or the criminal justice system, can hardly pretend to be writing from the superior perspective of an era that knows all the answers. Inevitably, twentieth-century attitudes are enmeshed with those of the past. This involvement accounts for much of the interest of eighteenth-century studies. But it can also lead to an emphasis on the inconsistencies, if not hypocrisies, of eighteenth-century thought. If the United States was founded on the principle that all men are created equal, nonetheless its founders managed to deny equality to many who happened not to be white or not to be male. One scholar might praise the ideal and the men who were able to conceive it; another might argue that the reality of American inequality unmasks the ideal as an illusion. But few scholars would disguise their commitment to the principle itself. Hence the eighteenth century (far more than any earlier age) remains contemporary, not least as a source of confusion and trouble. Dryden's politics, Richardson's novels, or Burke's arguments with Paine can still provoke outrage in readers who recognize the antagonisms as their own.

The acerbity of eighteenth-century scholarship has increased, in recent decades, as the modern consensus about the benignity of enlightened and civilized values has broken down. Scholars now come from more diverse backgrounds; they identify with the victims of "progress" as much as with its apologists; and they may consider themselves accusers rather than defenders of eighteenth-century England and its works. Moreover, the object of study has varied along with those who study it. For many scholars, eighteenth-century English literature no longer consists of a handful of eminent authors, trained in the classics and classic themselves, but potentially of *all* writing from the period—the more neglected and obscure, the more in need of retrieval. Even anthologies have taken in much writing that used to be outcast. *The New Oxford Book of Eighteenth Century Verse* (1984), edited by Roger Lonsdale, trims Addison, Pope, and Sir John Henry Moore to make room for "the vigorous, humorous, idiosyncratic verse of authors, many of them anonymous, who felt impelled at least to try to describe with some immediacy and colloquial directness the changing world they lived in, often for anything but a polite readership";[15] and almost all reviewers have approved this decision. But expansion is also divisive. Not all eighteenth-century scholars and critics now read the same primary texts, or think each other's favorite texts worth reading. In this way too the field of study has become continually more plural.

Nor do scholars agree about their methods of study. There have always been differences, of course, among the concerns of a textual scholar, a biographer, a literary or social historian, a linguist, and a critic, and the ways they study a text may have little in common. But those ways have multiplied lately. An old and new historicist, for instance, are likely to differ not only about how to interpret evidence, but about what constitutes evidence in the first place, and a traditional textual scholar and a poststructuralist may disagree about how to define a text. One method that seems particularly factious is a reading of the past in terms of its contradictions:

either the internal contradictions of a text or the historical and ideological contradictions that it manifests. To notice places where a work seems disjointed or perplexing is hardly new. One might argue that such places have long furnished scholars and critics with their most promising material, the cruxes they try to resolve. To understand a work at all, from one point of view, means precisely to show the larger pattern that knits all seeming contradictions into a complex whole. But scholars (especially though not exclusively Marxists) who define ideology as "false consciousness," or as the system of contradictions within societies and their discourses, may consider the "whole" a mere masking device or patchwork, contrived to distract attention from an incoherent reality. To understand a work thus depends on teasing out its contradictions, most of all when art has managed to disguise them. A scholar who adopts this method will emphasize exactly those features of a work of art that another scholar might think least significant; and each sort of scholar will regard the other as utterly superficial (one does not understand the wholeness of art or systems of thought, the other does not understand their social construction and dialectics). These differences seem irreconcilable. So do the scholars who follow such contrary methods.

The liveliest debates in eighteenth-century studies, however, pertain not only to method but to rival views of what the century and its texts have to offer. Not many of the issues seem settled. Even the "masterpieces" of the period still inspire controversy and dissent. It is not uncommon, for instance, for a critic who loves Richardson to dislike Fielding (or vice versa), for partisans of Pope or Blake to declare that Blake or Pope hardly qualifies as a genuine poet, or for devotees of Johnson and Hume to think the other writer not worth reading. And Rochester, Swift, and Boswell still draw violent personal reactions, pro and con, from scholars as well as the public. In this respect the eighteenth century continues to be a beleaguered and polemical era; the book on it has not yet closed. Perhaps that is also a sign of good scholarly health. Multiple eighteenth centuries keep being discovered.

IV

The discoverers also come from different places. One reason that scholars see such divergent eighteenth centuries may be that their vantage points are so far apart. This distance between perspectives should be understood literally as well as figuratively. Eighteenth-century English literature does not look quite the same when observed from England, the United States, France, India, or Australia (not to mention China or Peru). An emphasis upon theoretical and methodological disagreements too often slights geography and nationality. Even short distances can be decisive. To an outsider, the Scottish Enlightenment may seem uniform, but gaps appear when it is viewed from Aberdeen, Edinburgh, and Glasgow.[16] Similarly, a brief trip across the border from New England to Canada can alter one's sense of eighteenth-century colonial history beyond recognition, and *Oroonoko* and *Robinson Crusoe* take on different aspects south of the border. English literature does not belong to any one country or generation. The pluralism of eighteenth-century studies reflects their travels across time and space.

One oceanic rift in particular underlies the field: the gulf between America and Great Britain. From an American perspective, eighteenth-century English literature is a foreign country where they do things differently. Its politics, culture, ideas, and style require perpetual imaginative recreation. This gives the scholar a certain freedom, since the mental landscape of the century can always be rearranged by acts of the mind, as well as a heavy responsibility, since the scholar must look after dead authors who cannot take care of themselves. At its best, American eighteenth-century studies can be wonderfully fresh and inventive; the old bones speak again in a new world. But British eighteenth-century studies tend to assume a familiarity with literature of the period. Its relics survive and litter the world in which the scholar lives; its politics and cultural assumptions seem continuous with those of the present. From this perspective, a good deal of American scholarship appears fanciful or abstract. British eighteenth-century scholars often pride themselves on being down to earth, or on their intuitive acquaintance with nuances of region and party to which a foreigner might be blind (or pedantically attentive, through overcompensation). Sometimes their sympathy toward or aversion from an author seems intensely personal or class-conscious, as if in response to an objectionable accent. But the sense of continuity between the eighteenth century and the twentieth can vitalize scholarship. When the past is alive, whether as the weight of a tradition or as skirmishes not yet settled, no scholar can regard it with indifference.

At times the transatlantic rift may lead to pitfalls. If America and Britain are cultures divided by a common language, so the mirage of a common literature divides their scholars. On this side of the ocean, Samuel Johnson sounds to many like the voice of universal wisdom; on the other side, many praise him as the very model of an Englishman, John Bull incarnate, or damn his unreconstructed Toryism. Perhaps both images are misconceived, yet they retain their hold. Similarly, the broad issues of aesthetics or history of ideas that stimulate so much American scholarship can resolve, in the work of E. P. Thompson or Raymond Williams, into concrete and local matters of party, class, and power. Ideally these two sides can complement each other. If the danger of American eighteenth-century studies,

from a British point of view, lies in refining or vaporizing material practices into mere constructions of the mind, so the British scholar may be in
danger of finding old texts too familiar and forgetting how alien their assumptions are. Neither side has any reason to be complacent. Eighteenth-
century studies needs them both, if only to remind scholars that part of the
truth escapes them. The best contemporary eighteenth-century scholarship
often engages in traffic across the borders.

Closer to home, moreover, American scholarship seems internally divided, not only by theories and methods but by schools. Few differences
are so critical or so easy to overlook. Indeed, the history of eighteenth-
century studies could be written in terms of a handful of graduate programs, branching out into family trees and lines of succession. The influence of schools was more obvious at a time when the standard collections
of eighteenth-century essays were almost all festschrifts. Today the situation has changed. *The New Eighteenth Century* is not a festschrift, and
it views the scholarly past as a union or fraternity rather than a conglom-
eration of schools. But the four major critics it cites as representative each
came from a different place: Crane from Chicago, Wimsatt from Yale,
Wasserman from Johns Hopkins, and Brower from Harvard. That helps
account for how far apart they were. None of them, to be sure, can be
identified so simply with a school. Brower, for instance, had no Harvard
degree, and his long association with Amherst College as well as with contemporary techniques of close reading put him rather outside the Harvard
traditions (for example, the "New Humanism" and its focus on the history
of literary criticism) connected at one time with Irving Babbitt and later
with Bate. For some of his students, Brower represented a school within a
school, the better Harvard in Harvard. Yet that place had little to do with
Chicago, Yale, or Johns Hopkins. A similar story might be told about the
lovers' quarrels of Crane, Wimsatt, and Wasserman with their own institutions. Despite those quarrels, none of them is quite imaginable in another
school. And the legacy they left eighteenth-century studies—not only their
works but their students—splits off in four separate directions.

Other schools have invented their own eighteenth centuries. Though I
cannot pretend to be familiar with many, I might note a few other places
with characters of their own. Scholars with Princeton backgrounds (especially students of Louis Landa) have often paid close attention to the omni-
presence of Christianity in eighteenth-century writing (having taught at
Princeton for many years, I myself always notice the missing item, religion,
in the current fashion for studies of race, class, and gender). At Columbia, James Clifford's example spurred many students to an interest in the
details of daily life. Elsewhere the situation may be more complex, particularly as scholars become more mobile and transfer their horizons from

one place to another. My own graduate training, at Cornell, had a strong Chicago cast, imported by W. R. Keast. It cannot be coincidental that so many Cornell students, including myself, James Battersby, Robert Folkenflik, and Stephen Fix, have continued Keast's own work on Johnson's *Lives of the Poets*. Another eighteenth-century specialty, at several schools (i.e., Northwestern and Minnesota—though the line of succession could probably be traced back to Yale and the influence of Chauncey Brewster Tinker), is the sister-arts tradition. Some scholars view pictorialism as the key to understanding most poetry of the period; others are quite blind to it. It all depends on where the lookout is posted.

To write the history of eighteenth-century studies in terms of its schools or the genealogies of individual scholars would be impossible, even for someone with the patience of Namier. Nor would such a history do justice to the breaks between generations that also shaped the field. A hundred years ago, in the United States, quite a few eighteenth-century scholars were ministers; the faith of *Pilgrim's Progress* inspired them as well. Today an eighteenth-century scholar may well be Jewish, female, or generally irreverent. The history of the field represents no heritage or kinship, for many such scholars, but rather a nightmare from which they are trying to awake—insofar as they remember it at all. Institutional memories tend to be short, these days. Moreover, scholars who came of age in the 1960s are likely to analyze their fields, and their allegiances, in terms of generational conflict rather than traditions and continuities. Each decade or so brings out a new set of concerns. A history written on such assumptions is bound to be choppy, with one revolution of thought succeeding another. For all these reasons, a contemporary eighteenth-century scholar may feel cut off from the past. As the eighteenth century keeps being reinvented, so does the story of eighteenth-century studies.

That story is far from finished. If one use of a long view of the field is to perceive how adaptable eighteenth-century writing has been, how available to rival definitions, another is to suggest how much has escaped definition. No myth about the period stands more in need of correction than the myth of its stability. There never was a status quo in eighteenth-century studies. Though conservatives and radicals may equally want to claim the century as their own, neither vision can grasp more than a fragment of an era always in motion. Indeed, for many eighteenth-century scholars (of whom I am one), the constantly changing face of the century is precisely what makes it attractive. No era provoked better arguments; and those arguments still go on. The "mental fight" that Blake vowed to continue until his culture had been transformed is an eighteenth-century ideal. Modern scholars keep that fight alive.

Productive argument depends, however, on one condition: that the participants listen to each other. The diversity of eighteenth centuries and those who invent them does not preclude communications and negotiations among contending parties. Eighteenth-century scholars ought to be well trained, after all, in paying attention to the past, and the past includes the history of their own field. That history cannot be taken for granted. Whenever scholars identify their predecessors, they are also declaring their own biases and interests. Collectively, such interests make up the field, and there is no end to them. But a field consists of good conversation as well. That too is an eighteenth-century legacy; and as new eighteenth centuries continue to be invented, they will be tested by how well the past and the present manage to talk together.

Notes

1 Felicity Nussbaum and Laura Brown, "Revising Critical Practices: An Introductory Essay," in *The New Eighteenth Century: Theory, Politics, English Literature*, ed. Nussbaum and Brown (New York and London: Methuen, 1987), 5.

2 Compare Crane's essay "On Writing the History of Criticism in England, 1650–1800" (1953), reprinted in *The Idea of the Humanities* (Chicago: University of Chicago Press, 1967), 2:157–75, with Wimsatt's chapters 10–15 in *Literary Criticism: A Short History* (New York: Knopf, 1957). Though Crane takes J. W. H. Atkins as his target, his criticism of "a priori" history would apply to Wimsatt as well.

3 Nussbaum and Brown change the first word of the title of my own essay, "A History of the Future," to "The" (*New Eighteenth Century* 7, 276)—as if one could ever write *the* history, past or coming, of a field. I take this slip to be symptomatic (not mere carelessness, as when they get my name wrong).

4 Lawrence Lipking, "The Genie in the Lamp: M. H. Abrams and the Motives of Literary History," in *High Romantic Argument*, ed. Lipking (Ithaca: Cornell University Press, 1981), 136–38.

5 Matthew Arnold, "The Study of Poetry" (1880). This famous essay on touchstones, reprinted to open the second series of *Essays in Criticism* (1888), itself came to serve eighteenth-century scholars as a touchstone of fallacious criticism.

6 Louis A. Landa, Foreword, *English Literature, 1660–1800: A Bibliography of Modern Studies* (Princeton: Princeton University Press, 1950), 1:1.

7 R. S. Crane, "Philosophy, Literature, and the History of Ideas" (1954), reprinted in *The Idea of the Humanities*, 1:181. It should be noted, however, that Crane's references to Lovejoy in *Philological Quarterly* were admiring.

8 Donald J. Greene, "The Burdensome Past," *Studies in Burke and His Time*, 14 (Fall 1972), 81.

9 Ibid. Martineau's account of this meeting occurs in her *Autobiography*, ed. M. W. Chapman (Boston: Houghton, Mifflin, 1877), 1:298–300. Bate's reply to Greene appeared in *Studies in Burke and His Time*, 14 (Winter 1972–73),

163–68; and the following issue of the same journal contains Greene's rejoinder (14 [Spring 1973], 257–64).

10 Martineau's *Autobiography* 1:299.

11 Ibid. 1:300.

12 Arnaldo Momigliano, "Ancient History and the Antiquarian" (1950), reprinted in *Studies in Historiography* (New York: Harper & Row, 1966), 2.

13 On Warton's complex relation to ideas of literary progress, see René Wellek, *The Rise of English Literary History* (Chapel Hill: University of North Carolina Press, 1941), and Joan Pittock, *The Ascendancy of Taste* (London: Routledge & Kegan Paul, 1973).

14 The separation of professional historians from antiquarians and archeologists in Victorian England is the subject of Philippa Levine's *The Amateur and the Professional* (Cambridge: Cambridge University Press, 1986).

15 Roger Lonsdale, *The New Oxford Book of Eighteenth Century Verse* (Oxford: Oxford University Press, 1984), xxxvii.

16 For distinctions among different sorts of Enlightenment, see *Aberdeen and the Enlightenment*, ed. Jennifer J. Carter and Joan H. Pittock (Aberdeen: Aberdeen University Press, 1987).

2 *Leo Braudy*

Varieties of Literary Affection

I use affection here in a double sense—the literature that attempts to affect its readers through their feelings, their emotions, their sentiments (as distinguished from their intellectual understanding); and the literature that deals with one's feelings for other people and oneself—the literature of friendship, biography, and autobiography. Obviously I intend these two uses to be interwoven, and I would like to explore their connection in eighteenth-century English literature.

But I also want to talk about approaching literature as student, critic, and teacher. And so, together with the eighteenth century, I'd like to discuss a closely related topic—the affective fallacy, first described in an essay of 1949 by William K. Wimsatt and Monroe Beardsley that stands as the companion to their somewhat more notorious intentional fallacy essay of 1946. I have two goals here: first, since I want to explore the varieties of affective literature, I would like to focus on what for many was a decisive argument against calling affective works literature; and second, I want to examine the interest in this theoretical issue by a critic—Wimsatt—whose special field of historical interest was the eighteenth century. Since I studied introductory philosophy and aesthetics with Beardsley at Swarthmore in 1959–60, the Age of Johnson with Wimsatt at Yale in 1964, and later wrote a dissertation on eighteenth-century literature (although not with Wimsatt), that personal experience will no doubt permeate my description of their work.

Wimsatt and Beardsley were friends who had met while in graduate school at Yale. Both received their Ph.D.'s in 1939, Wimsatt in English and Beardsley in philosophy. Wimsatt took a position as instructor of English at Yale in 1939 and stayed there until his death in 1975. Beardsley began teaching at Yale, moved briefly to Holyoke, back to Yale, and then to Swarthmore, where he stayed from 1947 to 1969, when he took a job at Temple, where he remained until his death in 1985.

In their collaborative essays, Wimsatt and Beardsley essentially treat the poem, the literary work, as an object, a "verbal icon" in the title of Wimsatt's later collection. The poem, they say, is a literary action, "a linguistic fact," for critical attention (10).[1] Both an intentional approach (the assumption that the poem's true meaning can be derived from a study of the life and thoughts of the author) and an affective approach (the assumption that its true meaning resides in the emotional connection between author and audience) divert the critic from his own true vocation: "the public act of evaluating poems." As Wimsatt and Beardsley argue, "the evaluation of a work of art remains public; the work is measured against something outside the author" (10). Any other process contaminates "the verbal and hence intellectual composition that is the poem" (12).

In the light of their other writings, I believe that the main force behind the intentional fallacy article is Beardsley, while in the affective fallacy it is Wimsatt. In class Beardsley's arguments against intentionality and biographical interpretation were always much stronger than those he made against an emotional connection to the work. Even then, he usually tended not to attack intentionalistic arguments so much as show how nonintentional *language* should be substituted whenever possible (talking, for example, of the narrator rather than the author of *Tom Jones*).

Beardsley first made his philosophic reputation in 1950 with the publication of *Practical Logic* and *Thinking Straight*, whose titles indicate their approach to the question of meaning. Yet Beardsley, unlike many philosophers of his generation and outlook, was very interested in both art and politics. The crucial point in his *Aesthetics*, for example, comes toward the end, when he argues his belief in the instrumental rather than the intrinsic theory of aesthetic value. (He said it was the only point on which he and his wife, Elizabeth, for many years a member of the philosophy department at Howard University, disagreed.)

As befits a longtime member of the ACLU and the American Association for Legal and Political Philosophy, Beardsley's political outlook accorded with this emphasis on instrumental value, and I remember as well his mockery of the concept of *zeitgeist* (he particularly disliked "the baroque") for its repressive view of individual will. Aesthetic activity should be socially useful; good art ought to have good effects. The reader as well as the critic should therefore soft-pedal or deny the importance of the author, because the literary act, like the general good of liberal politics, ideally transmuted self-interest (read "intention") into citizenship.

In contrast, Wimsatt's book on Pope's portraits indicates his own interest in the biographical and even the intentional. Lacking Beardsley's activist social conscience, Wimsatt yet similarly wanted to deny the burgeoning authorial self, specifically its ability to transmit or inspire emotions. It was especially the specter of feeling that he wanted to dispel. I remember vividly his comment on one of my papers for his class. Next to where I had written "Fielding feels . . ." was testily penciled in "What's the matter with the poor fellow? Can't he think?" Clearly there was a hierarchy, and thinking was at the top. As he did in *The Prose Style of Samuel Johnson*, the 1941 book that had grown out of his dissertation, Wimsatt treated style as a personal construction deeply rooted in a submerged pattern of historically determined linguistic meaning (the Latin roots of Johnson's metaphors). He attacked what he considered to be the psychologism and emotionality of both intentional and affective criticism. Instead, he championed rhetorical training and often traditional, particularly Christian, standards of virtue as the best way to discover that web of ideal and determinable meaning underlying the uncertainties of individual psychology.[2]

Coming therefore from a quite different political perspective, Wimsatt's conservative distaste for the literature and criticism of ego and sensibility yet coincided with Beardsley's liberal distaste for any individualism expressed as bourgeois self-interest or fascist self-assertion. In their joint work they presented instead a method of analysis and evaluation that was democratically accessible to anyone with intelligence and an *Oxford English Dictionary* close at hand.

Although their approach did effectively prune the excesses of the impressionistic and anecdotal criticism Wimsatt and Beardsley were reacting against, it also led to excess and exaggeration in its turn, as eager explicators made it, until fairly recently, the major mode of critical discourse. In fact, this attack that the two friends made on the uses of feeling in literature and in literary criticism creates some intriguing paradoxes. To collaborate on the articles, there must have been affection between the literary critic and the philosopher. But in what they created, little of their own more endearing qualities emerge. The articles contain more of Wimsatt's moral demolition than Beardsley's whimsy, more of Beardsley's logic than Wimsatt's taste for the historical anecdote. Instead of affection enhancing the interplay of their ideas, the result was a canceling out—an implicit caveat to their theory.

The approach of Wimsatt and Beardsley thus aggressively asserts an ahistorical theory of literature when it is in fact historically bound to the periods in which it was developed—the prewar 1930s and the wartime 1940s—and in which it was promulgated, the cold war 1950s. Combining their political differences and personal affection, Wimsatt and Beardsley had found common intellectual ground in a cautionary theory of literary evaluation that asserted the irrelevance of the historical context, the author's biography, and the reader's emotional response. The only appropriate object of attention was the self-contained, self-justifying, and demonstrable structures of the work itself, uncontaminated as much as possible by author or audience.[3]

I contrast Wimsatt and Beardsley as disembodied writers and personally immediate teachers not only because their theories either dismiss or distance the role of emotion, expression, and affection in literature, but also because their methods are so strangely unsuited to understanding the literature of the eighteenth century and its later influence, on nineteenth-century English and American literature and on the popular culture of our own times.

Beardsley believed in the instrumental value of the literary work (or "aesthetic object" as it was often called). But literary theory has an even more obvious instrumental value: whatever a theory defines as literature is the kind of literature it is best suited to analyze and interpret. Wimsatt and Beardsley, for example, always use "poem" in their theory, never "novel," rarely "fiction." As Wimsatt says in his introduction, "I use the terms . . . 'poem,' 'poetry,' and 'poetic' relating to literature in its most intensive instances" (xv n1). At least four problems central to the study of eighteenth-century literature are thereby left out: the problem of the novel as a special mode of literature; the problem of associative structure in fiction and poetry; the problem of creating a literary language unindebted to literary tradition; and the problem of the poet, his nature outside the poem, his career, and his fame. Wimsatt and Beardsley speak disparagingly of the "incomplete verbal symbol" (16) that requires footnotes for full understanding. But, unless the willful formal incompleteness of much eighteenth-century literature is recognized as an aesthetic choice, we will be severely hampered from understanding the possible ways that incompleteness was defined—in special themes, motifs, characters, and values.

To emphasize the "verbal and intellectual structure that is the poem" glosses over the many attempts of eighteenth-century poets and novelists to connect emotionally and culturally with their audiences across the barrier of print. With the pamphlet literature of the civil wars and the propagandizing of a "Restoration," the assumption that a writer and his audience come from the same class and share the same beliefs was becoming harder and harder to maintain. Through the public poetry of the period runs the realization that the mere possession of poetic ability doesn't naturally incline you to any particular political position. Already with Dryden, the measured tones, the sense of shared knowledge, the ability to allude with confidence have become self-conscious acts of will. His and, later, Pope's effort to link aesthetic sensitivity with moral truth indicate how desperately they were trying to reach beyond a set of increasingly questionable analogies between class and taste to reach an audience with similar values, if not similar social positions. Pope's defense of himself and his satire in *Epistle to Dr. Arbuthnot* comes down to "Father, Mother, Body, Soul, and Muse"—indebted for his moral sense (and poetic power) to a father who took no part in faction: "Stranger to civil and religious rage / The good Man walk'd innoxious through his Age."

Just as such an aggressively antipolitical couplet highlights the actual factionalization that literature had undergone since the civil wars, so the rise of satire marks the appearance of a new, more affectively defined literary purpose. The older English satire castigated the social and political world from the standpoint of an isolated religious virtue. But the new satire rarely invoked religious or spiritual norms, even when it implicitly favored them. Its assertion instead was that only a few people in the kingdom were truly moral. It appealed to the feelings through the intellect, seeking to incite the morally outraged reader to *do* something, if only buy more of the works of Pope and Swift. Such satire assumes that literature can no longer justify itself as an elitist preserve. The older poetry tended to appeal to an audience whose social and intellectual beliefs were already known; the affective work begins, in Popean satire, to search for an audience of similar *sympathies,* out of which common beliefs might grow. Its appeal, therefore, is not to a class with specific traditions of literacy, but to a culture (and perhaps a nation) of those who share a common language and perhaps some common traditions and standards. All the balance and order of Pope's verse plays against his effort to break through to the reader's sensibility and make it his own, just as his magisterial voice in *Essay on Man* is balanced by the self-justifying, virtually autobiographical voice of *Arbuthnot*. Pope's ideal person is not some genealogically justified aristocrat or some conventionalized *vir bonus* but Ralph Allen, a good man. Through his taste and personal assertion, Pope's Allen has discovered his own moral standards and, perhaps not coincidentally, made his success by consolidating the English mail routes—a web of communication establishing a national coherence unindebted to either religion or class.

The essence of affective literature, therefore, is the way it attempts to build bridges between the work and its audience, so that the work can be contemplated for its effect as well as its affect, for what it makes the reader feel and do: satire for hate, sentiment for tears, pornography for erotic stimulation, gothicism for fear. Whether it is to hate Robert Walpole, have an erection, cry, or be scared, affective literature actively seeks to move its reader, to convey through literature something like the kinesthetic power of normal experience. Affective literature in the eighteenth century attempts to create and revive feeling that literature itself may have stifled, the feelings that were left out of life by the polite because of their fear of being labeled "enthusiastic."

How was this affective power communicated between author and reader? First, by breaking down the generic assumptions about the work's form; second, by breaking down linguistic and semantic assumptions about the work's language; third, by personalizing the author or speaker. The ultimate goal was to make the reader's response a fresh one, unmediated by or at least disentangled from what had been read before. No wonder that the categories of Wimsatt and Beardsley seem so irrelevant to the eighteenth century. The basic need of the eighteenth century, unlike that of the 1950s, was not to teach rhetoric, logic, and anti-affective rigor as a cure for an elitist sensibility of response. The eighteenth century knew its rhetoric all too well. Its problem was the inherited cultural baggage and literary language that were stifling the ability to see and write clearly. In collecting the ballads that make up his *Reliques of Ancient English Poetry*, Bishop Percy was convinced that he was in aesthetic alliance with the urbard who wrote the ballads and was therefore free to correct them. But Chatterton, Burns, Macpherson, and others knew that a surer way out of the impasse was to lie and cheat. The pure unfallen language was irretrievable. The only alternatives were to make up a language of your own—the way of literary fraud and the poetic insanity of Smart, Cowper, and Blake; or to create a new language from common usage—the way of the Romantics. This particular path—magically bringing back to language the incandescence of the old poetry—has been a rallying cry for poetic revivals and manifestos down to the present. Another way was the way of reality—the way of the novel—to write as much as possible in the way people actually spoke or to consider situations that people might plausibly experience or might at least want to hear about. Both ways were opposed to form and to authority; both told their stories in fragments, episodically, associatively. In one the coherence was the voice of the poet with his new language; in the other the voice of the fictional autobiographer and social observer.

Along with the renovation of language came the experimentation with form. The edited manuscript in Defoe, the discovered manuscript in the gothic, the fragments of Sterne and Mackenzie, the letters of Richardson—

all are efforts at a new kind of narration that will allow the reader to feel more directly. Forms that at least pretend to let us into their workings rely on a common responsiveness as much as a common set of generic assumptions. Defoe's fictional autobiographies parallel Pope's attempt to restore the presence of the author, who is *responsible* for what he writes and publishes. Dryden tried to express his distance from partisan conflict by a magisterial tone within the poem. The preface to *Absalom and Achitophel*, for example, talks about being above party and appealing to "the moderate sort of man." But when Pope includes a similar sentiment in the "Epilogue to the Satires" the effect is quite different. The detached voice no longer works for Pope. He must create his own.

How can the Wimsatt and Beardsley attack on intentional analysis be relevant at all to a century where one of the main issues is the assertion of the author, fictional or otherwise? The eighteenth century is the great era of secular autobiography, in which people tell their own stories because no one else will and because they want to know them themselves. The urge of a character to write bodies forth the urge of the author to connect the parts of his own fragmented self and to communicate with a rapidly growing and more anonymous audience. The older didacticism of moral and political ideas had developed into a didacticism of feeling. Fielding may still want to recapture the old epic elitist audience, but Richardson seeks to reaffect the unfeeling audience. In the course of the century, an unwillingness to have feelings (because they were associated with the submerged classes) developed into a desire to express and indulge them—as Smollett, say, moves from the harsh satire of *Roderick Random* in 1748 to the misanthrope turned sentimentalist in *Humphry Clinker* in 1771, where he reveals that the satirist's venom is always a mask for his tender feelings. Swift was reputed to have hardly ever laughed. But Matthew Bramble in Smollett's *Humphry Clinker* must finally embrace Humphry as his natural son.

Sentimental literature sets out to relearn and reexperience the world more directly, without the intermediaries of philosophy or tradition— or any distancing device, especially the hard-surfaced bulk of Wimsatt and Beardsley's hypostatized poem. Throughout the century the notion of authorial responsibility grows as literature becomes more and more personalized. If the satiric standard of *Essay on Man* is a secularized cosmology, sentimental literature contains a secularized ethics—of empathy and situation. The literature of tears says, "look within for the truth," even as gothicism shows the dark side of the personal: "it may be awful within, but it's certainly intriguing." Both gain their authority from the way they affect their audiences. Milton had been the last major representative of an intellectual tradition in which the spiritual and the secular represented complementary interpretations of the world; he could cite the

Zohar equally with Homer, Luke, and Copernicus. But by the eighteenth century the growth of society, the expanding economy and population, and the elaboration of political bureaucracy were causing the reflexive belief in an underlying spiritual cosmology to erode insensibly. Newton and Boyle may have thought that their scientific, mathematical, and theological works were equally valuable. But later admiration considered them primarily as minds, intelligences piercing the universe, transcending a world without transcendence.

The old cosmology had vanished—and the soul along with it. But in its stead there was a new cosmology, supernatural and psychical, bound to a numinous God and an omnipresent devil, no longer fighting for the kingdom but still easily summoned up by the latest fiction. Revealing the self had become a more complicated literary venture than revealing an idea.

With the social and the empirical establishing the guiding public cosmologies for the world of the eighteenth century, the interest in character and individuality became defined complementarily as the fascination with spirit, emotion, and sexuality—potential sources of nonscientific and private knowledge, perhaps even antiscientific and antisocial.

Character had been a basic seventeenth-century obsession. Character books, character sketches, the typing of vocation and habits of mind, the depiction of humours, the evolution of acting style—all were bent toward understanding the problem of personal style in both literature and life. The effort of the early eighteenth-century periodical essay was to establish a personal voice in close connection with the reader, to be reflected later in novelistic experimentation with the varieties of subjective narrative— first persona, epistolary, idiosyncratic detachment. In contrast to the desire to explain, typical of science and society, the novel tried to convey the nuances of feeling to its audience, to explore character, to understand what new character types were needed to meet the demands of the new age, and to discover at what cost these new natures would be purchased.

The novel thus explored the personal world, or more precisely, the world created by an individual perception of things. In a world of upheaval, an increasingly anonymous world in which old orders threatened to crumble in the face of new economic and political imperatives, individuals wondered how they would survive. With God, every being had a specific place, a foundation of existence; with society and perhaps without God came the possibility of role-playing and self-creation, and the necessarily accompanying anxiety: who am I really? Definition from the outside, through the eyes of others, became easier than definition from within. When Robert Burns writes that he wishes we all had the power "to see ourselves as others see us," he whimsically states a deeply felt preoccupation of his age, with its constant invocation of etiquette and the standard of others.

Sterne in *Tristram Shandy* brings together all of the basic character-istics of affective literature: its satire, its sexual reference, its attack on systematic knowledge, its emphasis on feeling unmediated or undistorted by language, its disdain for traditional literary form, its associativeness, and even its fascination with familiar and domestic settings. What Sterne so richly adds, aside from his virtuoso handling of these elements, is the most elaborate form of what I would call the restoration of the reader. *Tristram* is about the aesthetics of connection, not so much the quarrying of individual bits and pieces as the way they are held together. To enjoy it, you have to be committed to Tristram and his voice. The eighteenth-century novel is like a soap opera in its potentially infinite extension, and, like *Tristram* and *Clarissa*, it was frequently published that way. One of its main aesthetic elements is the sense of continuity, of journeying with the hero, in Fielding's stagecoach or inside Tristram's or Clarissa's head. *Tristram Shandy* continues as long as Sterne's life and is coextensive with it, because it is a restorative for his life, like the inked page that soothes the burn on Phutatorius' penis. The author is finally realized and justified through the work: if it is coherent, he is coherent. No artificial self has to be constructed according to any traditional standards. The goal of this litera-ture is to express, discover, and thereby cure a self within. The immediacy of the text, Tristram's willingness to include all possible present moments, undermines any belief that knowledge is timeless: who does wind your clock, he asks, and is it done only once a month? This is not the immediacy of Donne's "Batter my Heart, three-personed God," in which the violence of the language makes up for the keenly felt distance between the speaker and God. This is the immediacy of forgetfulness, of the casual moments of inattention, of what should be left out in any well-ordered world but is included instead. Every detail that conveys the insanity of Swift's narrator in *A Tale of a Tub* conveys Tristram's health—the willingness to be un-planned and unpremeditated. If the magic of the unfallen language cannot be restored to literature, at least the magic of the instant moment of time, the immediate response, the incautious emotion, can be.

Now I have come to two related issues: the first is the anti-affective counterstrain, the detached and magisterial pose that meets the problems of a more complex society by demanding further and further standards. I mean of course the question of Samuel Johnson. When Thomas Tyr-whitt attacks the authenticity of Chatterton's Rowley poems and Johnson attacks Macpherson's Ossian, standards are being brought to bear: consis-tency and regularity, not inspiration and affection, must justify the work. Neither Tyrwhitt nor Johnson ever asks whether a fake fifteenth-century work can nevertheless be real poetry. The second and connected issue is one that affective literature tries to deal with but essentially only palliates, the problem that arises when writers are no longer the possession of a class or a coterie and must sell themselves along with their ideas. I mean the problem of fame.

Fame, affection, and Johnson meet crucially in Johnson's *Life of Savage* (1744), a work that *must* be rooted in personal affection, for Johnson and Savage roamed the London streets together, and the *Life* is as close as we get to a full-scale depiction of someone for whom Johnson had deep feeling. But in it there is little of the passionate celebration of friendship that animates Pope's poetical tributes to Bolingbroke in *Essay on Man* or to Swift in the *Dunciad*. Even though Johnson is writing prose, he seems to have banished feeling, not only to hide his personal pain, but also to make clearer whatever lesson Savage's life has to offer. Savage becomes for Johnson essentially a type of the mad seeker for renown, possessed with a frenzy to succeed that ends only in disappointment and death. The critic stands aside, contemplates his antitype and watches, saddened but measured in his conclusions. Resignation and stoicism, as in "The Vanity of Human Wishes," seems to be the only answer. As Gray's "Elegy" implies, if the paths of glory lead but to the grave, it is better to be a mute inglorious Milton. Or, in Johnson's more elevated implication, the long view of critical abstraction is the escape from individual scrabbling, transience, and death. To repress his feeling for Savage is a small price for Johnson to pay for this wisdom. Unlike Pope's effort to define himself against Atticus, unlike Richardson's and Defoe's splitting into their various narrators, unlike Sterne's invention of the polymorphous Tristram, Johnson's goal is not to try to explore himself through others. He prefers impersonality. Thus, whereas all the work of Pope and the others in some way aims toward an affective synthesis, Johnson considers the work of criticism to be a work of repression or at best pruning, a way to stop the reader from doing things he would certainly do if Johnson were not around to wag a cautionary finger. The sense of the self in Johnson's writing is not an opening into variousness but a limiting, a consolidation for the harsh winter of real life: "life protracted is protracted woe." Even in the relentless questioning and probing that is part of his characterization in Boswell's *Life*, the end product is "Dr. Johnson," an icon uttering maxims.

Fame brings the basic problem of affective literature home to the reader because the ultimate end of personalizing the author and touching the reader with his story is to make the author in some way a model for the reader's own self-exploration. The spiritual autobiographers of previous centuries all followed essentially the same pattern. But in the eighteenth century the secular autobiographers, fictional or otherwise, made it an open market for possible new selves. These people could teach you to live in your own time, which their works implied you were probably having some trouble doing. In "The Vanity of Human Wishes," Johnson says that in the age of Democritus, "man was of a piece." Now, he implies, we need to find and assert the eternal values that will pull us together or at least plaster over the fragments.

The great eighteenth-century writers saw in literature a way of shaping the shards of private personality into a being made of words. So too they created the paradox—and when would it become destructive?— of an intellectual community that defined itself through an aesthetic of self-isolation. Johnson's career is instructive not least because his attitude toward the relation of literature and life and the proper function of critical discourse still so influences our own. Writing for Johnson seems to have been a structure of control stretched over what he believed to be his essential craziness. Empiricism had introduced uncertainty into the personal world at the same time that it seemed to introduce clarity into the external world. Both Locke and Hume subordinated the question of personal identity to questions of perception and causality. But what happens when the tabula rasa—the blank self on which the facts of experience wrote— was discovered to have elements sub rosa that experience didn't seem to account for, elements that in fact disrupted perception and the ability to understand the clear and distinct? Samuel Johnson embodies the materialist despair that was the dark side of empiricism: Man is totally matter and therefore there is an absolute gulf between man and God. Yet "The Vanity of Human Wishes," with its urge toward the eternal and its hatred of a world based on fame and money, its mockery of heroic aspiration, was also the first of Johnson's works to be published under his own name.

Writing was for Johnson an escape from an almost constant self-disapproval—his supreme effort to repress and control what he considered to be repellent parts of personality, from his love of chivalry to his tendency to sloth. Writing was not an expression of the self but a purification, and Johnson especially liked to write the lives of doctors and physicians, to explore the ways they had objectified and thereby subordinated their human frailties. As his creed guided him, so his critical precepts were meant to guide the fallible sensibilities of his audience, so rudderless without him. Fiction and the imagination were fraught with danger, for they appealed to the part of his nature over which he had no obvious control. His own inability to live up to his ideal vision of himself turned him against the possible benefits of affection, myth, and escape. Johnson thought that the construction of a monolithic and impersonal literary image insured his eternal transcendence of the mean world of the flesh. Richard Savage's fatal ambition to be recognized was a cautionary tale. He wanted to be seen as an individual, and the effort to be individual in that way marked you for disaster. To avoid the inconclusiveness of Rasselas' search for the appropriate and final choice of life, Johnson's choice of life was to become a literary critic, and finally, as Frances Burney reports, to speak *Ramblers* on request. But the main residue of Johnson's change from the anonymous writer of parliamentary debates to the magisterial rhythms of "Dr. Johnson" was something that by fighting against he had turned into—a famous person. Fame meant living more in words than in life, being a name rather than a person. Wittingly or not, Johnson himself had fallen victim to "the fever of renown."

To concentrate on the maxims of Johnsonian criticism without trying to understand why that style was created or what needs in his audience it served is like concentrating solely upon the anecdotal, the Boswellian Johnson. Both of these Johnsons, and they often appear in tandem, divert us from the actual confusions and uncertainties in Johnson's point of view. They adopt and even purify Johnson's practice, in *The Life of Savage* and elsewhere, of leaving feelings behind and concentrating instead on the eternal and the constant. No admirer of the Boswellian Johnson, no one whose choice of life has been nurtured under Johnson's solid shadow, is, for example, very comfortable with Mrs. Thrale's view of him. In a 1975 lecture, entitled "Images of Samuel Johnson," Wimsatt called her account "confused and inconsistent . . . without perspective and unredeemed"—in which Johnson speaks wisdom on one page and bangs his head against the table on the next. But the possibility remains that Mrs. Thrale's unblinking willingness to face Johnson's "inconsistencies" helps us understand the combat between personal eccentricity and magisterial self-control in the character that fascinated his contemporaries more clearly than does Boswell's view of his perpetually self-assured eminence.

Wimsatt and Beardsley might in these terms be considered not only as critical but also as psychical Johnsonians. Like Johnson, they try to ward off the unnameable and the unspecifiable, and make light of our efforts to resist their allure. "The affective fallacy," they write, "begins by trying to derive that standard of criticism from the psychological effects of the poem and ends in impressionism and relativism" (21). Like Clarissa, once the critic steps out of the garden gate of verifiable aesthetic objects and categories, she will become prey to emotions and fall to the bottom of the pit. Feelings are always the same; only the intelligence evolves. Affection and emotion, in other words, have no gradations. You either don't like someone or you go to bed with them. Perhaps this is a masculine critical attitude, or at least as masculinity was defined by the eighteenth century, with that need for control over otherwise destructive emotions. But what seems more certain is that it is an attitude that prevents us from understanding what much of eighteenth-century literature was trying to accomplish and therefore from understanding the nature of eighteenth-century culture.

I spoke of Wimsatt and Beardsley's mockery of the incomplete verbal object. But incompletion, willful incompletion, can express striving, the effort to grapple consciously with problems that finally prove too large to be pinned down on the page. One of Johnson's great fears was the imagination, a fear that arose from the incredible power of moral persuasion he ascribed to mimetic forms. Johnson's Don Quixote, unlike ours (or even Cervantes'), was trapped by imagination, not liberated by it to interpret the world for himself. Johnson is in this way a curious mixture of Swift and the narrator of *A Tale of a Tub* (as perhaps Swift was as well)—whose simultaneous fear and disdain of the aimless powers of the mind feed on each other in an incessant cannibalism. Johnson attacked romance and fiction because "they teach young minds to expect strange adventures." His own susceptibility to expectation, his own inability to live up to his vision of himself, turned him against imagination's possible benefits. The *Life of Savage*, like many of Johnson's other works, explores the fatal inability of the individual in early industrial society to live without expectations. Johnson's criticism affirmed the lesson. The choice of life, like Clarissa's step away from family and toward freedom, was foredoomed by the first step: "life protracted is protracted woe."

Johnson's primary defense against those expectations was his belief in eternity and objectivity. In his writings he created a special language, which Carey McIntosh in *The Choice of Life* has called "supercolossally splendid" and a special voice, which McIntosh whimsically describes as "a bardic-pathetic indoctrinating apparatus." [4] But Johnson's language, and the escape from the frailties of personality it implied, distanced him as well from the problems of maturity, choice, and ambivalence, for which the incomplete affective form was much more suitable. Johnson recoiling from the self-destructive Savage in 1744 must be faced by Boswell embracing the self-created Johnson in 1781. Instead of truly freeing him, his critical method imprisoned him more firmly—like Mrs. Thrale's chains— and spawned a line of literary critics constantly in fealty to the past and to their own self-imposed impersonality. [5] Whether one of these inheritors is the departmental "Johnson man," to invoke a prefeminist catchphrase, or wants to reveal "my Johnson," his attitude toward language is the same. The first inheritor has raised the umbrella of Johnson's words to ward off the shocks of an un-Johnsonian world, while the second has built his own Johnson from those same words to brandish it at others.

So I return to Wimsatt and Beardsley in another way, since my main interest here is the critics and students of the eighteenth century and how our knowledge of its literature and culture can be expanded. The paradox that I hint at is that it may be more difficult to tease out the mysteries of affective and intentionally created literature than it is to understand the works of intellectual and self-contained passion that seem to be the proper subjects of Wimsattian and Beardsleyan approval. There is a greater need for the critic's imaginative sympathy with a work, with its gaps and faults as well as with its successes. The need to evaluate and judge in terms of literary greatness must I think be replaced with an urge to understand. The works of the highest quality may be not the most perfect, but the ones that tease and challenge our understanding the most. The intention to affect needs to be explored, and the effort to move our feelings, our more involuntary emotions, should be given as much consideration as the effort to move our intellects. If we downgrade a work because it makes us feel, we are following the neo-Johnsonian assumption that feeling is necessarily a lower human activity. But why a work should make us cry and what that crying tells us about the similarities between our culture and the culture that produced the work seems to me to be a legitimate and fascinating critical issue. The writers and the works that attempt to get away from mere rhetoric, and launch a concerted attack on traditional forms in the name of a more directly expressed emotion, can not be properly investigated let alone judged by critical precepts that refuse consideration to emotion in either the author or the audience.

The problem is so acute, I think, not only because Johnson has been the model for most English-writing literary critics, but also because he has defined particularly the critic as moral teacher. Wimsatt and Beardsley confirm this assumption when they consider the main purveyors of the intentional fallacy to be "the introspective amateurs and soul-cultivators," while the main proponent of the affective fallacy is "the contagious teacher, the poetic radiator" (29). The teacher, in other words, should be as impersonal as the critic, as unauthored as the poem, with no obligation to acknowledge that he is an individual before an audience. Once again, we encounter a typical attitude toward teaching in the university: if you are smart enough, you can teach. What others might call the skills of teaching are for Wimsatt and Beardsley only the intellectually disreputable tricks of an entertainer and showman, meant to engage the emotions of the audience, not its mind. Appropriately enough, the villains of the affective fallacy article are equally Adolf Hitler and William Lyon Phelps.

But we now know or are beginning to know that teaching can be a craft and that there are many things to be learned that are not just drunk in with the great books. So we must also allow gradations to the feelings and the affections, in subject matter as well as presentation. Toward the end of the affective fallacy essay, Wimsatt and Beardsley point out that "all poetry, so far as separate from history, tends to be formulas of emotion" (37), as if emotion had no history and history no emotion. Our aim might be instead to try to understand why certain kinds of feelings (and not others) have

been reduced to formulas, how long such formulas last, what the characteristic formulas of different eras are, and how we may free ourselves from
the formulas we unknowingly accept. The urge to theorize and regularize
ignores the ways in which literature is a constantly evolving interchange
about the nature of cultural meaning. The eighteenth century is especially
bad hunting ground for such certainties because it marks the beginning
of a mass culture and a literature, too poorly understood, that made its
appeal not to people with the same class assumptions, but to a disparate
people, with different origins but similar fears and hopes. Johnson tried to
domesticate the imagination and replace the old elitist class with the elitist
Literary Club, and the Romantics followed suit by establishing an elitism
of feeling that may have reached a dead end in Hardy's Sue Bridehead—
"the epicure of the emotions." By the end of the nineteenth century the
self-conscious avant-garde had further institutionalized the separation of
popular from elitist art, at least as far as critics were concerned. In our own
time, those barriers have eroded considerably. Defensiveness is no longer
the only appropriate response; the first step into feeling no longer entails a
total fall.

Intention and Affection as negative categories, the appeal to the feelings
as opposed to the appeal to the intellect—such views have been promulgated by a criticism more interested in judgment and keeping up standards
than in understanding, a criticism constricted by the emotionally and historically ungrounded literary objects it chose to contemplate. Johnson has
been such a critical forefather for that tradition because he was willing to
tell his audience what they ought to appreciate and how they ought to go
about doing it. He constructed himself on the standards of eternity, with
as little debt to other human beings as possible, unless they had done the
same. And so he has left us a heritage of compartmentalized life and work,
cause and effect. By restoring his human complexity to him, and our own
to ourselves, we might better be able to end the bad effects of a literary
criticism so intent on finding answers and turn to one more attuned to
questions. Literary criticism stands between literature and life. It is up to
us all now, critics and audience alike, whether it is to be a bridge or a
barricade.

Notes

This essay is an expanded version of a lecture originally given at the University of
Rochester in 1974.

1 I quote from W. K. Wimsatt, jr., *The Verbal Icon: Studies in the Meaning of
Poetry* (Lexington: University of Kentucky Press, 1954). The title page refers to
the "*two preliminary essays written in collaboration with Monroe C. Beards-*

ley." They first appeared in the *Sewanee Review*, 54 (Summer 1946) ("The Intentional Fallacy") and 57 (Winter 1949) ("The Affective Fallacy"). A third collaboration, "The Concept of Meter: An Exercise in Abstraction," appeared in *PMLA*, 74 (1959), 585–98, as well as in Wimsatt's collection, *Hateful Contraries: Studies in Literature and Criticism* (Lexington: University of Kentucky Press, 1965), 108–45.

2 Not that Wimsatt thought the moral would be simple. "If it is possible . . . that a poem, even a great poem, may fall short of being moral—or to put it another way, if it is true that starting with the fixity of dogma we cannot hope to define the content of poems—it is yet true that poems as empirically discovered and tested do tend, within their limits and given the peculiar *données* or presuppositions of each, to point toward the higher integration of dogma. . . . The greatest poetry will be morally right, even though perhaps obscurely so, in groping confusions of will and knowledge—as *Oedipus the King* foreshadows *Lear*." See "Poetry and Morals: A Relation Reargued" in *The Verbal Icon* 100.

3 At the time that the essays originally appeared, the *Sewanee Review* was under the strong influence of the Fugitives. Few if any other academic literary journals would have been hospitable to such theoretical discussions of issues of evaluation and interpretation. Wimsatt's commitment to his theoretical polemic extended to his teaching as well. Typically he taught two graduate courses—the Age of Johnson and the History of Criticism, based primarily on the book *Literary Criticism: A Short History* he wrote with Cleanth Brooks (New York: Random House, 1957). Despite his own interest in historical detail that surfaced with *The Portraits of Alexander Pope* (New Haven: Yale, 1965), Wimsatt's often expressed view was that the criticism course was for "real" students, while the Johnson course was for antiquarians and harmless drudges. Authentic critical analysis, he implied, could not possibly be done on this material. The easiest way to get a good grade was therefore to do a straight New Critical reading of any text, even if, for most of those taking the course, it was hardly the most interesting topic to explore. Yet to do otherwise often invited ridicule. There are many such stories. But Peter Manning, who also took the Age of Johnson course, has reminded me of an incident I have totally repressed. Wimsatt was returning the graded version of a paper I had delivered in class the week before. Hurling it down the table at me, he said, "Another paper spattered with information, Mr. Braudy," as if the eternal monuments of poetry needed constant protection from the pigeon droppings of historical detail.

4 Carey MacIntosh, *The Choice of Life* (New Haven: Yale University Press, 1973), 97.

5 I refer here to Katherine Balderston's essay "Johnson's Vile Melancholy," in *The Age of Johnson*, ed. F. W. Hilles (New Haven: Yale University Press, 1949), 3–14, in which she presents evidence that Johnson and Mrs. Thrale had a compact by which, it seems, when Johnson was taken by fits, she would chain him to a kind of whipping post and beat him until the crisis subsided.

3 *Michael McKeon*

Cultural Crisis and Dialectical Method: Destabilizing Augustan Literature

My aim in the following pages is in part autobiographical. Twenty years ago, as a graduate student, I began the long process of coming to know and value Augustan literature with what now seems an authentic but ill-defined sense of resistance to the major assumptions that underlay its study at that time. Since then, I have gradually learned to identify the problem more clearly—not so much through the formulation of an alternative theory of Augustan literature, as by recognizing, in the way I have practiced its criticism over the years, certain threads of continuity. These threads suggest at least an alternative perspective on the texts and contexts of Augustan culture; my aim in this essay will be to try to give that perspective some coherence. For this reason, I will be referring primarily to the places in my own writings where, in one way or another, I have registered my understanding of an alternative. It should go without saying that I have often built upon the work of others (as the writings to which I refer will themselves acknowledge). My intention here is in any case not to claim authority, but to document the experience of one scholar who came of age at a time of imminent change (we can now see with hindsight) in the presuppositions of eighteenth-century studies.

I

In my experience, the central assumption of Augustan studies during the 1960s was of a pervasive stability that was taken to characterize not only the literary, but also the political, social, and intellectual activity of the time. Let me begin with the assumption of stability as it colored scholarship in these contextual fields, and then turn more specifically to literary studies.

During the period of my concern, the England that emerged from the Civil War and the Interregnum was generally understood to have embraced with gratitude the comforts and conveniences of a backward-looking reaction. And in a very general way, the assumption of an overarching stability after 1660 took its cue from what appeared to be the lesson of specifically political history. True, the Exclusion Crisis and the Glorious Revolution necessarily complicated that perspective. But certainly after 1688 it seemed possible to speak with confidence of a political stability grounded in a conservative respect for the balanced constitution, derived through a peculiarly English mollification of continental absolutism, and maintained by the managerial power of an ascendant Whig oligarchy. In social relations, the corollary of this view was a vision of a resurgent aristocracy, its normative values of honor, gentility, and patriarchal care tempered to fit the times. There was, of course, the problem of the rising middle class; but in the dominant view twenty years ago, the middle class enjoyed a harmonious coexistence with aristocratic culture at this time because its motivating impulse was to assimilate upward, to seek absorption within the aristocracy. In religion, the transformation of Puritanism into Dissent at the Restoration was seen to have dealt a fatal blow to its doctrinal and political efficacy; and this left the path clear for the via media of Anglican moderation and its forthright invocation of a providence benignly responsive to daily human needs. Finally, in the realm of learning, we were taught to associate the Restoration and early eighteenth century with a thoroughgoing revival of the forms and values of classical—especially Roman—antiquity. And in many respects, the resultant doctrine of "neoclassicism" codified, as normative values that literate contemporaries sought to conserve, precisely those conditions—of order, stability, and continuity—that scholars had found to characterize the period at large. In summary, this was not exactly the "Peace of the Augustans" of an older, Saintsburyan generation; nor did this view deny the continuing existence of conflict within these several realms of experience. Nevertheless, cultural crisis was seen in some definitive way to have been dissipated by the Restoration, replaced by the hard-won satisfaction with hierarchy that is expressed by these salutary, stabilizing exercises in reaction.

One obvious objection to this perspective on the period is that it distorts the broad diversity of Restoration and early eighteenth-century culture by trying to accommodate that diversity to a strictly "political" model. There is, however, a more profound objection to be made, one that also questions this insistence on the distinctness of the several realms of historical experience. This is the objection that by associating political order with the absence of sustained civil strife or effective party opposition, we limit the phenomenon of political instability to an implausibly ostensive model that renders invisible its more subtle (and perhaps, more subtly pervasive) manifestations—like ideological conflict that flourishes beneath or outside the realm of official policy-making. The major thrust of the objection is relevant to the treatment of nonpolitical phenomena as well. In other words, the real problem is not that political had dominated extra-political history, but that the range of activity that may be indicative of instability in any realm of historical experience is a great deal broader, and a great deal more susceptible to interpretation, than had been imagined. In fact—and this is my central point—even those exercises in reaction that I was taught to see as transparently representative of Augustan culture may themselves be subject to a radically alternative reading. The work I have done since graduate school has increasingly encouraged me to entertain this counterintuitive proposition, to question not so much the reality of these reactive movements as their effective meaning. Let me suggest what this might amount to by returning to the summary arguments on which the assumption of stability was based twenty years ago.

First of all, I have learned to see the truth of the thesis that the origins of conservatism, at least in its distinctively modern form, may be traced to Restoration politics. But I have also come to understand conservative thought as a self-consciously provisional and pragmatic affirmation of "tradition" not for its essential or intrinsic value—of which it remains skeptical—but for its political, cultural, and affective instrumentality. Conservatism therefore involves a contradictory sort of belief whose stabilizing motive to conserve what is given is predicated on a destabilized attitude toward what is entailed in that very "givenness." By the same token, it has become difficult to associate the absolutist rule Charles II restored to England eleven years after the epochal beheading of his father with a confident and straightforward doctrine of immemorial royal sovereignty. On the contrary, the Restoration aggravated what was from the outset a contradictory theory. "The dynamic tension that animates absolutism, and that is expressed in the tension between royal will and noble privilege, is the impulse to dissolve the limitations imposed by feudal social relations without also dissolving the implicit sanctions of feudal hierarchy." This is the unfulfillable impulse of absolutist doctrines like the divine right of kings and the patriarchal theory of political obligation, which, however ancient their ultimate sources, are strategic products of an early modern crisis in authority; and the very claim they make to a stabilizing continuity therefore bespeaks the apprehension of present instability and disorder. Indeed, the volatility of such doctrines may be seen in the fact that apologists in 1688 pragmatically justified not the sovereignty but the deposition of the king by reference to what they called "the divine right of providence."[1]

Again, the phenomenon of an aristocratic resurgence in early modern England is no mirage; but its meaning is disparate and problematic. What are we to make of the fact that institutions with which we are likely to associate the long-standing and tacit authority of the aristocracy—institutions like the visitations of the College of Heralds and their recording of genealogies, like sumptuary laws aimed at regulating dress according to social degree, like the legal recourse of *scandalum magnatum,* which empowered peers of the realm to vindicate their honor against the slander of their inferiors—what are we to make of the fact that these apparently "traditional" institutions were of rather recent invention in early modern England? The meaning of such developments—their status as signs either of a confident reaction or of a crisis of confidence—depends no doubt on the larger context in which they occur. And there is an enormous amount of evidence that during the Restoration and early eighteenth century the idea of aristocratic honor, and its attendant belief in patrilineal authority, were being criticized with unprecedented energy. So if there is any value (as some historians have claimed there is) in seeing the innovative political alliance of the latter part of this period as the rule of a "Whig aristocracy," it must also be seen to be suffused with progressive and capitalist values quite inimical to the traditional aristocratic ethos. As for the rising middle class, it is no longer plausible to understand this crucial but elusive phenomenon as the easy assimilation of a suddenly discrete social group. On the contrary, it makes more sense to see the rise of the middle class as inseparable from the rise of a class orientation toward social relations, an orientation that cuts across and transforms all traditional status groups, none more so than the aristocracy. The resurgence of the aristocracy, then, is an apparent continuity that masks discontinuity; and we approach closer to the contradictory heart of the phenomenon when we stress "how individualistic and class criteria are eating away, as it were from within, at a social structure whose external shell still seems roughly assimilable to the status model."[2]

Similar complications may be seen in the spheres of religion and learning. "The reestablishment of the Church of England in 1660 relieved Anglicans of the polarizing threat of a Puritan Commonwealth and encouraged them to embrace more openly those social implications of Reformation teaching which had always been central to Anglicanism, or which had by now been suffused throughout English culture by the radical solvent of Puritan activism." That is, the defeat of immediate and ostensible danger facilitated, at a deeper level, not reactive renovation but pervasive and irresistible innovation. Moreover, the middle way of liberal Anglicanism had more in common with the secularizing tendencies of Weber's "Protestant ethic" than with the church of Hooker or Laud. Evidence for this may be found, I think, in the ready invocation of providence during this period. On the face of it providential argument was a humble resubmission to divine will, but its "very vigor . . . , the polemical urgency and extremity of its presentation, signifies not faith but a crisis of faith." And although "ostensibly (and sincerely) an acknowledgment of God's unknowable power, the doctrine of providence also expresses the will to accommodate divinity to a plan more accessible to human rationality." The discovery that everything is providentially ordained prefigures the suspicion that nothing is. Finally, it is by now a commonplace that the English "Augustan" attitude toward Roman Augustanism was as much negative as normative. More generally, I have come to see English neoclassicism not as a simple renewal of classical standards but as their oblique modernization, a process that submerges the ancient past in a radically empirical and skeptical solution that leaves nothing unchanged. To understand the neoclassical, pseudo-Aristotelian "unities of time and place" we must look less to classical authority than to the empirical revolution in epistemology.[3]

Like the assumption of stability which it undertakes to revise, the foregoing account proposes summary positions on a broad and complicated range of historical developments. What are the principles that unite these disparate essays in revision? I think they can be described under two headings. First, a characteristic discovery implied in these several revisionist arguments is that what looks superficially like a revival of traditional forms, categories, or activities may better be understood as an unstable compound whose residual ties to past practices cannot conceal its distinctly innovative character. In the extreme instance, it might even be said that the systematic function of persistence is to facilitate change. Second, these arguments adduce evidence that the affirmation of tradition and stability is likely to be most insistent precisely at those moments when tradition and stability are most thought to be endangered. Both of these revisionist principles depend upon the contradictory insight that the symbolic enactment—through language and behavior—of a system of order signifies not order but crisis, implying through the very invocation of stability an effort to rectify a felt condition of instability. "The dangerously shifting ground of crisis is inseparable from the effort at ideological stabilization it evokes, which proclaims its persistent affiliation to crisis in the very attempt to overcome and negate it."[4]

What I have called here the "contradictory insight" into the proximity of order and crisis, of stability and instability, has been fundamental to my development as a student of Augustan culture. Over the years I have tried to give it theoretical substance and methodological flexibility by drawing upon, first writers in the Marxist tradition, then Marx himself. And in these terms, the disclosure of crisis within an apparently stable state is less a paradox than the effect of a dialectical method of reading history and its productions whose cardinal principle is the volatile partiality of all apparently stable totalities, and whose cardinal injunction is that historical products become intelligible only when they are resubsumed within the enabling and destabilizing contexts that produced them.[5] In a very real sense, then, dialectical method "would have us see all of history as 'unstable' and 'in crisis,' a contradictory unity divisible into antagonistic periods each of which replicates, in its 'own' domain, the tensions of dialectical process. At the same time, it encourages us to discriminate those crucial historical moments when crisis seems to be redoubled and intensified. Such moments can be known by the way the deep and perpetual contradictions of historical process force themselves to the surface of historical consciousness in the palpable form of warfare, social disruption, or the sort of cultural crisis . . . that entails the transformation of an entire system of cultural values."[6] In describing this transformative process, Marx has recourse to a metaphor according to which the enabling and seemingly natural "forms" of human intercourse come to appear as "fetters" upon it, comparatively accidental and arbitrary conditions of life susceptible now either to critical repudiation or to self-conscious reaffirmation, but no longer intelligible as tacit knowledge.[7]

II

In the years following my graduate study I have come to believe that a major cultural crisis of this sort occurred during the Augustan period. How were the more specifically literary manifestations of this crisis obscured by the dominant literary critical attitudes of the 1960s? Once again, the assumption of stability in literary criticism did not necessarily entail the denial of conflict. Rather, it operated through a consistent tendency to limit critical attention to that aspect of literary usage that seemed to bespeak a stabilizing and regularizing end. In the light of what I have already said, of course, the limitation could never be fully successful, since the evidence of instability was to some degree implicit in the very impulse of writers to diminish and contain it. And looking back, this was probably the most compelling argument against the dominant critical affirmation of an Augustan "order": the nagging sense that only a profound apprehension of disorder could have occasioned these remarkable exercises in defensive reinforcement. In fact, since the evidence of disorder was apparent in many Augustan writers even on the level of literary form, the assumption of stability required support by a range of critical strategies that provided for this evidence an ingenious counterinterpretation. These strategies may be discussed under two general headings.

The first of these strategies was needed to account for the extraordinary hybridization of generic form that took place during the Augustan period. At the center of this phenomenon was the ascendancy of ironic, parodic, and mock heroic forms, and they were nowhere more fully developed than in canonical authors like Swift and Pope. The arguments used to counter this disturbing evidence of unstable mixture were various and persuasive. For example, canonical mock heroic actually reaffirms the heroic orthodoxy (it was said) by mocking unworthy modern pretenders to it. The truth of this could be seen in the fact that writers like Pope used formal mixtures only in the substantive critique of modernist mixture. Thus the generic heterogeneity of *The Dunciad Variorum* (1728–29) might be explained as implicit parody of the mixed forms of the modernists, which also sustained more explicit attack in such lines as Pope's account of how, in the chaos of Grub Street writings, "Tragedy and Comedy embrace; / How Farce and Epic get a jumbled race."[8] On the other hand, works like *The Dunciad* (and *Absalom and Achitophel* before it) could also be felt, in their brilliance, to cross the invisible line between "mock epic" and the genuine epic of modernity, thereby laying claim in the end to a deeper generic unity and historical continuity.

But is it true, I wondered, that Augustan mock epic leaves the ancient epic untouched by its satire? Is it mistaken to hear a diminishing reflection on the *Iliad* in Swift's allusion to "Those Bully *Greeks*" in *A Description of a City Shower* (1710); or in the opening lines of *The Rape of the Lock* (1714): "What dire Offence from am'rous Causes springs, / What mighty Contests rise from trivial Things, / I sing—"?[9] How can we fail to detect, as at least one major element in Swift's mock pastorals, a furious assault on a tradition whose illusions were patently there from the very beginning? And what of those nonparodic hybrids, the verse essays, in which Pope took such earnest pride? Was it perhaps plausible to understand *An Essay on Man* (1733–34), with its nervous prose addition of prefatory "arguments" and explanatory footnotes, as an experiment in accommodating epic matter to an ineluctably alien age in which "poetry" and "philosophy" were beginning to enter into the modern mutual exclusion of verse and prose, the "imaginative" and the "discursive"? In graduate school I had learned that the proper question to ask of Pope's verse essays was not "Is it good philosophy?" but "Is it good poetry?" I was increasingly tempted to wonder, however, if their enervated thought and their volatile form both might owe to Pope's residual discomfort with the modernizing protocols he was in the process of internalizing. Once we juxtapose the verse essays not with the suprahistorical example of Lucretius but with the mock epic effects and the novelistic narratives with which they are contemporary, we can see them as generic experiments characteristic of a period of crisis.

In time I came to believe that by minimizing the profound ambivalence of the Augustans toward the classical forms, the criticism that had dominated my graduate education was also enabled to overlook their full participation in the vice of mixture which they castigated in their enemies.[10] I now think that the brilliance of the Augustans is fully a function of this unstable vulnerability, and that it cannot be appreciated apart from the crisis which contemporaries called the quarrel of the ancients and the moderns. The example of Swift and Pope teaches us that to be an effective "ancient" in a modern age is necessarily to be a cryptomodern, dedicated to the shoring up of tradition in the most innovative ways imaginable.

Because Augustan writers routinely voiced their positions on political, social, and religious matters, literary critics have been obliged to engage, at some level, many of the difficult "contextual" issues that I discussed above. The second of the critical strategies that dominated the reading of Augustan literature during my graduate education helped foreclose the difficulties entailed in this obligation by delimiting and stabilizing the personality—and the person—of the author. Here, too, the flowering of ironic and parodic forms is central to the problem of instability, since it was through the practice of such forms that Augustan writers encountered the necessity of impersonation.

Apparently, contemporary readers had some difficulty with this technique. In 1710, Swift added an "Apology" to *A Tale of a Tub* (1704) which sought to disarm his detractors by ingenuously observing (among other things) *"that there generally runs an Irony through the Thread of the whole Book, which the Men of Tast will observe and distinguish, and which will render some Objections that have been made, very weak and insignificant."* In fact, *"some of those Passages in this Discourse, which appear most liable to Objection are what they call Parodies, where the Author personates the Style and Manner of other Writers, whom he has a mind to expose."* [11] Certainly, modern critics have been disarmed by such disclaimers. Not that Swift's basic concern to disclose the operation of irony is suspect. But in Augustan studies, the wholesale deployment of the doctrine of the "persona" or "mask" had the effect of detaching the disturbing material expressed in satiric impersonation from the lived experience of the author. The doctrine of the persona reified impersonation as artistic technique: not really what the author is "saying," but an instrument he's momentarily "using" to artistic ends that may be segregated from the personality and personhood of the author himself. The problem with this critical strategy is that it seemed to require dispensing with the rhetorical (as distinct from the "artistic") motive for impersonation, leaving in its place an authorial personage sanitized into stability: a blandly unobjectionable Swift who never really meant to hurt anyone, a genial and placid Pope dispossessed of all meanness and paranoia.[12] From this perspective, authorial motives were paradoxically irreconcilable with the motives that authorized one's writing.

Yet in fact, Swift's impersonations have an uncanny way of evoking their author. In the appended "Apology" for the *Tale*, for example, Swift regrets the appearance in the same volume of the "Discourse Concerning the Mechanical Operation of the Spirit," "*a most imperfect Sketch with the Addition of a few loose Hints, which . . . was a sufficient Surprize to see . . . pieced up together*" by the printer.[13] But when we turn our attention from this apology to the epistolary "imperfect sketch" to which it refers, we find Swift impersonating the modern author with what he fatuously commends as "Modern Excuses, for Haste and Negligence": "I desire you will be my Witness to the World, it was but Yesterday, when You and I began accidentally to fall into Discourse on this Matter: That I was not very well, when we parted; That the Post is in such haste, I have had no manner of Time to digest it into Order, or correct the Style . . ."[14] Read in isolation, this passage may be felt to reinforce the familiar "order" entailed in the prospect of Swift the parodist dependably distinct from his Other. The juxtaposition of the two passages, however, dialectically transforms the prospect of "order" into one of "crisis," in which Swift and his Other are all at once on the verge of collapsing into sameness.

Understood in these terms, the crisis announced by the Augustan obsession with ironic impersonation—and effaced by the critical stabilization of personality—is one expression of the early modern crisis of the autonomous subject. Confronted by the specter of the spuriously self-sufficient individual, the cheerful modern who projects his own self-interest onto the world, the Augustan satirists responded with manifest loathing and repudiation.[15] And yet one of the things "masked" by the contempt implicit in the Augustan impersonation of modern selfishness is the deeply submerged but vitally accessible intuition of a shared vulnerability. Although I believe it is important, I do not mean by this only that Swift and Pope evince a wavering and tormented sense of their own implication in the substance of what they attack—that is, in the political, social, and religious individualism of their times. My main point is that even in the formal mode they adopted for this supreme act of alienation, they reproduced the very singularity and self-regarding individuation they meant to denounce.

Readers will already have recognized, in the foregoing account of the critical assumption of stable literary forms and unitary authorial persons, the familiar argument of "aesthetic" autonomy. Works that are authentically literary (it might be paraphrased) must instantiate generic forms that are unequivocally aesthetic in character, and must themselves be products of the activity of the author solely in his artistic capacity. Clearly, this aesthetic perspective on the nature of literary works would have been foreign to the well-known "moral," "rhetorical," and "didactic" concerns of Augustan writers. And it is to the credit of the eighteenth-century critics I read as a student that they tended to recognize the discrepancy between Augustan and modern attitudes toward the literary, even if they did not also acknowledge the problematic enactment of this discrepancy in their own critical procedures. To understand fully the crisis of the Augustans, however, we would be wrong, I think, to see them simply as having attributed to literature a function diametrically opposed to that of the modern, aesthetic perspective. Rather, Augustan literature is best seen as in transitional process toward the modern orthodoxy of aesthetic autonomy, evincing in subtle ways a precursory affinity for that as-yet-unformulated orthodoxy even as it ostensibly resists the notion of literature's separation from other human preoccupations and activities. Indeed, this view may allow the most direct access available to the contradictory instability of Augustan literature, and I will conclude my essay by exploring it in greater detail, limiting my attention for convenience to the paradigmatic case of Augustan satire and the relation between literature and politics it articulates. As might be expected, my discussion will recur to some of the concerns raised earlier in the essay.

III

Today no less than twenty years ago, the Augustan period is generally understood as one in which politics and literature enjoyed a close association. To put the case at its simplest and most persuasive, Augustan authors tend to write "about" political subjects, and their writings are suffused with a recognition—even, an insistence—that politics and literature are intimately connected to one another. My aim is not so much to challenge this understanding (since I share it), as to complicate it. My contention about Augustan literature belongs to a more general argument that the close association of politics and literature in eighteenth-century England is most instructively seen as part of a larger historical movement—the modern division of knowledge—that consists in their discrimination.[16] Eighteenth-century authors differ from their predecessors not in conceiving the relation between politics and literature (which is really a traditional if tacit point of wisdom), but in conceiving that relation with an unprecedented self-consciousness. This transformation—the change from a tacit assumption, to an explicit assertion, of the connectedness of politics and literature—signals a crisis in that relationship. By the same token, the characteristically emphatic didacticism of the literature of this period is a sign not of a confident politico-ethical engagement, but of a crisis in confidence whereby the tacit pedagogic function of literature is decisively thrown into question.

One way of describing this crisis would be as a function of the emergence of the categories "politics" and "literature" in their modern senses. For of course in a general sense, the world has always had both "politics" and "literature." What is distinctive about the modern status of these categories is that they are defined, dialectically, against each other. And so in another sense, "politics" and "literature" attain their recognizable, modern existence only when they are put in opposition. Henceforth the very effort to mediate and bridge the gap between them presupposes and reinforces their division. I will concentrate here on satiric literature because I think its very dominance during the Augustan period, although it would seem to challenge the claim that literature and politics now divide against each other, in fact should be seen as one sign of that growing division. But in order to vindicate this apparent paradox, I will begin not with the category "literature" but with "politics."

The crucial precondition for the separation of politics and literature in the early modern period is the Renaissance crisis of secularization, the foundational division of politics from religion. The Machiavellian separation of "is" from "ought" constituted politics apart from the spiritual standard to which it thus far had been subordinated.[17] The new language of political analysis in eighteenth-century England was that of "interest" quantified according to exclusively practical and material considerations. Now, it is clear enough that many contemporaries understood this new category of "politics" as the product of a destructive division, a mutilated part of a former whole. The pejorative sense of the "Machiavellian," for example, points to just such a perception. Sir Lewis Namier and his school taught an earlier generation of eighteenth-century historians to see political management, patronage, and the bartering of place and influence as the brand of politics peculiar to an age in which causes and principles had temporarily ceased to animate people's ambitions.[18] But it may be more accurate to see these self-conscious exercises in the administration of interest as the means by which first contemporaries, and then their historians, recognized the emergence of a distinct mode of human behavior: not a special brand of politics but "politics" as such. In this respect, the early eighteenth-century outcry against political "corruption" is really an outcry against politics—against the pursuit of practical and material self-interest conceived as an autonomous, and therefore self-vindicating, activity. It is in this extended sense that Fielding's Shamela is a "young Politician," and that Fielding's Jonathan Wild and Sir Robert Walpole converge in the memorable figure of the "great man," who employs "those great arts which the vulgar call treachery, dissembling, promising, lying, falsehood, etc., but which are by GREAT men summed up in the collective name of policy, or politics, or rather pollitrics. . . ."[19]

How is the ascendancy of satire, and more generally the constitution of the category "literature" itself, related to the emergence of this sense of the "political"? As the example of Fielding reminds us, early eighteenth-century writers are strenuously devoted to the treatment of political subjects. Yet the tendency of that devotion is, I think, to encourage the gradual disjunction of "politics" and "literature." The developing critique of the system of political patronage is a case in point, since it illuminated the outlines of the emerging literary system in two related ways. First, it helped spark the Augustan critique of literary patronage—the traditional means by which writing had been supported—as nothing more than a specialized version of political prostitution. The satire of patronage is an important theme in Pope's *Dunciad* even before he elevates the poet laureate—the national symbol of patronized corruption—to the role of King of Dulness in 1743. And the crucial difference between Pope's epistle "To Augustus" (1737) and the Horatian model it imitates so scrupulously is the implicit ludicrousness of seeking literary patronage from George II.[20] But the general critique of political patronage also sparked the conviction that modern writers, unlike modern court functionaries, had a clear alternative to political prostitution. This was the alternative of the literary marketplace, which promised to free writers from "politics" by making them independent of patronage. One of Pope's most trenchant criticisms of his Grub Street rivals is that they, unlike he, had experienced no success with the public.[21] So the decline of patronage amounted to a decline in the direct and visible relation between writers and what was increasingly seen as an alien political establishment.

But as *Peri Bathous* (1727) attests so brilliantly, Pope also knew (if others did not) that the dependence of the writer on the marketplace entailed its own sort of "political" subjection, a peculiarly modern corruption that seemed to him even more sinister and debilitating than the old system of patronage. The characteristic energy of Pope's later poems has something to do with his tireless struggle to escape this double bind, to define himself as a poet in a new way by delimiting a space apart from the politics of both patronage and publication. In the epistle "To Arbuthnot" (1735), this struggle takes the form of an alternating satire upon the amateur and the professional postures of the poet. What remains after their exclusion is the persecuted and irascible figure of Pope himself, seemingly above the fray of self-interested prostitution. True, by its end the poem has devolved into an exercise in strenuous self-promotion. But the mechanism is, in a sense, the very opposite of political corruption. For in the schemes of dependence that Pope resists, the telltale sign of corruption is a degrading self-interest that sells the poet's integrity to an alien power. But in the epistle "To Arbuthnot," integrity is indistinguishable from a positive sort of self-interest quite literally conceived as an unquenchable interest in oneself. Inexorably the figures of the world at large—Arbuthnot, Addison, Pope's father, even (with the aid of a crucial grammatical ambiguity) Lord Hervey himself—become partial projections of the poet's ample and richly transformative subjectivity. Dramatic dialogue collapses into monologue, Horatian epistle into self-address, rhetorical persuasion into self-expression. In the very typography of the later poems we see emblematized the psychological and aesthetic transcendence of the political world these poems purport to engage: above, the elegantly acerbic verse of the consummate tastemonger; below, the densely prosaic footnotes documenting the merely historical existence of his subjects—a history justly condemned, but for the poet's own exertions, to oblivion. In the prefatory material to *The Dunciad* Pope gives his own version of the topos of poetic immortality: "The *Poem was not made for these Authors, but these Authors for the Poem. . . . It is only in this monument that they must expect to survive. . . ."* [22]

   If it is true that Augustan poets write frequently and passionately on political themes, it's also true that their mode is overwhelmingly that of mock panegyric or directly satirical critique—or, as in Swift's "Satirical Elegy on the Death of a late Famous General" (written 1722), an impatient modulation from the one to the other. Increasingly, the only viable form of heroic poetry is a radical species of mock heroic whose mockery takes in not only the central object of attack, but also the putatively normative standard of heroism. Behind this development lies an extended crisis in the authority of public leaders. The celebrated ambivalence of Marvell's "Horatian Ode" (written 1650), for example, owes at least in part to the success of Cromwell in forcing upon England the difficult question of who is the *real* Caesar, a question Marvell propounds by self-consciously experimenting with an extraordinary range of poetic topics in praise of civic power. Once power is separated from its tacit authority and becomes an ad hoc possession, to be retroactively rationalized by any means available, the panegyric poet is left in an uncomfortable position. Marvell's ambivalence in the "Horatian Ode" most profoundly attaches not to Cromwell but to absolute power itself, and in his later poems to the Protector, the too-familiar figures of messianic kingship tread a thin line between the heroic and the mock heroic.[23] In the years that follow, and especially after the Hanoverian Settlement ostentatiously relinquishes the crucial principle of genealogical legitimacy, "poems on affairs of state" gradually abandon particularized advocacy and critique in favor of the wholesale attack on politics as such, and from a position necessarily defined apart from the realm of the political and its inevitable corruptions. What we think of as the great age of political poetry evinced an unprecedented conviction of the inapplicability of conventional panegyric topics to public figures. And in the early eighteenth century, the role of the "public" poet becomes that of the private excoriator of the public misuse of power. This is the enabling precondition for the later discovery, by Collins and then by Wordsworth, that the poet is possessed of a "Power" diametrically opposed to that of the statesman.[24]

But this is no doubt to pass too quickly over the topic of early eighteenth-century satiric reform, the great hallmark of Augustan literary culture and arguably the century's most compelling proof of its conviction that politics and literature are inseparable. Despite the plausibility of this belief, I would argue that Augustan satiric reform betrays the instability of an ambition not only to further, but also to replace by a literary substitute, the exercise of political power.[25] A case in point is the example of Fielding. When he announced the establishment of his literary "court of judicature," Fielding rationalized it as a needed supplement to the legal system, since "our lawes are not sufficient to restrain or correct half the enormities that spring up in this fruitful soil."[26] True, a supplement is not necessarily the same as a substitute, and Fielding worked long and hard as a magistrate as well as a novelist. But it is highly suggestive that his favorite persona as novelistic narrator is that of the benevolent magistrate, since his narratives typically consist of a protracted series of encounters with corrupt institutions, none more so than the law. And because the resolution of conflict is typically accomplished as a self-consciously artful effect of narrative manipulation and intervention, Fielding's achievement of literary reform tends to be experienced as an ideal alternative to what cannot be had on the level of political reality.

Fielding's court of judicature may owe something to Swift's notion, responsive to the impotence of the legal system, that "it was to supply such defects as these, that Satyr was first introduced into the World."[27] Like Fielding's, although in a different and darker way, Swift's vision of satire as a supplement to legal correction gets to the paradoxical heart of his satirical procedure. For the dignity and rectitude of writing to reform the world are inseparable, in Swift, from the foolishness and pride of expecting it to have any practical effect. Gulliver, it must be remembered, is nowhere more absurd than in having looked to his memoirs for the speedy accomplishment of what he calls "a Thousand . . . Reformations": "It must be owned, that seven Months were a sufficient Time to correct every Vice and Folly to which *Yahoos* are subject. . . ." And he is nowhere wiser than when he concludes that he has "now done with all such visionary Schemes for ever."[28]

Swift's greatest satires seem to depend on—to draw their peculiar power from—the quintessentially Swiftian belief that lies behind Gulliver's concluding vow: the desperate conviction that practical reform is largely unavailable. This conviction can be felt even in the distinctive formal procedures of Swift's satires. I am thinking, for example, of the studied extremity of *A Modest Proposal* (1729). The power of the piece lies not in its condemnation of an obviously inhuman proposal, but in its furious insistence that all supposedly practical reforms have been indifferently and inhumanly passed over. The desperate conviction can be felt, as well, in the fiendish difficulty of a tract like *An Argument against Abolishing Christianity* (1711), whose sinuous logic so challenges our need to pin down a normative stance and a practical response that we lose our way and wander at large within the voluminous folds of the argument. Again, we sense Swift's despair of practical reform in the way his impersonation of the enemy can become so persuasive that from time to time we lose all confidence in our ability to distinguish his voice from that of the Other. Most of all, the unavailability of reform is built into the bifurcated structure of Swift's implied audience in these several satires. On the one hand, Swift writes for his small circle of friends, the few "men of taste" who share his beliefs and can be counted on to follow closely his every rhetorical turn. On the other hand, he writes to the crude, ignorant, and prideful reader who often enough is embodied within the speaker's parodic personage. Yet the first sort of audience, eminently capable of understanding and responding to Swift's counsel, for that very reason does not need it (and in any case is far too few to make a difference); while the second, the great and vulgar mass that holds the future in its grasp, stands in appalling need of reform but for that very reason is unable to understand Swift's incitements to it. These two extremes pointedly exclude any middle range of readers who might respond to Swift's words with practical action, and the result is a literary economy that helps locate the power of Swift's rhetoric in the savage indignation of a call for reform that knows ahead of time the futility of its effort.

The difference between this familiar Swiftian fury, and the emotion associated with a rhetoric that undertakes a more recognizably practical act of persuasion, can be felt best by comparing Swift's most powerful satires with those few works of his that have a more genuinely "political" character. The most impressive of these is perhaps the first of the Drapier's Letters, written five years before *A Modest Proposal* and concerned with the same political crisis that animates that much more celebrated work.[29] In some respects the two tracts also share the same formal techniques—most obviously, the impersonation of another and the implication of a common, vulgar audience. But in the first of the Drapier's Letters, the speaking voice is clearly normative; the despised other is sharply differentiated and made accessible to a definitive repudiation; and the implied audience, however vulgar, appears the object of a sincere persuasion. What this audience is to be persuaded of is one of those practical expedients—a boycott of English currency—whose silent disregard provides the occasion for the impractical outrage of *A Modest Proposal*. All of this is only to say that the first of the Drapier's Letters seems an instance of what I have claimed is a rare species in Augustan satire, a literary work that is also a recognizable effort at political reform.

But precisely because of its recognizably political motive, the first of the Drapier's Letters must be said to be relatively deficient—by aesthetic standards that Swift's contemporaries were only beginning to formulate and that we moderns have thoroughly internalized—in just those features that characterize great Swiftian satire. Although its form is mock epistolary, for example, it is so only to the practical end of plausible communication, and there is no reflexive attempt here (as there is, say, in "A Discourse Concerning the Mechanical Operation of the Spirit") to ironize epistolary form itself as one sign of the projecting enemy. Most important, however, the speaker's indignation is held tightly in rein, economically fueling the argument at suitable points without ever spilling over into that dark extremity of rage we learn to recognize as the subjective signature of Swift's greatest work, a riveting affective power that flourishes only in the absence of practical power. For these reasons, the first of the Drapier's Letters helps throw into relief, by its difference, a truth about Swift's major canon as well as Augustan satire at large: that it marks both the golden age of politically concerned literature in England, and an early stage in the dialectical constitution of "literature" as that to which we turn our attention in the face of political impotence.

The succeeding stage in this process—the restabilizing formulation of an explicit doctrine of aesthetic autonomy during the latter half of the eighteenth century—is another story. Rather than begin that story here I will conclude this one by observing some of the apparently irreversible consequences of the cultural crisis I have just recounted, the foundational disjunction of "politics" and "literature."

Because they are motivated by its first appearance, efforts to overcome the disjunction of "politics" and "literature" may also be taken to date from the eighteenth century. We have come to acknowledge such efforts (Pope's *Peri Bathous* is a good example) under the general category of the theory of ideology: the demystification of apparently universal, autonomous, or "natural" modes of thought by showing their entanglement with and their dependence upon particular power dispensations. To locate the rise of ideology theory in the Enlightenment is not to say, however, that the Enlightenment is distinguished from earlier periods by its conviction of the connectedness of cultural and political activity. On the contrary, ideology theory exists to insist explicitly upon a connection that in former times was tacitly assumed to be true. And in the very need for insistence it presupposes and concedes that gulf between the "political" and the "cultural" which it was mobilized to refute.

I would like to suggest a relationship between the theory of ideology and that other child of Enlightenment crisis, the theory of literary realism. The early provenance of realism bears a double message. Replete with the conviction that "the world" is accessible to literary representation, realism is, by the same token, unthinkable apart from the apprehension of a constituting estrangement between "literature" and "empirical reality." It first emerges as a highly contradictory strategy of literary reform. Repudiating the incredible fictions of "romance," writers like Defoe and Richardson reflect the influence of empiricist epistemology by claiming the empirical veracity—the literal historicity—of their narratives, in order to achieve better the announced purpose of religious improvement. In time, realism learns to turn the claim to literal historicity into the claim to being history-like, and to modulate its religious into a more decorously ethical ambition.[30] But these early instabilities of the realist mode are not so much a youthful aberration as a chronic condition, since the central motive of realism is to reconcile two standards of truth that are defined precisely by their irreconcilability. The sophisticated abandonment of the claim to historicity succeeds only in concealing this contradiction. And in its subsequent history, realism continues to enact in other terms the original paradox of a mode that reinforces the division of the literary and the empirical in its very effort to hold them together.

The suggestion with which I will close is that the theory of realism recapitulates, in a different mode, the contradictory movement of the theory of ideology with respect to the disjunction of "politics" and "literature." In fact, it may be useful to see the theory of ideology and the theory of realism as not simply intellectual children of the Enlightenment, but as fraternal twins whose patent dissimilarities cannot conceal a profound and uncanny resemblance. What principally distinguishes them is the respectively negative and positive approach each takes to the common problem of disjunction. Ideology theory exists to expose (and only thereby to reform) the illusory separation of culture from its empirical circumstances; whereas realism seeks to reform (and only instrumentally to expose) that separation, to represent circumstance by a faithful simulacrum. What draws them together most strikingly is what they share with the contradictory structure of crisis that has been my concern in this essay: namely, the way the powerful promulgation of each theory reinstates and signifies the disjunction each exists to overcome. It is as though modern vigilance earnestly, but with a fatal irony, invents not one but two methods of achieving the same decompartmentalizing end. For the diligent redoubling of the effort, with one method proper to the "political" realm and the other to the "literary," only reinstates the disjunction at another level. In this way, the cultural crisis that lay secreted in the ostensibly stabilizing order of early eighteenth-century culture has become an inalienable bequest to the modern world.

Notes

1 See my *The Origins of the English Novel, 1600–1740* (Baltimore: Johns Hopkins University Press, 1987), 169–71, 208–11 (conservatism); 177–82 (absolutism) (quotation 178).

2 *Origins* 150–59 (critique of aristocracy); 159–67 (middle class); 167–69 ("Whig aristocracy") (quotation 167).

3 See *Origins* 198–200 (liberal Anglicanism) (quotation 198); 124–25, 181–82 (providence) (quotation 124); 126–27 (neoclassicism).

4 Michael McKeon, "Historicizing *Absalom and Achitophel*," in *The New Eighteenth Century: Theory, Politics, English Literature*, ed. Felicity Nussbaum and Laura Brown (New York: Methuen, 1987), 39.

5 For an attempt at a theoretical elaboration of these ideas in conjunction with the reading of an exemplary Restoration text, see my "Marxist Criticism and *Marriage à la Mode*," *The Eighteenth Century: Theory and Interpretation*, 24, no. 2 (1983), 141–62.

6 "Historicizing *Absalom and Achitophel*" 39.

7 E.g., see Karl Marx and Friedrich Engels, *The German Ideology*, ed. C. J. Arthur (New York: International Publishers, 1970), 86–89.

8 *The Dunciad Variorum* 1. 67–68, in *The Dunciad*, ed. James Sutherland, 2d ed. (London: Methuen, 1953), 68.

9 "A Description of a City Shower" (1710), line 49, in *The Poems of Jonathan Swift*, ed. Harold Williams (Oxford: Clarendon Press, 1937), 1: 139; Alexander Pope, *The Rape of the Lock* (1714), lines 1–3, in *The Rape of the Lock and Other Poems*, ed. Geoffrey Tillotson (London: Methuen, 1962).

10 See my *Politics and Poetry in Restoration England: The Case of Dryden's*

Annus Mirabilis (Cambridge: Harvard University Press, 1975), 5–11; "Historicizing *Absalom and Achitophel*" 24–25, 39.

11 Jonathan Swift, "An Apology for the, &c.," in *A Tale of a Tub*, ed. A. C. Guthkelch and D. Nichol Smith, 2d ed. (Oxford: Clarendon Press, 1958), 8, 7.

12 See the critique of the doctrine of the persona in *Politics and Poetry* 14–15.

13 "Apology" 17.

14 Jonathan Swift, "A Discourse Concerning the Mechanical Operation of the Spirit," in *A Tale of a Tub* 263.

15 For a discussion of the modern emergence of the autonomous subject within a specifically socio-economic context, see *Origins* 200–205.

16 For a discussion of the seventeenth-century preamble to this movement, see my "Politics of Discourses and the Rise of the Aesthetic in Seventeenth-Century England," in *Politics of Discourse: The Literature and History of Seventeenth-Century England*, ed. Kevin Sharpe and Steven N. Zwicker (Berkeley and Los Angeles: University of California Press, 1987), 35–51.

17 On the late medieval and Renaissance emergence of "politics" see Sheldon S. Wolin, *Politics and Vision: Continuity and Innovation in Western Political Thought* (Boston: Little, Brown, 1960), chap. 7; Quentin Skinner, *The Foundations of Modern Political Thought* (Cambridge: Cambridge University Press, 1978), Vol. 2: *The Age of Reformation*, "Conclusion."

18 See Lewis B. Namier, *The Structure of Politics at the Accession of George III*, 2d ed. (London: Macmillan, 1957); *England in the Age of the American Revolution*, 2d ed. (London: Macmillan, 1962).

19 Henry Fielding, *An Apology for the Life of Mrs. Shamela Andrews . . .* (1741), in *Joseph Andrews and Shamela*, ed. Martin C. Battestin (Boston: Houghton Mifflin, 1961), 299 (title page); *The History of the Life of the Late Mr. Jonathan Wild the Great* (1743), ed. J. H. Plumb (New York: Signet, 1961), 89 (II, v).

20 See Alexander Pope, "The First Epistle of the Second Book of Horace Imitated" (1737), printed with Horace facing in *Imitations of Horace*, ed. John Butt (London: Methuen, 1939), 189–231.

21 E.g., see *Dunciad Variorum*, "A Letter to the Publisher" 14–17.

22 *Dunciad Variorum* 205, 8 ("Preface" to the ed. of 1728, "Advertisement" to the ed. of 1729).

23 For a related and fuller treatment of these poems and their political context, see my "Pastoralism, Puritanism, Imperialism, Scientism: Andrew Marvell and the Problem of Mediation," *Yearbook of English Studies*, 13 (1983), 51–59.

24 I'm thinking, for example, of the Wordsworth of the "1801" sonnet ("I grieved for Buonaparte").

25 Compare my argument that the Augustan doctrine of poetic justice rationalizes not the representation but the replacement of divine authority (*Origins* 124–25).

26 Henry Fielding, *Champion*, 2 vols. (1741), Dec. 22, 1739, 1:112.

27 Jonathan Swift, *Examiner*, no. 38, April 26, 1711, in *The Examiner and Other Pieces Written in 1710–11*, ed. Herbert Davis (Oxford: Blackwell, 1940), 141.

28 Jonathan Swift, "A Letter from Capt. Gulliver, to his Cousin Sympson," prefixed to *Gulliver's Travels* (1726), ed. Herbert Davis (Oxford: Blackwell, 1941), xxxiv-xxxv, xxxvi.
29 Jonathan Swift, *To the Tradesmen, Shop-Keepers, Farmers, and Common-People in General, of the Kingdom of Ireland* (1724).
30 See *Origins* 118–22 and part I passim.

4 *John Bender*

A New History Of The Enlightenment?

Anthony Giddens has remarked that knowledge cannot situate itself within the same framework as its object of study because the result is nothing more than recapitulation.[1] I understand this to mean that if knowledge is to escape tautology it must conserve its own systems of reference and its own contemporaneity. Equally inadequate, on this understanding, are both the fiction of positivist historicism that the specificity of ages past can be immanent to the inquirer as if to a divinely comprehending eye, and the Hegelian fiction that the spirit of each age, comprehended philosophically, participates in a teleologically directed causal order. In the first case, abstractive analysis is delimited because the minutiae of the past are recapitulated ideologically within the historian's tacit assumptions. In the second, a theoretical system overwhelms the particular and eradicates dissonant facts or subsumes them into abstract dialectical patterns.

These observations need not call forth an excursus on historiography. Rather I wish to reflect here upon Giddens' notion as it touches the reception that certain historically observant, theoretically alert modes of inquiry have received in American eighteenth-century studies. I shall focus in particular on the related if loosely defined, and sometimes overlapping, movements usually known as new historicism and cultural materialism as well as on the feminist rewriting of eighteenth-century literary history. I shall concentrate more upon the affinities among the new movements than upon their manifold differences, though I recognize the imperfect coherence of any categorization that attempts to contain their diversity. I aim to move away from content-specific consideration of these movements toward the question of systemic function. For this reason, the argument is intentionally broad, aiming at more general points than a survey of current research could accommodate (a brief bibliography is included as a guide to readers inclined to sample some of the innovative scholarly projects that mark eighteenth-century literary studies today).

My basic claim is very simple: until recent revisions of critical methods by feminism, new historicism, and cultural materialism, Anglo-American investigation of eighteenth-century literature proceeded largely within deep-rooted postulates—within a frame of reference—that fundamentally reproduced Enlightenment assumptions themselves and therefore yielded recapitulation rather than the knowledge produced by critical analysis.[2] The early parts of this essay lay the groundwork for a central section reviewing four indicative Enlightenment categories that have underlain the critical enterprise: the categories of aesthetic autonomy, authorship, disinterestedness, and gendered sexuality. Along the way, I shall offer some conjectures about why the new movements have arrived belatedly in eighteenth-century studies and, in the case of new historicism, displayed mutant characteristics. I shall close with some speculations about the new historicism as a symptomatic feature of the legitimation crisis under way in academic literary studies at large, a crisis especially germane to the eighteenth-century field because this period, more than any other, produced the assumptions that have structured modern literary study.

None of this will be to urge that anyone discard the findings of previous—or present-day—scholarship: the project of recapitulation has immense value in preserving, ordering, and systematizing the traces of the past, selective though the transcription may be. Nor do I wish to imply that attempted recapitulation—or even seeming repetition—can ever be neutral. The old historicist ideal of value-free scholarship seems increasingly a delusion even in the case of works like catalogs, much less editions and biographies. Choices grounded in various interests and assumptions must be made even in simple listings or topologies, and, to this extent, the most anatomical scholarship is ideologically conditioned. But whereas editions or catalogs arguably might benefit from an unselfconscious subsistence within the framework of the objects they preserve, critical knowledge, as Giddens defines it, must pay the price of ceasing to be knowledge at all.

I

New historicism in the United States, cultural materialism in Britain, and feminism in both have provoked so much notice—and hostility—because they have changed the frame of reference. They have denaturalized and transformed into historical phenomena a range of assumptions fundamental to mid-twentieth-century Anglo-American literary study. Retreat to the previous status quo now seems unlikely though reassertions of the old values are bound to continue. It will be a long time before inaudibility overtakes the graciously phrased echoes of that orderly, well-reasoned, fundamentally hierarchical vision of Augustan England so brilliantly epitomized in Maynard Mack's 1950 introduction to the Twickenham Edition of Pope's An Essay on Man and, during the same period, in his essays entitled " 'Wit and Poetry and Pope': Some Observations on His Imagery" and "The Muse of Satire." Secure in its vision and at peace with its classical and Renaissance heritage, this "eighteenth century" held the bastions against modernity through the wit, common sense, and good taste of gentlemen like Swift, Pope, Fielding, and Johnson. To be sure, these men sometimes gave way to rage, spite, despair, or even to madness or obscenity but only upon extreme provocation. And even their outbursts occurred in finely wrought styles that yielded riches when assayed with the precision instruments of disciplined formal and rhetorical analysis. Irony, the master trope in New Criticism's lexicon, chimed loud and clear in this Augustan eighteenth century. Whatever injury the others may have done through its brilliant misuse, Johnson more than counterpoised by refining their techniques and turning them to the service of high moral seriousness.[3]

Having been trained myself in graduate school during the 1960s on a combination—uneasy to be sure but then customary in American English departments—of historical philology and formalist poetics (chiefly those of the New Criticism), I have personally undergone the change of referential framework I am describing. And so it may be useful, though I risk the appearance of self-regard, to illustrate the shift by serving as my own witness: by portraying the contrasting methods and operative premises of my own work about the relationship between the eighteenth-century realist novel and the technology of reformative imprisonment. If this work fits into any one of the movements I have singled out, it would probably have to be the new historicism. No single book could display every vital sign of the new framework, but several indicators are indeed present in Imagining the Penitentiary:[4] the dust jacket blurb by Stephen Greenblatt; the subject inspired by Michel Foucault; the dissolution of boundaries between venerated aesthetic objects like novels or paintings and tracts, pamphlets, or legislation; the reading of institutions as "texts"; the treatment of subjectivity as a socially constructed—and therefore historically changing— phenomenon rather than as a permanent feature of human nature; and, perhaps above all, the view that manifestly fictional texts like plays and novels are culturally constitutive—not mere reflections of a "reality" that exists prior to and outside them.

Questions about the formulation and maintenance of power would have to figure in any work on prisons. And, broadly speaking, I do join Foucault and the new historicists in viewing transgression and lawlessness as structural positions—as necessary elements—in the fluid and contestatory scene within which power is defined and arrayed. Power cannot exist merely as a possession of governmental authorities. Instead, it lives in reciprocation with—and partially shared by—the alien, resistive, disorderly, and criminal elements that seem to define "otherness" in any given society. I argue, for example, that when Henry Fielding became a judge at mid-century he adopted systems for controlling information about crime that were devised in the 1720s by the underworld figure Jonathan Wild. Power is all too often treated as if it were a fixed commodity rather than a range of complex discursive practices which alter so radically over time that they are scarcely recognizable from one era to another. The constant is not power but rather discourse as the structuring principle of human social formation. The languages of different eras may be mutually unintelligible as to grammar and diction but they still establish discursive order in any given society at any given moment.

What, then, are the broad, definitional traits of new historicism? Such work, it seems to me, needs as a rule to maintain three simultaneous postures: (1) an active awareness and employment of theory, including a certain self-reflexiveness; (2) a fairly pervasive use of original sources both literary and nonliterary, with similar methods of analysis being employed on both and with a minimum of the old-fashioned background/foreground opposition; (3) a redefinition through rereading of some canonical work, or previously uncanonized work, as a culturally operative text rather than as a strictly aesthetic object. With this general description in view, I see no reason to stress the methodological differences between my work and Greenblatt's, or indeed that of many others working in Renaissance studies where the movement began. But I shall enter one large qualification: any talk about new historicism in eighteenth-century studies must notice the immense changes in governmental, social, and cultural forms between the reigns of Elizabeth and the first two Georges (often, and significantly enough, called the reign of Walpole).

These changes are worth contemplating here. The revolutions of 1641 and 1688 altered fundamental assumptions about the monarchy. The settlement of 1689, in particular, not only established a succession that brought

foreigners to the throne, but reinscribed the monarchy as a contract with
Parliament. Rule by party—a practice unthinkable to Elizabeth I—became
ever more central to both the theory and the exercise of English government. On the social front, a vociferous critique of traditional aristocratic
display and arbitrary authority accompanied the increasing appropriation
of aristocratic forms by commercial magnates seeking broader social and
political power than commerce alone could sustain. Meanwhile, the management even of long-held landed estates was breaking with conventional
patterns and laying more stress on commodified production. Finally, in
matters of religion, the settlement of 1689 definitively institutionalized the
Protestant hegemony in England and worked both to diminish sectarian
differences among non-Catholics and to broaden the reach of the Anglican establishment. Religious concerns remained vital but would become
less urgently political with each passing decade of the eighteenth century.
Whether or not by reason of the dominant Protestant consensus, cultural
arenas opened within which questions about ethics, morality, psychology, and human institutions that previously had to be considered within
highly overdetermined religio-political contexts could be viewed in a secular light. If Foucault taught us anything, it is that power is never a fixed
object but a multiplicity of relationships and techniques that have con-
tinuously to be reproduced, and therefore changed, in order to maintain
themselves. Power and authority usually are conceived as transhistorical
abstractions, but their nature alters according to social and cultural struc-
turation. A fully historicized, fully theorized practice of eighteenth-century
studies, therefore, must have a distinctive profile because of the necessarily
dialectical relationship between an object of study and its apprehension by
criticism.

II

I shall return now to my earlier assertion that criticism prior to the new
movements was tacitly founded on Enlightenment premises—first adding
a disclaimer that the term "Enlightenment" is used here not to define a
strict historical period but rather as a marker to signify a large, somewhat
rough-edged phase in European culture. *Webster's* singles out the usual
attributes when it notices that the movement is marked "by questioning of
traditional doctrines and values, a tendency toward individualism, and an
emphasis on the idea of universal human progress, the empirical method
in science, and the free use of reason."[5] A longer essay might encompass
a more subtle definition of the Enlightenment not as a monolith in which
certain categories of thought emerge or become definitive but rather as a
period structured by its production of and operation within certain charac-

teristic diadic oppositions such as reason versus sentiment, practical versus aesthetic, public versus private, the masculine versus the feminine, and so forth. Such an account also would accommodate resisting individuals and even institutions at variance with prevailing forms. I have in mind a writer like Swift or, if one may call it an institution, the amazingly persistent and powerful coalition of loyalists supporting the Pretender.

Peter Gay echoed Kant when, some years ago, he dubbed the Enlightenment the "age of criticism." Gay sees the period's thought as fundamentally unified by the informality of its social and literary forms, by its stress on utility, and by its confidence in critical method. Gay sums up his view by quoting Gibbon's encomium to criticism: "All that genius has created, all that reason has weighed, all that labor has gathered up—all this is the business of criticism. Intellectual precision, ingenuity, penetration, are all necessary to exercise it properly."[6]

Although Peter Hohendahl speaks out of a tradition very different from Gay's—the Frankfurt School—and stresses institutions rather than individuals, he too marks the Enlightenment as the founding era of criticism as we know it:

Seen historically, the modern concept of literary criticism is closely tied to the rise of the liberal, bourgeois, public sphere in the early eighteenth century. Literature served the emancipation movement of the middle class as an instrument to gain self-esteem and to articulate its human demands against the absolutist state and a hierarchical society.[7]

Both Gay and Hohendahl refer to the eighteenth-century formulation of an independent—seemingly autonomous—intellectuality of the kind typified by Addison's *Spectator* and by coffeehouses, clubs, and societies where, in contrast to literate exchange within the traditional courtly milieu, external marks of rank were laid aside and aristocratic patronage was displaced by a paying literate public. Especially in the earlier phases, aristocratic privilege everywhere penetrated the new intellectual institutions, nor was the kind of education necessary for entry into the realm of critical discussion available to anyone beneath what were called the "middling sort," if indeed to many of them. But this was not the point. A powerful convention had come into being: the convention that ideas are equally accessible to educated men and that, in the realm of public discussion, men are judged by the degree of their information and the quality of their ideas, not by rank, office, or wealth. I refer advisedly to "men" here, for the Enlightenment, though a source in the long term of powerful arguments and institutional formations supporting educational and social equality for women, not only was a male possession, but worked to efface the question of gender in the public sphere by idealizing impartial neutrality.[8]

Criticism framed in this way presumes a whole stance toward reality that became coherent during the earlier eighteenth century and that increasingly was naturalized as the truth of reality itself. Romanticism and various later movements would challenge Enlightenment culture, the early phase of which Addison exemplified and promulgated. Over time, this culture would be reproduced within a broad range of institutions that at once deeply held its values and in many ways altered their nature. Still, these values and the reality they postulated—this sense of the nature of things—endured as foundational presumptions. I single out four of these postulates below because of their specific relevance to literary study. But more broadly, this naturalized reality presumed above all the existence of an integral subjectivity expressing personal individuality. This subjectivity was validated in any number of ways, including a revised conception of the imagination which also was broached by Addison in his influential papers on "the pleasures of imagination."[9] Other naturalized presumptions included the division of social life into private and public realms; the division of labor along lines of class, profession, and gender; as well as the construction of middle-class ideology in general, and of sexuality in particular, as self-reproducing social forms that enforced these divisions.

Perhaps I may digress to give just one example of the perdurance of Enlightenment presumptions through various periods and institutionalizations. Friedrich Schlegel importantly redirected attention away from evaluative obsession of Enlightenment aesthetics when he argued that criticism should reveal the immanent nature of the work of art, whose attributes "one can learn to understand only from itself."[10] The critic assists, indeed guides, art in its move toward fulfillment through his contemplation of specific works and through empirical study of their attributes. The various institutions that reproduced thinking like this across the nineteenth and twentieth centuries stressed different features within it. The organicist aspect flowered into *l'art pour l'art,* informed writing in literary periodicals, and flowed into aestheticism—ultimately to be lodged in the mid-twentieth-century academic establishment as the New Criticism. The historicist aspect, having joined in an *entente cordiale* with nationalist Romantic philology, much earlier found its path into universities in the disciplinary shape of literary history conceived as an account of forms and types derived not from classical or conventional generic concepts but deduced from art itself—from the productions of genius.

The afterlife of ideas of the kind we identify with Schlegel might be cast into some different story. Obviously I have told it a certain way to suit my purposes here. But any account would have to notice the endurance of an Enlightenment presumption that individual subjectivity can be willfully suspended and reconstituted, according to certain rules, as disinterested objectivity in service of purposive ends—be they the ends of literary criticism, of justice, of education, of scholarship, or any other constructive order. The persistence of the Enlightenment framework is scarcely surprising in view of the institutionalization—delineated by Hohendahl—of the critical stance as a defining feature of middle-class consciousness. This institutionalization has been especially potent in the United States, where a liberal arts education in colleges and universities has long been central to the middle-class definition of success and where this education in itself has worked to preserve among faculties as well as among the general public the very Addisonian ideals to which Hohendahl refers.

Such is the general background. But when it comes to academic inquiry, I would observe, further, that eighteenth-century studies have worked under a kind of double jeopardy. Let me clarify. It seems to me that students of each historical period—be it the Renaissance, the eighteenth century, or Romanticism—have tended quite strongly to adopt the terms of reference and points of view within which their respective periods beheld themselves. Earlier Renaissance critics joined the Elizabethans in glorifying Elizabeth I or Renaissance humanism, and, as Jerome McGann and Clifford Siskin have shown, study of the Romantics has worked largely within that period's epistemology and terminology.[11] But since, as Hohendahl argues, the whole institution of criticism has been built upon Enlightenment foundations, at least critics of the Renaissance or the Romantic period could benefit from a certain cognitive dissonance that provided openings for genuine analysis. In eighteenth-century studies, however, the institution of criticism and the object of study are far more congruent. The field's often remarked "conservatism" reappears, in this light, as a historically determined systemic function. In any case, an absence of the kind of congruence between criticism and its object that I believe to have prevailed in eighteenth-century studies must be one reason why the new historicism arose among academic critics of sixteenth-century English literature—a period at once temporally adjacent to and yet at the largest possible ideological remove from the post-Cartesian world of the Enlightenment.

Conversely, the double jeopardy I have just been describing can explain the new historicism's jump to Romantic studies prior to its emergence in the eighteenth century, where scholars not only work within the larger institution of criticism as founded in the Enlightenment but, further, are prone for reasons of specialization to adopt its terms of reference. It is axiomatic, too, that Romanticism sought in numerous ways to define itself in opposition to Enlightenment values. And it follows from my argument that Romanticism's radical critique of its immediate forebears must, so to speak, have opened a circuit that much later enabled the new historicism to arc across the eighteenth century. Nonetheless, all of the categorical assumptions I shall shortly treat in fact are strengthened by fuller articulation and institutionalization during the Romantic period though usually with some distinctive reorientation. Even the category of disinterestedness, which might seem to have sunk in the *Sturm und Drang* of Romantic subjectivism, lives on as the everyday groundwork—the contextually normative "other"—in opposition to which Romantic and post-Romantic creative aestheticism define themselves. Aestheticism reconstitutes disinterestedness and puts it in the service of art but preserves it still.

Recently, however, we are seeing scholarly books that explicitly analyze—even attack—the Enlightenment framework. I have in mind, for example, Jerome Christensen's *Practicing Enlightenment*, in which the author specifically says that he is approaching Hume's literary career from a Romantic perspective. Or Nancy Armstrong's *Desire and Domestic Fiction*, which opens with a chapter on the need to denaturalize the eighteenth-century constitution of gender in order to arrive at an unblinkered history of the novel.[12] Interestingly enough, in view of my suggestion that some kind of double jeopardy or overdetermination may have been at work in eighteenth-century studies, several of the books that operate within the new framework, including Christensen's and Armstrong's, are by authors with marked affiliations to periods other than the eighteenth century. Christensen started as a Romanticist, and Armstrong has strong scholarly interests in the Victorian period. Cathy Davidson, whose *Revolution and the Word* deals in substantial part with the eighteenth century, is an Americanist based largely in nineteenth-century studies. I also think of Peter Stallybrass and Allon White's cultural materialist work, *The Politics and Poetics of Transgression*, even though it deals only in part with the eighteenth century, because their other writings have attended, respectively, to the Renaissance and to fiction in the two following centuries.[13]

III

There is space here to describe just four assumptions characteristic of the Enlightenment framework within which criticism has proceeded. The new historicism, cultural materialism, feminism, and deconstruction (or at least deconstruction's original impetus in Derrida) have challenged and largely denaturalized this framework.[14] Although I lay stress on those assumptions that most obviously concern literary criticism, the elements I identify are in fact interdependent parts of a large cultural system and should not be thought of hierarchically or teleologically.

First let us take up the Enlightenment invention of the aesthetic as an autonomous discursive realm. Literature, along with the other arts, became in this construction a disclosure of sensate experience produced and arranged according to principles entirely different from those governing other forms of knowledge. Now it was a specialized department in a system, conveniently epitomized by d'Alembert's *Preliminary Discourse to the Encyclopedia*, a system that categorized human endeavor by correlating it with the physiological and psychological faculties.[15] Literature was ideologically, if not actually, confined to the realms of sense, intuition, and imagination where previously it had comprehended virtually everything written. The new late twentieth-century movements work, at least tacitly, to reestablish the previous state of affairs by challenging the autonomy of the aesthetic domain and reconstituting it as a historical phenomenon subject to critical analysis.

The Enlightenment constitution of the aesthetic delineated one major axis in a complex geometry—a division of knowledge into disciplines that not only separated the arts from the historical, scientific, and argumentative discourses but led to sharp distinctions among the arts themselves such as we find in Lessing's *Laocoön* and its English predecessors. This division of knowledge had large material consequences as it was institutionalized over time and yielded, for example, not merely the various professions with which we are familiar but the concept of professionalism itself. In universities, where to be sure learning had for centuries been parceled into broad areas, the ultimate repercussion of the new division of knowledge by faculties was the emergence of separate departments not only of philosophy, history, political theory, and economics but of music, the visual arts, and literature.[16]

The new movements under discussion here often are described as innovative because they reach across the customary boundaries between literary study and the visual arts, history, anthropology, sociology, law, and so forth. Certainly interdisciplinary criticism existed and was thought desirable well before the new historicism, cultural materialism, or feminist literary history. In fact the American Society for Eighteenth-Century Studies originated under a banner of interdisciplinarity that it continues proudly to fly.[17] But the word itself implies the preservation of traditional disciplinary boundaries and provokes one to think of the critic either as a fugitive living dangerously in the no-man's-land between nations or as a kind of extraordinary ambassador moving without portfolio from one sovereignty to another. Interdisciplinarity in itself does nothing to denaturalize the category of the aesthetic.

It is one thing to compare literature with the other arts or with—shall we say—philosophy, conceived as uniquely structured disciplines, and quite another to treat novels, paintings, buildings, logical treatises, legislation, and institutional regulations all as texts participating in the complex and contestatory processes through which societies define and maintain the structure not only of their institutions but of human entities. (We usually call the human entities that live within and largely constitute society "persons," though we might more properly use some analytical nomenclature like that of narratology and label them "actants.") The new approaches might better be called "transdisciplinary" because they work to erode presumptions on which the existing disciplines are founded. They are so disturbing, I believe, because they challenge not merely ways of thinking about the "aesthetic" but ways of disciplinary existence that are deeply engrained within the schools, museums, universities, and other educational establishments of our own society. The discourse of the aesthetic disguises the constitutive role that symbolism plays in social life at large and founds institutions that segregate the arts both physically and mentally from other social processes. Professors of literature have been earning a fair living perpetuating this segregation.

Authorship is a second category of Enlightenment belief at once central to orthodox criticism and challenged by the new historicism and other movements. Here, again, Foucault helped us to understand the historicity of a phenomenon that had been taken for granted. He describes the "author function" as a culturally variable designation used at times to affiliate certain texts and to lend them authority by attributing their production to a historical person like Virgil or to an imagined individual like "Homer." An "author" in the modern era is, above all, a simulacrum to which are assigned traits that allow its interpretive construction as a personal subject who creates a unique world of thought in a manner that usually has been considered to be universal but is in fact confined to the post-Cartesian West. An author's uniqueness is manifest in the "work" and confers identity upon it.[18] Once the category of creative authorship exists, it influences not only scholarship and criticism but literary production itself. The anchoring of discourse in sponsoring subjectivity that began in the seventeenth century and was naturalized in the eighteenth is noticeable, for instance, in works like the Ossian forgeries or in the emergent construction of Shakespeare as an artistic personality. The category of authorship was consolidated in the Romantic era, when it was sanctified as an attribute of the creative personality and written definitively into copyright laws throughout Europe.[19] Authorship was progressively institutionalized in the nineteenth century, when the study of literature was gaining its place among the university disciplines. It is hard to think of even one major canonical English work after the early Tudor period that is *now* designated as anonymous. Of course what Foucault called the "author function" can be assigned to anonymous works (as has routinely happened in medieval and Renaissance art history), but it says much about the strength of our presumptions about writing that such has seldom been the case in literature.

Although the new historicism and, to a large extent, cultural material-ism have been strongly affixed to the authorial canon—most especially to Shakespeare—in practice they also have challenged the centrality of the canon by placing an enormous array of anonymous or collective social texts on an equal footing with acknowledged masterpieces. Legislation, legal documents, press reports, and conduct books, for instance, now have standing as *texts,* not just as background or underpinnings. Feminist scholarship has gone very much farther in altering the canon despite—or possibly even because of—the preservation of sponsoring subjectivity in some versions of feminism. The point here is not so much the imperfect execution of theory: after all we still live in a culture that places enormous value on the category of subjectivity, a culture in which biography is about the only type of academic writing on literature that trade publishers or the general public will touch. The point is, rather, that the comfortable and repetitious gentlemanly discussion of a few masterpieces that typified the New Criticism is almost over. Certainly in its early years the New Criti-cism had to struggle against the old orthodoxy of philology, and, perhaps as a way of vaccinating my own essay against the charge of Whiggishness, I want to note that the astounding speed with which the new movements seem to have become standard in Renaissance and Romantic studies causes me to be curious what new "isms" may overtake them. In any case, femi-nism, new historicism, and cultural materialism have forced the up-to-date critic—like Marvell's lover—to contemplate a vast eternity of primary texts. Indeed, while the frequent accusation that the new historicism takes an anecdotal view of the past puts a negative spin on the question, it may well be true that the issue of selection poses any method's single biggest theoretical quandary.[20]

A third definitive category of Enlightenment belief within which sub-sequent criticism has operated is faith in transparency, neutrality, and disinterestedness as ideals of critical discourse. Related to and produced by this category is the definition—epitomized by a work like Dr. John-son's *Dictionary*—of a public language against which all others may be judged. Kant is the eighteenth-century figure who most fully theorized the already existent ideal of critical communication in a public sphere free of special interests—whether personal, political, or religious.[21] In this ideal sphere only the spirit of impartial rational inquiry is supposed to guide research, the findings of which are examined by an equally impartial audi-ence, improved by further analysis, and eventually perfected not merely into knowledge but into truth. This disinterested dialogue is technically ungendered but it of course turns out to be presumptively male.

New historicists have not been as thoroughgoing in their challenge to the category of disinterested inquiry as to those of the aesthetic and of authorship. They have consistently treated history as a narrative function relative to the historicity of the historian. And certainly they have broken with the idea of history or any other form of knowledge as empirical representation. But, self-reflexive introductions and conclusions notwithstanding, new historicism on the whole has preserved the *voice* of disinterested inquiry and, despite the fascination with Elizabeth as a woman exercising the power of monarchy, all too often has treated humanity as if it were ungendered.[22] More explicit have been the cultural materialists in Britain: the temporal, geographical, and political position of their historical criticism has been extraordinarily precise. For them, the stress on Shakespeare goes beyond any question of residual aesthetic admiration to become a contest with established ideology (and especially with Thatcherism) over the significance of a playwright at once deeply embedded in the British system of education and central to an outworn and delusionary nationalism. More explicit still have been feminists who find the canons of disinterestedness and impartiality to cloak the old male patriarchy in a new garb that is part of its adaptation to emergent capitalism.

This brings us to the fourth and final category I can discuss here, that of gendered sexuality. Foucault's late work, *The History of Sexuality*, presents a conveniently available, eloquently argued case for the general proposition that while the biological traits of the sexes remain constant over long periods of time, sexuality is constructed socially and operates differently in each historical period.[23] He maintains, specifically, that the delineation of sexuality as at once constitutive of personality and subject to scientific mapping, surveillance, and social consciousness is an attribute of modern existence that took initial shape as its features emerged across the eighteenth century and that became fully operational in the nineteenth. Feminist literary scholars, already having built upon historical studies of the family that draw, however generally, upon Marxist categories, have taken further impetus from Foucault. They have retold the story of the eighteenth century to disclose the ideological implications of writing for and by women. They have stressed above all the operative place of narrative writing in an emergent system of gendered sexuality within which the male moves as wage earner and speaker in the open realm of a public sphere where disinterested discourse reigns while the female is confined to the closed realm of the family where she works without wages to reproduce the moral, educational, and psychological orders that at once enable capitalism to function and ideologically disguise its real exploitation of labor through the maintenance of the categories of class, race, and gender. Nancy Armstrong's *Desire and Domestic Fiction* and Felicity Nussbaum's *The Autobiographical Subject* present forceful versions of this feminist critique of eighteenth-century gender construction as it works through literature. Their arguments also exhibit attributes of the new historicism and cultural materialism as well.[24] Ludmilla Jordanova's *Sexual Visions*, a book that displays affinities with cultural materialism despite its authorship by a professional historian, is one of a growing number of historical studies that document the social construction of gender in the eighteenth century. Such work in the history of gender makes it seem increasingly artificial to discuss literary study as a separate discipline.[25]

IV

My observations thus far have deemphasized the differences that separate the new historicism from cultural materialism and feminism by grouping them together. Now, in conclusion, I want to suggest one way in which the new historicism may be different—not rhetorically or as a method but functionally in today's academy. This difference does not imply superiority on the part of new historicism. On the contrary, I consider the long-range significance of feminism to be far greater. I simply want to engage in an episode of systemic thinking in order to consider the force of recent debates about the new historicism. The catalytic role the following analysis assigns to new historicism in the discipline of English at large can work with my description of eighteenth-century studies—as a field operating under double jeopardy because of the resonance of its assumptions with those of its objects of study—to explain in systemic terms the field's belated acceptance of the new historicism and other new movements. On the account that follows, the Englightenment framework's legitimating force simply endured somewhat longer in eighteenth-century English literary studies than in the early modern, Romantic, nineteenth century, and modern period specialities.

The role of the new historicism in the American academy of the 1980s can be understood with reference to Jürgen Habermas' discussion of legitimation crises, which depends in turn upon his theory of communicative competence. The theory goes like this in the convenient summary offered by Habermas' translator, Thomas McCarthy:

a smoothly functioning language game rests on a background consensus formed from . . . different types of validity claims that are involved in the exchange of speech acts: claims that the utterance is understandable, that its propositional content is true, and that the speaker is sincere in uttering it, and that it is right or appropriate for the speaker to be performing the speech act. In normal interaction, these implicitly raised validity claims are naively accepted. But . . . situations arise in which one or more of them becomes problematic in a fundamental way. In such cases . . . specific forms of problem resolution are required to remove the disturbance and restore the original, or a new, background consensus. Different forms are needed for each type of claim. But the validity of problematic truth claims or of problematic norms can be redeemed . . . only . . . by entering into a discourse whose sole purpose is to judge the truth of the problematic opinion or the correctness of the problematic norm. . . . The speech situation of [such] discourse represents a break with the normal context of interaction in that, ideally, it requires [the suspension] of all motives except that of a willingness to come to an understanding.[26]

The purpose of this special form of interest-free discourse is to reestablish the working fiction under which normal communication proceeds: namely, the fiction that speakers understand the beliefs and norms under which they operate and can, if called upon, justify them in good faith. Of course this fiction of accountability is counterfactual and can be stabilized, to quote Habermas, "only through legitimation of the ruling systems of norms" and through systematic barriers to bad-faith communication. These barriers have contradictory effects because they both "make a fiction . . . of the reciprocal imputation of accountability, [and] support at the same time the belief in legitimacy that sustains the fiction and prevents its being found out." This, says Habermas, "is the paradoxical achievement of ideologies."[27] Legitimacy is, thus, an effect of ideology. The specialized, interest-free discourse Habermas describes allows escape from ideology through entry into what he calls a "reciprocal supposition" that enables the critique of systematically distorted communication (ideology) and provides guidelines for rational institutions. In short, and to return in another form to the proposition from Giddens with which I began, escape to genuine knowledge.

How does this apply to the new historicism? I think it does whether or not one rejects as impossible the ideal of interest-free discourse. Ever since the 1960s, and possibly before, the academic literary disciplines in the United States have responded to challenges to their prevailing norms by entering into discourse and attempting to assimilate representative dissenters. For a time this strategy worked to sustain the disciplines and their communicative norms, but the very process of taking in dissenters, not to mention the emergence of challenge by converts from within, broadened and varied the community that had to reach consensus in order to maintain legitimacy and thereby energized the crisis anew.

It is tempting to view the new historicism as another challenge to disciplinary ideology. This is how I have described it in this paper, and this is one of the ways in which it has functioned. Tempting also is to view its odd amalgam of various theories and methods as a new orthodoxy. My introduction of Habermas lends a certain plausibility to this interpretation. The new historicism seems in many ways to bear the marks of a new groundwork of norms, a new consensus within which communication can proceed. If the movement indeed has the makings of a new ground of assumptions working to legitimate the discipline, this can explain its having become an object of attack by other challengers because, in fact, the discourse used to reestablish a new ground of legitimacy for speech acts can never really be interest free.

On the other hand, the very quality of the new historicism that has been most attacked by feminists—its tendency to slide into a neutral, authoritative, putatively interest-free voice—may be a mark of the actual role it is playing in a legitimation crisis under way in the literary disciplines because such a voice, on Habermas' reading, would be a feature of the very discursive mechanism the system of communication produces to confront crises in legitimation whether or not new consensus actually emerges. In this light, I consider the new historicism not as a newly legitimated consensus—not really a new orthodoxy or even a prototype of one. Rather, it is a discourse produced by a discipline in crisis, with a view to finding a new ground that may or may not resemble it. This, I believe, explains the overwhelming volume of commentary about it. By one count the 1988 Modern Language Association meetings alone included thirty papers on the subject.[28] This, too, is why some of the movement's leading practitioners have attained such high profiles. They are not merely standard-bearers of a new orthodoxy. Through no premeditation of their own they have become the visible signs of a sweeping and profound process in which whole institutions are at stake. By the logic of this process, new historicists, feminists, and cultural materialists alike become necessary players and find themselves in demand. Whether this process leads to new forms of disciplinary legitimacy, which is to say to a new ideology of literary study, or to a sustained critical discourse yielding genuine knowledge in Habermas' or Giddens' sense, remains to be seen.

V

Locke asserts in the Introduction to *An Essay concerning Human Understanding* that he wants to find the "horizon . . . which sets the bounds between the enlightened and dark parts of things."[29] Social theorists at least since Durkheim—not to mention contemporary critical movements—have found the quest for such a division to be as delusionary as Locke considered metaphysical and religious speculation to be. And the Enlightenment, thanks to Horkheimer and Adorno's *Dialectic of Enlightenment,* has long been seen to have its own dark side: that is, the instrumental usage of reason to control and dominate rather than to emancipate.[30] Indeed, the revelation that the neutral inquirer's reasonable stance is not only historically and ideologically constituted but potentially threatening to human society can be traced through Horkheimer and Adorno back to Nietzsche and Marx. This genealogy's venerable antiquity when viewed from any number of late twentieth-century vantage points shows that my central contention about the tenacity of Enlightenment assumptions in eighteenth-century studies may be surprising but not, I believe, historically inaccurate.

In a sense, Anglo-American literary criticism is just catching up with the rest of the world, a world in which not only the Frankfurt School but, for example, the *Annales* group in France stretches back for generations. The opening to literature and to what we may call "cultural studies" came, however, with the revelation, which arrived in this country under the rubrics of structuralism and poststructuralism, that human endeavor is discursively constituted—whether this endeavor happens like literature to lie under the discredited rubric of the aesthetic or in some other disciplinary domaine like history, philosophy, or politics—and that this discursive constitution is historical. These, I believe, are the basic insights within which the new movements—including new historicism, cultural materialism, and feminism—work and which not merely eighteenth-century studies but the whole discipline of literature must confront.

Notes

1 Anthony Giddens, West Memorial Lectures, Stanford University, April 1988. A written version of these extempore lectures has appeared as *The Consequences of Modernity* (Stanford: Stanford University Press, 1990). The basic idea to which I refer here is developed, much less explicitly than in the lectures themselves, on pp. 10–17 and pp. 36–45.

2 Criticism of eighteenth-century English literature by Raymond Williams is a conspicuous exception; see, for example, *The Country and the City* (New York: Oxford University Press, 1973). See also Arnold Kettle, *An Introduction to the English Novel* (London: Hutchinson University Library, 1959. Williams, Kettle, and other Marxist literary critics in England such as Christopher Hill have operated as a minority, largely outside the dominant trends I am describing in this essay.

3 These works are conveniently gathered in Maynard Mack, *Collected in Himself: Essays Critical, Biographical, and Bibliographical on Pope and Some of His Contemporaries* (Newark: University of Delaware Press, 1982). Mack says, for example: "Against this Renaissance background, a number of important elements in the *Essay on Man* stand out in their full significance. In fact, it may not be unfair to say that while Pope's poem is in all its surface aspects a work of the Augustan period, its underlying themes have much in common with the kinds of meaning Renaissance poets constructed. . . . Readers of Shakespeare, for example, have long sensed in several of the plays a structural pattern that asserts some form of equilibrium or order, usually with reference to the universal order, which is then violated in one or several ways, and reestablished at the close. . . . It is also, of course, and particularly, the theme of Milton

in *Paradise Lost*. As every one knows, the central conflict in Milton's epic is
that between the hierarchical order, coherence, law, love, harmony, unity, and
happiness of a world created and sustained according to God's purposes, and
the chaos, rebellion, dissension, hatred, and misery brought into it by man's
and Satan's unwillingness to be contented with these purposes and their part in
them" (221). In an essay from the same time, Louis I. Bredvold's "The Gloom
of the Tory Satirists," one reads: "Good satire may be withering, it may be
dark anger, it may be painfully bitter; but it cannot be great satire without
having at its core a moral idealism expressing itself in righteous indignation.
The *saeva indignatio* which Swift suffered from is radically different in quality
from a morbid *Schadenfreude*. Once that distinction is admitted we have the
essential justification for our pleasure in satire, as well as an understanding
of the fellow feeling with which the satirists sustained one another." Quoted
from James L. Clifford, ed., *Eighteenth-Century Literature: Modern Essays in
Criticism* (New York: Oxford University Press, 1959), 11; originally published
in Clifford and Louis A. Landa, eds., *Pope and His Contemporaries: Essays
Presented to George Sherburn* (Oxford: Clarendon Press, 1949), 1–19.

For a survey, from a contemporary theoretical perspective, of postwar eighteenth-century literary study in English see Felicity Nussbaum and Laura
Brown, eds., *The New Eighteenth Century* (New York and London: Methuen,
1987), 1–22. William H. Epstein's "Counter-Intelligence: Cold-War Criticism
and Eighteenth-Century Studies," *ELH*, 57 (1990), 63–99, appeared after this
essay was written. He connects the tacit collaboration of the New Criticism and
positivist literary history with strategies of concealment and personal efface-
ment characteristic of counterintelligence as practiced during World War II and
during the cold war by several members of the Yale School of eighteenth-century
studies.

4 John Bender, *Imagining the Penitentiary: Fiction and the Architecture of Mind
in Eighteenth-Century England* (Chicago: University of Chicago Press, 1987).
See also "Prison Reform and the Sentence of Narration in *The Vicar of Wake-
field*," in *The New Eighteenth Century* 168–88.

5 *Webster's New Collegiate Dictionary* (Springfield, MA: G. & C. Merriam
Company, 1980).

6 Peter Gay, *The Enlightenment: A Comprehensive Anthology* (New York:
Simon and Schuster, 1973), 16–18. Gay quotes Gibbon's *Essai sur l'étude de
la littérature* from the *Miscellaneous Works*, ed. John, Lord Sheffield, 2d ed.,
5 vols. (1814), 4:38.

7 Peter Uwe Hohendahl, *The Institution of Criticism* (Ithaca: Cornell University
Press, 1982), 52.

8 Even the French Revolution refused women an active political role. Indeed,
Joan Landes argues in *Women and the Public Sphere in the Age of the French
Revolution* (Ithaca: Cornell University Press, 1988), in many ways women had
more influence under the old regime. Addison does welcome female readers
in paper number 10 on the *Spectator*'s desired audience. Having condemned
"ordinary" women as engaged in trivial and irrational amusements, he wel-

comes the "Multitudes . . . that join all the Beauties of the Mind to the Orna-
ments of Dress" and hopes to increase their number "by publishing this daily
Paper, which I shall always endeavour to make an innocent if not an improv-
ing Entertainment, and by that Means at least divert the Minds of my female
Readers from greater Trifles." In context, the hyperbole of "multitudes" and
the characterization of the *Spectator* as a trifle seem to me to take back at
least as much as they grant. See also the treatment in numbers 37 and 92 of a
lady named Leonora who possesses a remarkable library. See Donald F. Bond,
ed., *The Spectator*, 5 vols. (Oxford: Clarendon Press, 1965), 1:46–47, 152–59,
389–93.

9 See *The Spectator* 3:535–82. The papers appeared between June 21 and July 3,
1712, as numbers 411–21; the conventional title comes from Addison's announcement in number 409 of an impending "essay on the pleasures of the
imagination."

10 Quoted by Hohendahl, *The Institution of Criticism*, 59, from *Kritische
Friedrich-Schlegel-Ausgabe*, ed. Ernst Behler (Paderborn: Schöningh, 1958–
80), 2:133. My discussion of Schlegel is inspired by Hohendahl though it moves
in somewhat different directions.

11 See Jerome McGann, *Romantic Ideology* (Chicago: University of Chicago
Press, 1983), and his essay on "Ancient Mariner" from *Critical Inquiry* 8
(1981), reprinted in *The Beauty of Inflections: Literary Investigations in His-
torical Method and Theory* (Oxford: Clarendon Press, 1985), 135–72; Clifford
Siskin, *The Historicity of Romantic Discourse* (New York: Oxford University
Press, 1988).

12 Jerome Christensen, *Practicing Enlightenment: Hume and the Formation of a
Literary Career* (Madison: University of Wisconsin Press, 1987). Nancy Arm-
strong, *Desire and Domestic Fiction: A Political History of the Novel* (New
York: Oxford University Press, 1987).

13 Cathy N. Davidson, *Revolution and the Word: The Rise of the Novel in
America* (New York: Oxford University Press, 1986). Peter Stallybrass and
Allon White, *The Politics and Poetics of Transgression* (Ithaca: Cornell Uni-
versity Press, 1986). I too run in this pack of interlopers since my own first
book was *Spenser and Literary Pictorialism* (Princeton: Princeton University
Press, 1972).

14 Although Rousseau, in particular, figures importantly in the writings of Jacques
Derrida and Paul de Man, the movement did not have a widespread impact in
the field of English eighteenth-century studies. See Derrida, *Of Grammatology*,
trans. Gayatri Chakravorty Spivak (Baltimore: Johns Hopkins University Press,
1976), and de Man, *Blindness and Insight: Essays in the Rhetoric of Contemporary Criticism* (New York: Oxford University Press, 1971). Important among
the exceptions are William B. Warner, *Reading Clarissa: The Struggles of Interpretation* (New Haven: Yale University Press, 1979), and William Dowling,
Language and Logos in Boswell's "Life of Johnson" (Princeton: Princeton
University Press, 1981). I mention deconstruction here because certain of its
features and procedures have been absorbed by other new movements.

15 Jean le Rond d'Alembert, *Preliminary Discourse to the Encyclopedia of Diderot*, trans. and ed. Richard N. Schwab (Indianapolis: Bobbs-Merrill, 1963). The original title was *Discours préliminaire des éditeurs* in the first volume of the *Encyclopédie* (Paris: Briason et al., 1751).

16 On the historical constitution of the aesthetic and on its ideological significance see David E. Wellbery, *Lessing's Laocoon* (Cambridge: Cambridge University Press, 1984), especially chapter 2, and Terry Eagleton, *The Ideology of the Aesthetic* (Cambridge, MA: Basil Blackwell, 1990).

17 On ASECS and its reinforcement of "the traditional relationship between literary and historical study" see Nussbaum and Brown, *The New Eighteenth Century* 7–9.

18 Michel Foucault, "What is an Author?" in Josué V. Harari, ed., *Textual Strategies: Perspectives in Post-Structuralist Criticism* (Ithaca: Cornell University Press, 1979), 141–60.

19 See Henrich Bosse, *Autorschaft ist Werkherrschaft. Über die Entstehung des Urheberrechts aus dem Geist der Goethezeit* (Paderborn: Schöningh, 1981), 8–9. David Wellbery called this work to my attention and summarized its chief points. See also Mark Rose, "The Author as Proprietor: *Donaldson v. Becket* and the Genealogy of Modern Authorship," *Representations*, 23 (1988), 51–85.

20 On the intrinsically anecdotal character of history writing see Joel Fineman's brilliant, posthumously published essay, "The History of the Anecdote: Fiction and Fiction," in *The New Historicism*, ed. H. Aram Veeser (New York and London: Routledge, 1989), 49–76.

21 Immanuel Kant, "What Is Enlightenment?" *On History*, ed. and trans. Lewis White Beck (Indianapolis: Bobbs-Merrill, 1957), 3–10. On reason as a regulative principle in Kant, see also Roger Scruton, *Kant* (New York: Oxford University Press, 1982), 54–55.

22 An important exception is Stephen Greenblatt's "Fiction and Friction," which appears as chapter 5 of *Shakespearean Negotiations: The Circulation of Social Energy in Renaissance England* (Berkeley: University of California Press, 1988), 66–93.

23 Michel Foucault, *The History of Sexuality*, trans. Robert Hurley, 3 vols. (New York: Pantheon, 1978–86).

24 See in addition to Armstrong, *Desire and Domestic Fiction*, and Felicity A. Nussbaum's *The Autobiographical Subject: Gender and Ideology in Eighteenth-Century England* (Baltimore: Johns Hopkins University Press, 1989), Armstrong's "Introduction: Literature as Women's History," *Genre*, 19 (1986), 347–69.

25 Ludmilla Jordanova, *Sexual Visions: Images of Gender in Science and Medicine between the Eighteenth and Twentieth Centuries* (Madison: University of Wisconsin Press, 1989). See also Jordanova's "Natural Facts: A Historical Perspective on Science and Sexuality," in *Nature, Culture, and Gender*, ed. Carol P. MacCormack and Marilyn Strathern (Cambridge: Cambridge University Press, 1980), 42–69, and her "Naturalizing the Family: Literature and the

Bio-Medical Sciences in the Late Eighteenth Century," in *Languages of Nature: Critical Essays on Science and Literature*, ed. Jordanova (New Brunswick, NJ: Rutgers University Press, 1986), 86–116.

26 Jürgen Habermas, *Legitimation Crisis*, trans. Thomas McCarthy (Boston: Beacon Press, 1975), xiii–xiv. See also McCarthy's *The Critical Theory of Jürgen Habermas* (Cambridge: MIT Press, 1978). My discussion of a legitimation crisis in literary studies is broadly inspired by Jean-François Lyotard's application of Habermas' term to the entire system of intellectual production in *The Postmodern Condition: A Report on Knowledge*, trans. Geoff Bennington and Brian Massumi (Minneapolis: University of Minnesota Press, 1984). After this essay was written, I became aware of Jerome J. McGann's rather different use of Habermas on the question of legitimation in *Social Values and Poetic Acts: The Theoretical Judgment of Literary Work* (Cambridge: Harvard University Press, 1988).

27 Quoted in McCarthy's introduction to *Legitimation Crisis* xv.

28 The flood of publications is comparable. For comprehensive bibliographical references on the subject see the annotations to the essays in Veeser, *The New Historicism*; since this book's publication a substantial, exhaustively annotated essay by Alan Liu has appeared, "The Power of Formalism: The New Historicism," *ELH*, 56 (1989), 721–71. In addition, the title "History and . . ." recently marked *New Literary History*, 21 (1990), an entire issue devoted to the subject. See also David Simpson, "Literary Criticism and the Return to 'History,'" *Critical Inquiry*, 14 (1988), 721–47.

29 John Locke, *An Essay concerning Human Understanding*, 2 vols., ed. Alexander Campbell Fraser (New York: Dover Publications, 1959), Introduction, section 7.

30 Max Horkheimer and Theodor W. Adorno, *Dialectic of Enlightenment*, trans. John Cumming (New York: Herder and Herder, 1972); originally published as *Philosophische Fragmente* (New York: Institute for Social Research, 1944).

Select Bibliography

Armstrong, Nancy. *Desire and Domestic Fiction: A Political History of the Novel.* New York: Oxford University Press, 1987.

Barrell, John. *The Political Theory of Painting from Reynolds to Hazlitt.* New Haven: Yale University Press, 1986.

Bender, John. *Imagining the Penitentiary: Fiction and the Architecture of Mind in Eighteenth-Century England.* Chicago: University of Chicago Press, 1987.

Brown, Marshall. *Preromanticism.* Stanford: Stanford University Press, 1991.

Carnochan, W. B. *Gibbon's Solitude: The Inward World of the Historian.* Stanford: Stanford University Press, 1987.

Castle, Terry. *Masquerade and Civilization in Eighteenth-Century English Culture and Fiction.* Stanford: Stanford University Press, 1986.

Christensen, Jerome. *Practicing Enlightenment: Hume and the Formation of a Literary Career.* Madison: University of Wisconsin Press, 1987.

Damrosch, Leo. *Fictions of Reality in the Age of Hume and Johnson.* Madison: University of Wisconsin Press, 1989.

Davidson, Cathy N. *Revolution and the Word: The Rise of the Novel in America.* New York: Oxford University Press, 1986.

De Bolla, Peter. *The Discourse of the Sublime: Readings in History, Aesthetics, and the Subject.* New York: Basil Blackwell, 1989.

Doody, Margaret Anne. *The Daring Muse: Augustan Poetry Reconsidered.* Cambridge: Cambridge University Press, 1985.

Eagleton, Terry. *The Ideology of the Aesthetic.* Cambridge, MA: Basil Blackwell, 1990.

Epstein, Julia. *The Iron Pen: Frances Burney and the Politics of Women's Writing.* Madison: University of Wisconsin Press, 1989.

Erickson, Robert A. *Mother Midnight: Birth, Sex, and Fate in the Eighteenth-Century Novel.* New York: AMS Press, 1987.

Hunter, J. Paul. *Before Novels: The Cultural Contexts of Eighteenth-Century English Fiction.* New York: W. W. Norton, 1990.

Landry, Donna. *The Muses of Resistance: Laboring-Class Women's Poetry in Britain, 1739–1796.* Cambridge: Cambridge University Press, 1990.

McKeon, Michael. *The Origins of the English Novel, 1600–1740.* Baltimore: Johns Hopkins University Press, 1987.

Marshall, David. *The Figure of the Theater: Shaftesbury, Defoe, Adam Smith, and George Eliot.* New York: Columbia University Press, 1986.

Mullan, John. *Sentiment and Sociability: The Language of Feeling in the Eighteenth Century.* Oxford: Clarendon Press, 1988.

Nussbaum, Felicity. *The Autobiographical Subject: Gender and Ideology in Eighteenth-Century England.* Baltimore: Johns Hopkins University Press, 1989.

Nussbaum, Felicity, and Laura Brown. *The New Eighteenth Century: Theory, Politics, English Literature.* New York and London: Methuen, 1987.

Paulson, Ronald. *Breaking and Remaking: Aesthetic Practice in England, 1700–1820.* New Brunswick: Rutgers University Press, 1989.

Pollak, Ellen. *The Poetics of Sexual Myth: Gender and Ideology in the Verse of Swift and Pope.* Chicago: University of Chicago Press, 1985.

Richetti, John. *Philosophical Writing: Locke, Berkeley, Hume.* Cambridge, MA: Harvard University Press, 1983.

Rousseau, G. S., and Roy Porter. *Exoticism in the Enlightenment.* Manchester: Manchester University Press, 1990.

Rousseau, G. S., and Roy Porter. *Sexual Underworlds of the Enlightenment.* Chapel Hill: University of North Carolina Press, 1988.

Stallybrass, Peter, and Allon White. *The Politics and Poetics of Transgression.* Ithaca: Cornell University Press, 1986.

Todd, Janet M. *The Sign of Angellica: Women, Writing, and Fiction, 1660–1800.* London: Virago, 1989.

5 *William H. Epstein*

Professing Gray: The Resumption of Authority in Eighteenth-Century Studies

This essay is an adumbration of some of the arguments in a chapter of a book I am writing on the professional practice of eighteenth-century studies in America from 1925 to 1975. That chapter deals with the criticism of Gray's "Elegy" in the late 1940s and early 1950s, and most especially with Frank H. Ellis' long 1951 *PMLA* article, "Gray's *Elegy*: The Biographical Problem in Literary Criticism," which promulgated the "Biographical Fallacy," induced the so-called "Stonecutter Controversy," and remained a crucial document in Gray criticism for the next twenty years or so.[1] Ellis' article was also the critical text that introduced me (and, I suspect, many other graduate students) to Gray scholarship, when I studied under James Clifford at Columbia in the mid 1960s. Clifford believed in what he called "teaching through controversy," a pedagogical approach stressing "topics where during recent years there have been heated arguments and fundamental disagreements," through which he hoped to "rouse interest and increase involvement."[2] In a sense, I suppose, I am extenuating this approach in my explorations of the professional practice of our period specialty, except that for me these controversies are not merely interesting instructional examples tacitly reinscribing the agreements-to-disagree so characteristic of academic criticism conceived as a humanistic enterprise of democratic pluralism—but unbridgeable gaps revealing and concealing the ongoing processes of misrecognition through which a professional practice assumes and resumes authority. I begin my exploration of this difference with a description of a methodological term—a familiar gambit in critical discourse that I hope you will recognize as a mere gesture.

The term is, in fact, the word *gesture,* my use of which is more or less authorized (though not induced) by Neil Hertz's question, in an essay interrogating the graduate instruction he received in eighteenth-century studies in the 1960s, "What can be made of the gestures by which a teacher places himself somewhere between his subjects and his students?"—and by Stanley Fish's answer to the question "What Makes an Interpretation Acceptable?"—"The basic gesture, then, is to disavow interpretation in favor of simply presenting the text; but it is actually a gesture in which one set of interpretive principles is replaced by another that happens to claim for itself the virtue of not being an interpretation at all."[3] The discursive practices of interposition, disavowal, and misrepresentation invoked by Hertz and Fish are, as we shall see, embodied in my deployment of the word *gesture*—which I am defining as a way of sanctioning critical activity under the cover of some other activity. That is, the critic authorizes his or her interpretation by attributing it to someone or something supposedly outside or to the side of professional practice, such as the text (or, for example, textual structure), the author (or authorial intentionality), the reader (or readers' expectations), the culture (or cultural background), the genre (or generic conventions), etc.

A deeply embedded and unavoidable tactic of professional practice, gesturing is a positioning and attitudinizing, a metaphorical placement and movement of the body that expresses thought or feeling by appearing not to do so. That is, because practice is inarticulate and can thus be expressed only in and through the mutual displacements and inadequacies of alternative articulations, gesturing, a nonlinguistic semiotic operation, seems to be a way of signifying something but "not in so many words." Moreover, because gesturing attempts to transfer authority (or at least the temporary site of authority) from a human body (the critic's) moving through and contextualized within cultural space-time, to a reified sign (the author, the text, etc.) seemingly stabilized within an autonomous, disciplinary matrix, it is also a way of *misrecognizing* the participation of individual critics in the community of professional practice. If practice is, as Pierre Bourdieu has suggested, a contingent, temporal group activity poised on the margin between discursive and nondiscursive behavior that can only be "misrecognized," then gesturing is one of the characteristic forms of this behavior—"a truth whose sole meaning and function are to deny a truth known and recognized by all, a lie which would deceive no one, were not everyone determined to deceive *himself* [or herself]."[4] Thus gesturing is a critical tactic (of which we are all more or less aware, but which we are also determined to misrecognize) that characteristically shifts interpretive authority out of the context of everyday human and social activity (what I am calling professional practice) and into a timeless, independent, already constituted and structured realm of subjects, works, ideas, and linguistic patterns (what I have called a disciplinary matrix).

This is roughly the distinction Stephen Toulmin draws between an "intellectual profession" and an "intellectual discipline," [5] except that, unlike Toulmin, I do not ultimately believe in this difference. In my view, "the professional" drives "the disciplinary," although it must not appear to do so—thus such tactical operations as "the gesture." This is not to say that "the professional" is itself a reified, autonomous, stabilized, and stabilizing structure of formalized relationships. As John Guillory has recently remarked, deploying a Bourdieuvian analysis somewhat as I have done, "The profession is not an institution, any more than criticism is: it is the self-representation by means of which teachers misrecognize their relation both to their discursive practices and to the institution of the school." Of course, as I'm sure Guillory would agree, "the profession" is other things as well, but the point here is that it is *never* a mere substitution for "the discipline" or "criticism" or other "older institutional structures [that] serve to legitimate and stabilize what is always illegitimate and unstable— the momentary conjunctural order." [6] In other words, "the professional" is a way of naming (if imprecisely situating) the embedded social strategy of misrecognition and its deployment through such authorizing tactics as "the gesture."

Ellis' article more or less thematizes this tactic by calling into question what he calls "the practical aspect of a larger, theoretical problem: the relation between a written work and the biographical experiences of the writer" (971), specifically, the interpretive gesture that treats a poem as "an autobiographical document" (971) and that assumes "that an exact, one-to-one correspondence exists between the person who is imagined to be speaking the lines of a poem (the Spokesman) and the historical personage who is known to have written the poem" (988). In characteristic New Critical fashion, Ellis labels this gesture "the biographical *fallacy*" (971, 988, emphasis added) and asserts that he will restore "the poem itself, the product as distinguished from the process of composition" (972), to critical discourse, which now "can *resume* its original Aristotelian function of rhetorical analysis, instead of pretending to dictate terms to poetry or to serve as a substitute for it" (1008, emphasis added). Of course, in recognizing and naming this gesture, a deeply embedded tactic of professional practice that he calls one of "the more persistent fallacies in literary criticism" (988), Ellis is himself practicing to deceive, for (as you may have noticed) he replaces it with another gesture.

Yet Ellis should not be chastised for this replacement, for he could not do otherwise: the general authority that a critic assumes and the specific tactics whereby he or she exercises that authority must always seem as if they are outside or to the side of professional practice. Accordingly, Ellis returns to "the poem itself": that is, he adopts an interpretive strategy enabling "the problem of the poem's structure [to] be *resumed* without prejudice" (971, emphasis added). Of course, this is a familiar critical gesture, reinscribed (as we have just seen) at both the beginning and end of Ellis' article as a mode of "resumption," a way of starting over or being paid back, or, more specifically (in British law), "the action, on the part of the Crown or other authority, of reassuming possession of lands, rights, etc., which have been bestowed on others" (*OED*). In this sense criticism is (explicitly for Ellis and implicitly for the rest of us) an ongoing activity of resumption—of repossessing a text, author, genre, theme, literary period, or whatever, from other critics or scholars who have misused it or (just as likely) used it too well to their advantage.

Moreover, resumption entails a return to "original" possession (e.g., to "resume its original Aristotelian function of rhetorical analysis"), a nostalgic, sentimental approach that presupposes a situation in which authority is unquestionable and unquestioned, in which (as Bourdieu would have it) there is no "field of opinion"[7] and hence no need to explain, defend, or assert our assumption (indeed, possession) of interpretive authority. This too is a familiar gesture in Anglo-American cultural discourse (e.g., under the cover of "returning to the original constitution") and generally in Western culture—thus Bourdieu's (self-consciously) "nostalgic" description of the collective group practice of "ancient societies," where "there is a quasi-perfect correspondence between the objective order and the subjective principles of organization" and where consequently "the natural and social world appears as self-evident."[8] This sense of a self-evident, quasi-perfect correspondence returns us not only to a crucial "starting point" in American cultural discourse—the Declaration of Independence's "we hold these truths to be self-evident"—but also to Ellis' article, which, on behalf of deauthorizing one mode of resumption ("an exact, one-to-one correspondence" between Spokesman and author), sanctions yet another mode of resumption ("the problem of the poem's structure resumed" through criticism's "original Aristotelian function of rhetorical analysis"). The latter approach, of course, posits just such a self-evident, quasi-perfect correspondence between the poem and the critic: in Ellis' words, "The job of criticism then becomes to make it as clear as possible what these ["intellectual and emotional effects" of the poem's "calculated rhetorical structure"] are . . . on the critic himself" (1008).

Now, the assumption or resumption of interpretive authority through the assertion of such a correspondence is a familiar gesture often (although, of course, not exclusively) associated with the New Criticism, which, when Ellis' article appeared in *PMLA* in 1951, was coming to share professional space in the academy with traditional historical/bibliographical scholarship. This is the ground upon which W. Powell Jones, in a 1952 *PQ* review of Ellis' article, praises and appraises Ellis' argument and links him to "other 'new critics,' "[9] and through which the many other scholars who participated in the 'Stonecutter Controversy' over the ensuing two decades mapped what we might call the citational topography of Ellis' article.[10] As Ralph Rader observed in the early 1970s, "for the better part of two centuries it never occurred to anyone to suppose that the agent of the words in the poem was anyone but the poet Gray in his own proper person, but the interpretive possibilities opened up by modern theory have led some in recent years to the view that the speaker is to be entirely dissociated from Gray."[11] As we shall see, Ellis deploys several strategies, not all of which are consonant with conventional notions of the modern theoretical program sponsored by New Criticism, but which, collectively, delineate an approach that instrumentalizes one way we can write or rewrite the discourse of the professional practice of eighteenth-century studies in America in the late 1940s and early 1950s.

For Ellis' article can be treated as a kind of "bug in amber," a preserved moment in this discourse when an alliance of textual and institutional politics was being formed between the New Criticism, which was more or less a-, non-, or anti-historical, and traditional historical scholarship, which was more or less a-, non-, or anti-theoretical/critical. Traditional scholarship produced the biographies, historical accounts, and (most especially) "standard" texts which the New Criticism transformed into impersonal, autonomous, decontextualized, rhetorically and formally structured artifacts. Ellis' article offers a kind of fossilized record of this moment in professional practice when, as near the end of the Napoleonic Wars, antagonistic powers waged war and negotiated peace simultaneously. Deflecting threats from both the Left (revolutionary Marxist explanations of events) and the Right (McCarthyism's suspicion that intellectual labor was alien and seditious), mid-century American cultural discourse (in general) and academic literary criticism (in particular) actively sponsored either historical descriptions that were resolutely capitalist and untheoretical, or theoretico-critical descriptions that were formally unhistorical and apolitical (although, it is often claimed, the latter were Tory, Anglo-Catholic, and corporatist in their early promulgation by such figures as T. S. Eliot and John Crowe Ransom, whose conservative politics, "objective correlatives," and concept of "Criticism, Inc." were crucial features of New Criticism's formation).

Ellis resumes his authority from both of these contending powers, indeed, from a kind of uneasy, temporary alliance between them that was,
as I have suggested, characteristic of textual politics at this moment. The
first part of Ellis' essay "attempts to reconstruct, in as much detail as
printed documents permit, the biographical experiences which went into
the composition of the *Elegy*" (971), the kind of historicist project habitu-
ally associated with traditional scholarship, which seeks, as does Ellis, "to
recapture something of the atmosphere in which the poem originated"
(971–72). As we know, this "reconstruction of biographical experience"
and "recapturing of original atmosphere" induce the interpretive strategy
of resumption, which is emplotted as a narrative scheme of nostalgic re-
possession. Ellis pursues this familiar strategy by distinguishing himself
from those commentators who, he charges, have misused biographical
evidence and thus misinterpreted the poem. Invoking the authority of "external documents" (1007)—"external" in the sense that they are treated as
"outside" the poem, thus preserving the New Critical distinction between
"extrinsic" and "intrinsic"—Ellis nostagically repossesses original experience through a creative rereading and rewriting of Gray's correspondence
and the first draft of the *Elegy*, also referred to as the Eton manuscript,
which Gray apparently described in a letter as "a few autumnal Verses"
and titled *Stanza's wrote in a country church-yard* (976).

Interweaving passages from the *Stanza's* with others from Gray's correspondence and from a collection of state trials, Ellis tries to show that
Gray's witnessing and contemplating "the trial and execution of the Scottish rebel lords" (972) during the summer of 1746 induced an emotional
and intellectual crisis from which emerged Gray's decision to abandon
the study of law and embrace "the profession of poetry" (982), a decision and state of mind encoded in the intensely personal verses of the Eton
manuscript. These *Stanza's*, Ellis maintains, "were originally an 'artless
Tale' about Thomas Gray, not about 'the [poem's] unhonour'd Dead'"
(981). Only some years later, in June 1750, when he revised and expanded
these unpublished verses, did Gray "depersonalize them entirely" (983).
Writing "himself out of his poem," he shifted pronoun references, can-
celed and combined some of the original lines, and added sixteen stanzas
introducing "a dramatic situation involving four characters" (984–85),
one of whom is "a completely generalized Spokesman who is simply the
vehicle of the poem" (986), which can now be referred to as "the *Elegy*"—
"'almost a part of the national consciousness'" (988), an autonomous,
apolitical organism marked by impersonality, "'anonymity'" (986), and
"a calculated rhetorical structure" (1008).

I have no real desire or need to evaluate the interpretive power of Ellis'
biographical and bibliographical resumption of Gray's state of mind and

the circumstances surrounding the composition of the *Elegy* in its various versions. This is more appropriately a task for Gray scholars, for
whom this ongoing evaluative process is a crucial, constantly changing
activity of their professional practice, one which, of course, they consistently misrecognize as occurring within and contributing to an already
constituted disciplinary field. What interests me here is how Ellis' article
so obviously and specifically reproduces the general situation in textual
politics at mid-century. Sharing and contending for interpretive space in
Ellis' article, as they were in journals, conference panels, undergraduate
curricula, graduate programs, and other venues of literary criticism in the
American academy at this time, are two powerful projects of professional
practice: a biographical/bibliographical approach, for which the poem is
a personal and historical record of Gray's "experiences" (982) and "imagination" (990–91), and a formalist approach, for which the poem is an
anonymous, impersonal, ahistorical structure of rhetorical, stylistic, and
thematic "effects" (1008). In the "plot" of Ellis' article, as in presumptive,
New Critical narrative schemes depicting contemporary textual politics,
the formalist seems to be superseding the biographical/bibliographical, despite (indeed, because of) its reliance upon traditional scholarship for the
establishment of such stable, "disciplinary" propositions as the biographical subject and the provenance of the text. The *Stanza's*, unpublished,
incomplete, and "intensely personal" (983), are both the product and the
emblem of traditional scholarship; the *Elegy*, "*a thing with an end to it*"
(980) (Gray's description in a letter to Walpole, cited approvingly by Ellis),
is a perfectly realized, impersonal, literary artifact expressing national (indeed, international, transcultural) consciousness, and, as such, is both the
product and emblem of New Criticism.

Apparently bridging the gap between these two seemingly irreconcilable
strategies of professional practice and their dissonant tactics of resuming
interpretive authority is yet another gesture in Ellis' article that I have so
far neglected. This is his persistent deployment of Milton's poetry, a familiar tactic involving an appeal to the authority of a great writer who, it can
be shown, worked in a similar mode and whom the author (treated here
ambiguously as both biographical subject and implied underwriter) must
have read. "It is evident from this [Ellis writes] that Gray's experience in
reading *Lycidas* was of equal importance in the composition of the *Elegy*
with the varied experiences of the holiday in London and Stoke Poges [dur-
ing which Gray saw the trial and reexamined his life]" (982). The indefinite
reference of the word "this" and the assumed self-evidence of the interpretive tactic (both expressed in the phrase "It is evident from this") are
symptomatic of the slipperiness of such gestures. Although "this" could
refer to the argument citing lines from *Lycidas* in the previous paragraph,

Ellis has elsewhere conspicuously interwoven passages from Milton and Gray, most dramatically perhaps on the preceding page, just as the argument is shifting from the *Stanza's* to the *Elegy*. "The *Stanza's* wrote in a country churchyard were originally an 'artless Tale' about Thomas Gray, not about 'the unhonour'd Dead,' just as *Lycidas* is essentially a 'Doric lay' about John Milton, not about the 'Unwept' Edward King. Both poems are concerned with the same themes: the alienation of the Poet from his audience, or the conflict between the aesthetic values of poetry and the materialistic values of 'the World'" (981). Later, Ellis will use Miltonic authority to complete this transition from *Stanza's* to *Elegy*: "Gray has shifted the bearing of the poem from the conflict of the Poet with an alien world [as in the *Stanza's*] to the triumphant persistence, or continuity, of poetry despite this hostile world [as in the *Elegy*]. And this is what may be implied in the concluding line of *Lycidas*" (987), which he then quotes.

As we have seen before, Ellis' treatment of the *Stanza's* derives its authority from and acts on behalf of traditional scholarship, which, he finds, has failed to resolve "the conflict between the aesthetic values of poetry and the materialistic values of 'the World,'" a common charge leveled against this professional project by Eliot, Ransom, Allen Tate, and other influential promoters of Anglo-American formalism. The New Criticism, they claimed, characteristically transcended this conflict by asserting "the triumphant persistence, or continuity, of poetry despite this hostile world," a conservative reaction against modern culture that depicts literature and literary criticism as an autonomous, apolitical, decontextualized, saving remnant. Interestingly, and significantly, Milton's *Lycidas* can imply both situations, can (as Ellis claims) "[remain] the model even for this wholesale revision of the poem" (986), and can thus function as the crucial gesture apparently bridging the gap between the two parts of Ellis' argument.

How can it do so? Simply because this invocation of authority (in every instance it is invoked) is a *mere* gesture: a misrecognized act of professional practice through which interpretive authority is resumed by attributing it to a disciplinary authority (a mode of scholarship, biographical subject, textual provenance, rhetorical structure, generic convention, canonized author or work, et al.) that is always and only a transient, inarticulate tactic of professional practice. In this respect, Milton acts as Ellis' "spokesman," for he becomes not only the momentary agent of authority through which Ellis articulates his resumption of Gray's *Elegy* but also the pattern for Ellis' celebrated and notorious vehicle of this articulation—the Stonecutter.

According to Ellis, the Stonecutter is a deceased village epitaph writer ("there must now be imagined some semi-literate artisan on whom the village would rely to frame 'Some frail Memorial'" [984]), a crucial figure in the poem, unimagined or unappreciated by two centuries of criticism, to whom the Spokesman (the narrating "me" of line 4) refers in "For thee, who mindful of th'unhonour'd Dead / Dost in these Lines their artless Tale relate" (985). The Stonecutter now also becomes the subject of the "hoary-headed Swain" 's inscribed narrative detailing a local pastoral poet's life and death, and of the poem's concluding Epitaph, written by the Spokesman and read by yet another imagined figure, a "melancholy wayfarer" or "Enquirer" (the poem's "Some Kindred Spirit"), to whom the old swain tells his tale (985, 1003). The consequences of this rather elaborate plot can be traced in the transition, monitored by Milton's poetry, from *Stanza's* to *Elegy*, a transition which can now be seen as also marking the movement of the Stonecutter from a shadowy marginal figure to a centrally positioned major character: "In the original *Stanza's*, the narrator, with whom Gray identified himself, occupied the central position of the 'uncouth Swain' who mourns for Lycidas. But in the completed *Elegy*, the Spokesman is relegated to the position of the anonymous elegist whom the 'uncouth Swain' in *Lycidas* momentarily invokes, and the central position is occupied by the village Stonecutter who mourns 'th'unhonour'd Dead' " (987).

The Miltonic analogy enabling Ellis' exposure of the Stonecutter is also induced and sustained by the Spokesman's conjecture that among the country church-yard's "unhonour'd Dead" rests "Some mute inglorious Milton." Thus Ellis proposes: "The Stonecutter is not Milton, of course, but he may have been a 'mute inglorious Milton,' and he was, in a sense, a poet" (986). Milton and yet not Milton: we are back to the *in*exact, quasi-perfect, one-to-one correspondence between biographical subject and poetical spokesman, as between calculated rhetorical structure and critical sensibility, which we noted previously. Let me imitate the manner of this remark: "The Stonecutter is not Milton is not Ellis, of course, but, after all, this is the figure by which Ellis is most well known in Gray criticism and eighteenth-century studies; constrained (as are we all) from speaking for himself in his creative rewriting (which is also a resuming) of this poem, and thus limited to expressing himself through nonlinguistic gestures, Ellis may be considered a 'mute inglorious Milton' and he is, in that sense, a poet." In other words, Ellis *is* the Stonecutter: not only in the sense that he is (still) identified with this interpretive formulation but also because the trope of the "mute, inglorious Milton," after which the Stonecutter is modeled, is a traditional way of characterizing the literary critic in Anglo-American discourse—the 'silent' marginal figure who is not formally there but whose (seemingly inevitable if resented) emergence and articulation become crucial to (if not constitute) the production or reproduction of meaning. Thus, like the Stonecutter, the critic is a poet who is not a poet—Milton and yet not Milton.

Reencountering one's own interpretive gestures is an inevitable consequence of participating in cultural discourse. There is no privileged position from which to explore the professional practice of period specializations like eighteenth-century studies or interpretive movements like the New Criticism. As I remarked at the beginning of this essay, practice is inarticulate and can thus be expressed only in and through the mutual displacements and inadequacies of alternative articulations. Nor is reflexivity, an instance of which I am about to use in an attempt at closure, a solution to the problem: it merely displaces one kind of gesture with another; the second may be more fashionable than the first but it is no less permanent or definitive. Nevertheless, everybody has to be someplace, if only temporarily and provisionally. Thus I close by asking you to remember my claim that Ellis' article can be treated as a kind of "bug in amber." Besides the cultural currency of this familiar phrase and the interpretive logic by which I associated it with "a preserved moment in textual politics," how can I authorize such a crucial gesture in my own professional practice? Taking my lead from Ellis, I cite a generally recognized influential precedent—in this case, a passage from Alexander Pope, the figure who has dominated the twentieth-century American academy's professing of early and mid-eighteenth-century poetry.

In the *Epistle to Arbuthnot* Pope's so-called poetic spokesman is, as usual, belittling literary critics: "Each Wight who reads not, and but scans and spells, / Each Word-catcher that lives on syllables, / Ev'n such small Critics some regard may claim, / Preserv'd in *Milton's* or in *Shakespear's* name. / Pretty! in Amber to observe the forms / Of hairs, or straws, or dirt, or grubs, or worms; / The things, we know, are neither rich nor rare, / But wonder how the Devil they got there?"[12] Preserved in Milton's or in Shakespeare's or in Pope's name, we word-catching critics can always be observed as if we were grubs or worms or bugs in amber, forms neither rich nor rare, whose misrecognized articulations of professional practice are a constant source of wonder. How the devil did we ever get there? The study of the professional practice of a period specialization is always gesturing toward answers to that vexing question.

Notes

My much longer article on a similar topic appears in the Spring 1990 issue of *ELH*, although this essay does contain some material not in the *ELH* piece.

1 Frank H. Ellis, "Gray's *Elegy*: The Biographical Problem in Literary Criticism," *PMLA*, 66(1951), 971–1008; references cited parenthetically in text.
2 James L. Clifford, "Argument and Understanding: Teaching through Controversy," *Eighteenth-Century Life*, 5, no. 3(1979), 1–2.
3 Neil Hertz, "Two Extravagant Teachings," *Yale French Studies*, 63(1982), 63;

Stanley Fish, *Is There a Text in This Class? The Authority of Interpretive Communities* (Cambridge, MA, and London: Harvard University Press, 1980), 353.

4 Pierre Bourdieu, *Outline of a Theory of Practice*, trans. Richard Nice, Cambridge Studies in Social Anthropology 16 (1972; Cambridge: Cambridge University Press, 1977), 133.

5 Stephen Toulmin, *Human Understanding: The Collective Use and Evolution of Concepts* (Princeton, NJ: Princeton University Press, 1972), esp. chaps. 2–4.

6 John Guillory, "Canonical and Non-Canonical: A Critique of the Current Debate," *ELH*, 54(1987), 498.

7 Bourdieu, *Outline* 168; emphasis dropped.

8 Ibid. 164.

9 W. Powell Jones, "Review of Ellis' 'Gray's *Elegy*,' " *Philological Quarterly*, 31, no. 3(1952), 274; Jones's review of the article is especially interesting because he also "recommended it for publication" (274).

10 There are many ways of mapping such a citational topography. Steve Nimis' recent work on the reputation of Wilamovitz in classics studies seems more or less appropriate in this instance. At first, citing Ellis is a necessary gesture underwriting interpretations that must support, attack, or emend his argument; eventually, citing him becomes a quaint gesture revealing a desire to be thorough but dismissing his article's privileged status in Gray studies. See Steve Nimis, "Fussnoten: Das Fundament der Wissenschaft," *Arethusa*, 17, no. 2(1984), 105–34.

11 Ralph W. Rader, "The Concept of Genre and Eighteenth-Century Studies," in *New Approaches to Eighteenth-Century Literature*, ed. Phillip Harth, Selected Papers from the English Institute (New York and London: Columbia University Press, 1974), 93.

12 Alexander Pope, "An Epistle from Mr. *Pope*, to Dr. *Arbuthnot*," in *Imitations of Horace with An Epistle to Dr Arbuthnot and The Epilogue to the Satires*, ed. John Butt, The Twickenham Edition of the Poems of Alexander Pope, Vol. 4, 2d ed. (1939; New Haven: Yale University Press; London: Methuen, 1953), 108, 11. 165–72.

6 *John Richetti*

The Legacy of Ian Watt's
The Rise of the Novel

In a recent review essay surveying the year's work in eighteenth-century studies for 1987, Robert D. Hume remarks that most of the century's fiction is "eminently comprehensible, and the future for explicative criticism seems dim indeed." One way out, says Hume, is for a critic to "work in the broader regions of psychology and sociology" and thereby to "get us out of the rut dug by a generation of in-text critics."[1] Leaving aside the metaphorical riddle of what it means to work inside or outside a text, part of what Hume says is true enough, since eighteenth-century fiction in all of its varieties seems largely overt in its designs and purposes, limited as later novels are not by the moral and social functions it claims to serve. Moreover, Defoe, Richardson, Fielding, and Smollett do not seem especially troubled by what we nowadays call the problematics of representation, although in the case of Richardson especially recent critics have found a lot to trouble them. And yet it is just this forthrightness and formal transparency of eighteenth-century fiction that is the difficult issue, especially so now that literary criticism has made itself acutely self-conscious of the artificiality of all re-presentation. Like the amazing pictures recently beamed back from the far reaches of interplanetary space that are constructed from millions of bits of digital information, what we think of as naively realistic presentation is upon examination a hugely complicated artifact, visible as a plausible simulacrum only when processed within a cultural framework almost as complicated if far less exact than NASA engineers' digital technology. So the critical task is to reveal the artifice behind the seeming transparency of eighteenth-century novels—by means of an analysis directed toward their cultural and historical functions to dismantle their surfaces and show just what they are really up to in appearing so open. Moreover, Hume's dichotomy or division of critical labor is exactly wrong, since the text as it appears in its transparency must be serving just those psychological and sociological functions or meanings he says critics should be looking for.

Hume's remarks are prompted by his discussion of two recent books that have renewed interest in the perennial question of the origins of the novel in the eighteenth century: John Bender's *Imagining the Penitentiary: Fiction and the Architecture of Mind in Eighteenth-Century England* (1987) and Michael McKeon's *The Origins of the English Novel, 1600–1740* (1987). They are especially welcome, says Hume, because Ian Watt's *The Rise of the Novel* is now virtually discredited; "taught as gospel" twenty-five years ago, it is now "widely understood" as offering "a grossly misleading historical model."[2] Hume doesn't have time in his long review essay to elaborate on so serious a charge, and in fact I think he is completely wrong, grossly misleading himself not only in his assessment of Watt's book but in implying that Bender and McKeon have somehow definitively corrected or indeed dismissed *The Rise of the Novel*. Certainly, it is a book that has drawn hosts of envious detractors because of its success, but that success seems to me richly deserved, precisely because Watt turned students of the novel away from the very sort of narrow-minded positivism Hume has in mind when he speaks of in-text criticism. Watt in fact also did much to rescue literary history from a dominant simplistic evolutionary view of the development of the novel and made possible by his example a richly psychocultural understanding of its emergence in the eighteenth century, offering a model of the very sort of extrinsic and contextual criticism Hume admires.[3]

The Rise of the Novel made a generation of readers aware, as never before, that the transparency and overtness of eighteenth-century fiction that Hume thinks render it uninteresting were means to sociocultural ends rather than self-explanatory phenomena. Watt's book is thus nothing less than a foundational critical work that in Bender's and McKeon's brilliant books has provoked the latest of a line of worthy successors. But as much as I value their books, I think neither McKeon nor Bender (nor, for that matter, other recent students of the beginnings of British fiction) negates or discards the insights about the beginnings of the novel Watt articulated so memorably. A comparison of his work and theirs is, I think, useful to show how whatever progress has been made since his work in critical understanding of the evolution of the novel is essentially indebted to his enduring example. Such a comparison may also be interesting for showing a few of the ways in which literary history has changed since the late fifties, and more specifically the way one aspect of eighteenth-century studies has reacted to recent trends in styles of critical discourse.

As Watt explained in a tongue-in-cheek retrospection twenty years after his book first appeared, *The Rise of the Novel* began its existence as a theoretically informed attempt to use the "hypothetico-deductive method," as he then called it, in order to inquire by means of close textual analysis how the novel differed "from the prose fiction of the past" and "why those differences appeared when and where they did." [4] The first question is primarily formal, the second historical, and the special achievement of Watt's book is that in his critical practice these issues are never separated. The novel as he describes it is always a unique formal effect of new and equally singular historical circumstances. Watt's rendition of those circumstances is sometimes necessarily comprehensive, perhaps overgeneralized. The novel appears as a parallel manifestation of "that vast transformation of Western civilization since the Renaissance which has replaced the unified world picture of the Middle Ages with another very different one— one which presents us, essentially, with a developing but unplanned aggregate of particular individuals having particular experiences at particular times and at particular places." [5] But in the next paragraph Watt zooms in from that panoramic shot to tight focus on the "distinctive narrative mode of the novel," a circumstantial view of life which imitates not the philosophers but the "procedures of another group of specialists in epistemology, the jury in a court of law" (31). The "formal realism" he goes on to describe is very much a convention located within a constellation of particular social practices, as we have learned to call them, and Watt's emphasis throughout this influential discussion is on the historical distinctiveness of those practices, "a more largely referential use of language than is common in other literary forms" (32), visible as such only within the context provided by a comparative critical experiment such as this. In other words, Watt's presentation of the unique formal nature of the novel can be read, proleptically as it were, as a response to Robert Hume's challenge and as a negation of the opposition between formal and historical approaches. As Daniel R. Schwarz pointed out a few years ago in an assessment of *The Rise of the Novel*, Watt provides "a model for reading literature in terms of contexts without sacrificing formal analysis of a work's imagined world." [6]

The eighteenth-century novel's realistic transparency is from the first identified by Watt as a response to cultural circumstances and not as a move, as some of his critics think, toward an improved access to some sort of transhistorical realm of actuality. It is certainly true that he has what some have called a "teleological" bias, and he does trace a progression in the refinement of realistic narrative technique that culminates in Jane Austen. But that progression is always viewed in pretty rigorous historical terms, since, as Schwarz puts it, Watt believed that "the principles of scientific and historical inquiry can be applied to the humanities and that valid hypotheses can be developed for studying literature as cultural phenomena."[7] Watt's effort, in the context of the heightened historical awareness of the postwar decades when he was working, constitutes a deliberate modification of the Leavisite or humanist evaluative moral and aesthetic standards that still dominated criticism and literary history. As he said in his retrospective essay on *The Rise of the Novel*, he was out to explore the "historical, institutional and social context of literature" as well as its relationship to "philosophical ideas" and thereby to protest against what is still the prevalent tendency "to write as though both ideas and novels existed independently of each other."[8] To be sure, Watt looks old-fashioned to high-flying contemporary academic Nietzscheans because he did not abandon humanist values and the belief that literature manifested human agency and will; he offered, in retrospect, a highly original and exemplary blend of new critical styles that allowed him both to historicize and to make moral and aesthetic judgments. His series of particularized readings of the central eighteenth-century novels is part of the sharpened attentiveness to the text of Anglo-American "New Criticism" of the time.[9] But behind the fine-grained textual analysis of particulars that Watt offers to sustain his thesis there are the broad brush strokes of generalized sociology (Weber, Durkheim, Pareto) and intellectual history in the grand manner, perhaps derived specifically from the Frankfurt School: Richardson's narrative mode is part of "a much larger change in outlook—the transition from the objective, social and public orientation of the classical world to the subjective, individualist and private orientation of the life and literature of the last two hundred years" (176).

   If one looks at the criticism and literary history that immediately precede Watt's book, such an effective and theoretically consistent merging of history and criticism is simply not there. As good and still useful a book as A. D. McKillop's *The Early Masters of English Fiction* (1956) just assumes that there is significant continuity of narrative theme and technique between later novelistic achievements and the work of these "early masters." McKillop, for example, praises Richardson and Sterne for coming "to such a close reckoning with inner experience as makes them the forerunners respectively of tragic and comic intransigence as the basic themes of the later novel."[10] For McKillop eighteenth-century writers inhabit a rhetorical world that, through the force of genius, they modify and improve as narrative edges closer in their best work to representational efficiency and adequacy. In certain passages in Richardson and Sterne, "we can realize the importance of a tendency to use in place of these stock attitudes and expressions a more minutely particularized account of spontaneous mannerisms and gestures" (23). At moments like these, McKillop was paying special attention to the details of the craft of fiction, and his book is still valuable for its descriptions of the technical advances (from the point of view of the mid-twentieth century) in narrative fashioning to be found here and there in the eighteenth-century masters. Send a student to McKillop's chapters and she or he will probably read these writers with sharpened interest and appreciation. McKillop is informative because he is modest and relatively undemanding, requiring only the local historical and biographical knowledge that he himself supplies, recounting literary history as a movement toward the special expressiveness and completeness of the modern novel. History is there in McKillop's pages, but it is a neutral medium, material for the novelist to work with and not essentially distinct, only different in its details, from later or earlier history.

Read in sequence, Watt adds to McKillop's informative presentation and progressivistic view of the development of prose narrative a self-conscious historical-theoretical framework, lucidly and indeed wittily presented but nonetheless ambitious and comprehensive. His general argument is too well known to need detailed summary here, and much of what he said was in its broad outlines hardly original, as he later admitted.[11] Linking developments in epistemology with those in the social and economic spheres, Watt sought to show how the novel expressed the emerging "individualism" and privatization of experience to be found in the early eighteenth century. To some extent, he echoed Weber and Tawney and identified this individualism with the "middle classes," but his use of that notoriously loose designation has been exaggerated by his critics. Most of the time, he employs the term only to label certain values and habits that deserve the tag. He never claims, as some critics assert, that the "middle classes" constituted a dominant or even coherently self-conscious social group. And who can deny that most of the novels in question promote "bourgeois" virtues and denounce "aristocratic" vices? Whatever one's views on the proper ideological labels, it is more important to see that Watt kept before his readers the controlling insight that individualism, whether "middle class" economic or epistemological or literary, was the result of forces larger than particular individuals. Defoe, Richardson, and Fielding may indeed have been the inventors of modern narrative, but they "could not have created the new form unless the conditions of the time had also been favourable" (9).

Among those critics who have attacked Watt's views on these socioeconomic foundations of the novel, Maximillian Novak, the preeminent

Defoe scholar of the last thirty years, is notable for the cogency of his objections. A recent book by Bram Dijkstra, *Defoe and Economics*, has defended Watt against Novak in spirited and I think essentially accurate terms. Dijkstra finds in *The Rise of the Novel* "a new level of sociological awareness and historical specificity" entering the mainstream of Anglo-American literary scholarship. More contentious is Dijkstra's charge that in challenging Watt's interpretation of economic history Novak was in fact promoting an ahistorical understanding of Defoe's fiction, specifically and especially *Roxana*.[12] The point of Novak's challenge, he says, was "to make a case for a Defoe whose moral and economic ideas contained none of the freewheeling, predatory, 'modern' elements his characters' actions exhibited, and whose notions about trade were indeed conservative and regressive rather than accurately reflective of the dominant attitudes of this time toward economic development" (161). In the special case of *Roxana*, Dijkstra charges with some real anger, the result has been to reject the heroine's subversive economic notions and attempt to make her story a moralized case history in which Defoe dramatizes the necessity of rejecting what he in fact deeply believed.

Dijkstra's polemic is somewhat overstated, and he makes Novak sound like someone carrying out a secret vendetta. In fact, Novak has been quite generous and straightforward in his disagreement with the governing thesis of *The Rise of the Novel*. As he says in a recent gathering of his essays on Defoe, Watt's book was written with such "great intellectual force and equal critical power that it is hardly surprising that it has become the orthodox way of reading" the eighteenth-century novel.[13] Yet Dijkstra has a point, for Novak's most important objection to *The Rise of the Novel* is not that Defoe is an economic "mercantilist" whose views do not really line up exactly with the protocapitalist ideology that Watt finds in the novels. Instead, Novak offers a positivist and "old historicist" objection when he protests that Watt's "homology between external developments and fictional events is almost impossible to prove" (6). In the long run, Novak's formidable scholarship and unrivaled command of Defoe's works and times are mobilized precisely to complicate the historical record, to particularize it so minutely that generalizations of the sort required for sociohistorical analysis are rendered impossible or invalid. Novak's scholarship is ultimately concerned to rescue Defoe's works from the larger ideological forces criticism like Watt's invokes in order to promote an author who was fully and absolutely in control of his writing within its specific historical contexts. For Novak, Defoe is a thinker, not a profound one but "perhaps the most versatile and prolific creator of systems in his age" (13). This may indeed be true, but Novak's skepticism about the "homologies" Watt proposes (and as he renders them they are not really that) represents just the sort of traditional Anglo-American historical positivism *The Rise of the Novel* challenged.

Many critics are nowadays, as far as I can tell, embarrassed by talk of individual genius. Watt, of course, felt no such inhibition, and *The Rise of the Novel* speaks often of the special talents and insights of these novelists and of what he calls "literature," another term now banished from polite critical usage. This combination of sociohistorical rigor and enthusiastic appreciation for individual achievement, even if it is in some sense provoked by or derived from circumstances, seems to me to save Watt from the special pleading and the cult of personality that still operate among some eighteenth-century scholars who specialize in particular authors. Such scholars become, to some extent, fans, celebrants of the unique genius of Johnson, Pope, Defoe, or Fielding. Watt pointedly avoided that sort of curatorial relationship to his authors, but his blending of historical distance and respect for the abilities of the first novelists is what allows *The Rise of the Novel* to face (if not to resolve) issues that some of his successors do not always engage frankly.

As McKeon's and Bender's studies make clear, there are two main issues that can be defined as central in the current critical climate for those who aspire to revise or replace Watt's book as the standard account of the emergence of the novel: a working definition and historical location for the amorphous category we call the novel and, once that's settled, the genre's relationship to cultural and ideological change. Both issues raise problems of literary value and canonicity and the more general question of the relationship between literature and social conditions and why the novel should have an especially intimate connection with the life that surrounds it. In choosing his triumvirate of writers, Watt more or less accepted posterity's verdict, but he did see himself as revising the canon to the extent that he was taking fiction with special seriousness and promoting Richardson over Fielding as the greatest of the eighteenth-century novelists. But in practice, Watt was not concerned with justifying either his choice of texts or his method of sociocultural analysis; his book is not out to trace the ultimate origins of fiction or to prove that fiction and society are closely interrelated but rather to see how narrative functions in relationship to its determining historical moment. He was not at all concerned with tracing in detail the immediate literary antecedents in the seventeenth and early eighteenth centuries of the three major writers he chose. His aim was to examine and to judge their narrative skills not just as the epiphenomenal results of altered historical circumstances but as an exceedingly coherent and meaningful set of responses by three writers to the challenges offered by those new circumstances. Although his definition of the novel is open to the challenges since presented, it was in fact no more than what was (and still is) generally assumed about the novel, and that confident set of assumptions allowed him to get on with the business of historical description and critical analysis.

Defoe and Richardson, especially, were awarded high marks for managing in different ways to render what we now would want to call the problems and indeed the contradictions built into an emerging early modern consciousness. In the chapter called " 'Robinson Crusoe,' Individualism and the Novel," for example, Watt links Defoe's "Puritanism" with his achievement as a novelist: "Defoe's importance in the history of the novel is directly connected with the way his narrative structure embodied the struggle between Puritanism and the tendency to secularisation which was rooted in material progress" (83). The centrality of *Robinson Crusoe* as Watt outlines it in this chapter lies in Defoe's control of narrative possibilities in order to respond to contradictions like those and to produce a work that is culturally dense and mythically resonant for its historical moment, a moment defined as crucially distinct from the past. Defoe's adaptations of traditional narrative—"a treatment of the individual's psychological concerns that was a tremendous advance in the kind of forensic ratiocination which has previously passed for psychological description" (85)—have their origins in the ideological, both religious and socio-economic, pressures of the moment, and *Robinson Crusoe* is the beginning of the English novel because it responds to those pressures with a completeness and complexity that other works of the time could not manage. Defoe's novel, at one and the same time in Watt's analysis, renders with new vividness Crusoe's consciousness and also "departs from psychological probability in order to redeem his picture of man's inexorable solitariness" (88). The book thus renders what its author sees as the varied reality of contradictory experiences and feelings and thereby promotes what we are in a position to see as an ideology. Much the same pattern is the secret to Richardson's achievement in *Clarissa*, as he takes the "most apparently implausible, didactic or period aspects of the plot and the characters" and brings them "into a larger dramatic pattern of infinite formal and psychological complexity" (238). Richardson's novel resonates with a richly historical orchestration of themes, and the heroine represents "all that is free and positive in the new individualism" as she combats "all the forces that were opposed to the realisation of the new concept—the aristocracy, the patriarchal family system, and even the economic individualism whose development was so closely connected with that of Puritanism" (222).

Obviously, all narrative from this period properly considered has similar historical resonance and ideological purpose or at least some effect in that direction. There is a substantial mass of narrative from the first forty years of the eighteenth century that Watt ignored. Most of that, as

I know from painful if instructive personal experience, is of little interest to a modern reader, and I remember my own struggle during the long dark afternoons I spent twenty-five years ago reading those novels in the British Museum to sustain my wandering attention and overcome a longing for hot liquids. My difficulties in concentrating grew, however, only in part from a preference for the sort of coherence and narrative control that we have learned to value from the established tradition of canonical writers, especially those from the nineteenth and early twentieth centuries. The "popular" or noncanonical narratives that I was attempting to read lacked as well just that cultural density, that mixture Watt had identified of protorealistic technique and ideological intensity to be found in the canonical writers. That is to say, Manley, Haywood, Aubin, Barker, and other women writers of novellas both scandalous and pious, the anonymous producers of religious autobiographies, the writers of travel narratives, real and imaginary, and the compilers of criminal and rogue stories, constitute a body of work that we can say was more or less secreted by its cultural moment, expressing various sorts of pressing concerns and ideologies but lacking, with only rare exceptions, the complexity, density, and authorial singularity of Defoe's or Richardson's novels.[14] That complexity is no doubt the result of some imponderable that deserves to be called genius, and aesthetic achievement is also the result of certain, mostly male, authors' having full access to the means of cultural production. As Watt renders it, genius is always and instructively situated between ideological significance and aesthetic achievement. Or to put it another way, *The Rise of the Novel* taught a generation of critics that the formal achievement of the early novelists is inseparable from their ability to render their unique and strenuous situation in the midst of cultural complexity as opposed to the ideological simplicities and formulae of popular fiction. The canonical works of the new genre, then, are defined by their bringing to something like full expression what other contemporary narrative for whatever reasons could only sketch out clumsily and partially. By omitting them, Watt is clearly implying that these predecessors and forgotten coevals are the origins of the novel only in that they provoke by their incompleteness and lack of distinctive authorial signature the full achievements of the writers who used to be called the early masters.

Something like that, in much more theoretical language and conception, is Michael McKeon's point in his magisterial study, *The Origins of the English Novel, 1600–1740,* which continues and indeed enormously expands and complicates Watt's analytic effort. Using the difficult Marxian dialectical notion of "simple abstraction," McKeon argues that those narratives that precede the mid-century masters create the "pre-givenness" out of which the novel springs. By virtue of their rehearsal of issues (retrospectively recognized as novelistic), such narratives establish a climate or history of "novelistic usage" into which the major writers can insert themselves and conceive of their own projects as an advanced development even as they see their rudimentary predecessors as their own undeveloped but enabling difference.[15] This is a brilliant and wholly original analysis, but in the end it emphatically preserves the canonical writers as creative geniuses who managed as no other writers could to master the dialectic McKeon discovers. Indeed, McKeon has given offense in some quarters because he fails to fulfill the promise of his massively analytical framework and terminology to enlarge the canon by treating all novelistic texts as in effect equal characters in the large historical story he has to tell. On the one hand, McKeon's only standard for qualifying a narrative as part of the mediating cultural action fiction performs is a chronological one, but on the other hand, he in practice excludes from extended analysis the work of numerous noncanonical writers, who are simply part of the prenovelistic floundering that plays its subordinate if essential role in the grand dialectic that produces the novel. In fact he concludes with six chapters on six canonical male writers: Cervantes, Bunyan, Defoe, Swift, Richardson, and Fielding.[16]

Where Watt's project was to some extent local and limited by what might be called the prevailing canon of eighteenth-century novelists (his book was subtitled "Studies in Defoe, Richardson, and Fielding"), McKeon aspires to provide a totalizing, global explanation that places the rise of the novel exactly at the resolving center of the most important cultural changes of the early modern era. The shift in emphasis is crucial and is partly a result of changing intellectual and academic fashions whereby literary criticism has been granted (by whom, I am not quite certain) an interdisciplinary authority and ambition to produce the sort of intellectual syntheses that were once the province of the greatest historians. Certainly, Watt used a large historical framework as a backdrop for performing delicate and exceedingly specific acts of literary criticism that explored the issue of the relationship between the formal features of the new fiction and the sociocultural situation. But Watt observed the disciplinary boundaries, building on the work of social thinkers and historians, deferring in fact to their formulations and subordinating, without falling into base/superstructure simplifications, the role of fiction to larger forces of which fiction was only a part and from which fiction took its shaping impetus. He conceded, implicitly, the limitations of literary-historical and critical discourse, exploring what the novels in question looked like from his own historical vantage point, and granting by the whole drift of his discourse that formal realism was a historical development and to that extent a determined and contingent one.

In what may be a rhetorical miscalculation, McKeon rehearses for his readers nothing less than the shifting relationship between narrative and truth in the two millennia from antiquity to the English late seventeenth century. He proposes to trace the emergence of skeptical and empirical modes in Western thought and to register in detail how that emergence affects narrative. The result of such a comprehensive inquiry is both impressive and ponderous, as well as melodramatic in speaking of a century and a half of "epistemological crisis, a major cultural transition in attitudes toward how to tell the truth in narrative" (20). In the end, however, he still depends upon the historical formulations that Watt invokes more economically if rather less self-consciously: the novel for both of them is a response to new conditions produced by socio-economic and epistemological circumstances peculiar to the early modern period. In his ambitious sweep, McKeon may be reacting to the historical thinness of recent literary critical discourse, in which a newly trumpeted linguistic and rhetorical instability of all discourse has too often licensed the free play of uninformed cleverness that revels in the yawning gap between the text and historicity. His immense learning is in one sense a tribute to *The Rise of the Novel*, a return to the example of a founding text as well as an attempt to displace it. Perhaps the consciousness that literary critical discourse, in spite of its totalizing pretensions, has been even further marginalized since Watt wrote his book makes McKeon raise the historical stakes and define the novel as a central force at the highest level of cultural significance. The novel, he says

> attains its modern, "institutional" stability and coherence at this time because of its unrivaled power both to formulate, and to explain, a set of problems that are central to early modern experience. These may be understood as problems of categorical instability, which the novel, originating to resolve, also inevitably reflects. The first sort of instability with which the novel is concerned has to do with generic categories; the second, with social categories. The instability of generic categories registers an epistemological crisis, a major cultural transition in attitudes toward how to tell the truth in narrative. (20)

In formulating and explaining, reflecting and resolving, the novel for McKeon has "unrivaled power," and he says it can be "understood comprehensively as an early modern cultural instrument designed to confront, on the level of narrative form and content, both intellectual and social crisis simultaneously" (22). Although he never quite admits it, McKeon thus commits himself to the same premises that underlie Watt's work, for the only writers who measure up to the cultural power he describes are the canonical few. His whole thesis, in fact, depends upon the special genius of these founding fathers, in particular Richardson and Fielding. McKeon's elaborate theoretical apparatus upholds and tries to explain the power of these two writers, for he finds in what I think is his most original critical move that the key to the full development of the novel is the emergence of the aesthetic as an autonomous category.

Derived, as he notes, from Aristotle's separation of history and poetry in the *Poetics* ("a time bomb in the cultural unconscious of the West until its 'discovery' by Renaissance modernity" [119]), belief in such a sphere takes place when realism "gathers up and sophisticates the scattered themes of verisimilitude and probability that Renaissance writers had teased out of the *Poetics*" (120). The novel as we know it originates, says McKeon, in that category, which enables a shift away from the problematic of representing truth and virtue and toward the novel's various kinds of confident realistic transparency, which are actually forms of egocentric assertion, the projection of individual imagination, now a fully abstracted ideological possibility or new form of culturally licensed "truth." As McKeon puts it, the claim to historicity and its subversion remain part of the novel after Richardson and Fielding establish the novel in the 1740s, but both claim and subversion "end in the triumph of the creative human mind," the mind of Richardson's protagonists and the mind of Fielding's playful and omniscient author (418–19). That is to say, the defining problem of narrative before 1740 is transcended by drastically reformulating questions of truth and virtue, as the category of history separates from "literature" and the private self with its internalized virtue separates itself from society and its status categories. The issue has shifted from truth to aesthetic effect, as human nature (and the moral-social world such a notion implies) is now a settled question, and readers can now turn their attention to what sort of narrative technique best delivers these now-established truths.

All this is quite brilliant if perhaps too schematic to be swallowed whole.[17] It does, of course, modify our view of the origins of the novel, deepening, extending, and refining but not essentially altering Watt's description of its cultural functions. Implicitly for McKeon, the superiority of Fielding's novels and those of the others is nothing more or less than their cultural density, which produces their aesthetic value and thus their manifest superiority to thinner earlier narratives. Value as such is not denied but massively relocated, shifted from moral-aesthetic structures to cultural construction that employs those structures. McKeon thus attempts to balance two normally opposing conceptions whereby, as John Guillory has recently observed, the "value of the work as representative of a given constituency and its 'values' can always be set against the value of the work as aesthetic artifact." At the extremes of these positions, literature as a category disappears into "a purely anthropological domain" or into a realm of pure aesthetic values that "mask by their transhistorical prestige the value of aesthetic value itself to particular strata of a given social formation."

But value, as Guillory points out, is always value for someone and involves social relations in "real historical societies."[18] Despite what some critics see as his "humanist" prejudices, Watt's discussion of the values projected by these novelists illuminates precisely the ways in which their works are valuable for particularized if hypothetical eighteenth-century readers and for actual twentieth-century readers, like himself. He thereby admits implicitly what recent critics of McKeon's book like Homer Obed Brown have said: that we can only read the eighteenth-century novel retrospectively from our own belief in the categorical stability of the novel as a genre.[19] Watt's study is openly retrospective in its critical values, working from post-Jamesian novelistic standards and therefore radically selective, as he admits. That openness is part of Watt's strength as a critic, although it can provide an opening for an attack on his scholarship.

Moreover, the superiority of Richardson and Fielding, a value judgment that McKeon simply offers as obvious, is authorized by the cumulative force of traditional literary evaluations such as *The Rise of the Novel* was especially influential in authorizing and perpetuating. Where Watt offers both judgment and such illustrations of quality as textual analysis can provide, McKeon can only reaffirm within his historical account of fiction's ideological functions the values and hierarchies of the critical tradition. He is a brilliant historian of ideas and a superb dialectician, but his textual analysis operates almost exclusively at the level of intellectualized plot summary that tends to treat narrative as a relatively inert medium for ideas. The choice of Fielding or Richardson rather than a lesser writer remains undefended. It is no disparagement of McKeon's richly perceptive discussion of, say, Fielding in *The Origins of the English Novel* to complain that it never fully engages the text in all of its playful richness, even as he depends upon that aesthetic richness for a key part of his argument.

Although he never uses a loaded term like "aesthetic value," John Bender in *Imagining the Penitentiary* overtly revalidates canonical works for a similar sort of ideological density, and like McKeon Bender has a comprehensive thesis that puts the novel at the dynamic center of its cultural moment. His book's special strength is precisely its historical specificity and particularized analysis not only of texts but of a wide range of cultural practices that are treated as if they were texts. Both novel and penitentiary, says Bender, are related "social texts," and indeed the penitentiary is itself a corollary for the largest text of all, society itself.[20] Where McKeon is necessarily abstract and hugely generalized, Bender is focused by virtue of his concentration upon the single historical fact that the modern prison and the penal theories that led to its establishment began to emerge during the middle decades of the eighteenth century. His thesis, startling in its originality as well as in its cogency and aptness, is that the novel from Defoe to Goldsmith is part of the process of cultural production that enabled the turn from the traditional prison to the modern penitentiary, and more generally that the novel is an active component of the regulating mechanisms that help to form the emerging modern state.

In spite of this quite remarkable originality, Bender's book is overtly an *hommage* to Watt, his colleague at Stanford, and he is always scrupulous about noting his indebtedness to *The Rise of the Novel*, whose "definition of the realist novel's literary phenomenology has not been supplanted" (257). In some sense, Bender's emphasis on the novel's part in the social reorganization of individuals made possible by the new urban scene grows out of some of Watt's obiter dicta and brief aperçus on such matters.[21] Overall, *Imagining the Penitentiary* is a work of masterly synthesis, matching the learning of McKeon's tome and marshaling insights from a wide number of fields—cultural anthropology, history of law and jurisprudence, art history, social history, linguistics, political science, and sociology are the main ones—into the original but thoroughly grounded interdisciplinary thesis of the enabling relationship between the novel and the penitentiary. In that synthetic gathering, Bender imitates Watt, bringing him very much up to date (just as Watt was up to date and interdisciplinary in 1957) but not altering his mode of understanding fiction. The crucial insights with which he begins are precisely those from *The Rise of the Novel* about the departure from traditional modes of narrative understanding that Watt called formal realism.

Bender himself points to the few differences he has with Watt when he says, in a footnote, that his "treatment of realism turns out to be less formalist than Watt's and my view of the novel's instrumental role in cultural formation more activist" (257 n. 19). This activist notion of fiction's role whereby "formal innovation in the novel becomes a mode of action" (139) is especially convincing in Bender's chapters on Fielding, who was of course crucially active in his career as a magistrate in reforming the enforcement of the law in the eighteenth century. Along with Defoe's energetic involvement in the ideological ferment of his time, Fielding's activism gives Bender's book a human dimension and a narrative line of its own that McKeon's lacks. For McKeon, history is an overarching set of determinants within which social and political action are viewed in abstract terms and are subordinate in any event to the seismic movements of the dialectic.

And yet Bender himself is curiously bloodless if not abstract in his approach to a topic that might be enriched by engagement of some sort. Although he uses Marxist categories for their "highly developed theoretical accounts of the interaction between literary form and social institutions" (256 n. 13), he also inevitably if implicitly offers a Foucauldian critique of the emerging supervisory and thereby repressive bureaucratic power structures of the modern state. It is hard to say whether Bender thinks the emergence of systematic confinement as a replacement for the carnivalesque atmosphere of the old "liminal" prison was a real improvement. On the face of it, he seems to agree with a full fledged Foucauldian like D. A. Miller who says without qualification that the "liberal subject" traced by the novel recognizes "himself most fully only when he forgets or disavows his functional implication in a system of carceral restraints or disciplinary injunctions."[22] But Bender keeps his analytic distance and is exceedingly careful in all this to separate himself both from Foucauldian outrage about modern repressive power and from those Marxists who retain their belief in the "economic bases of production" as the "ultimate causal, or at least explanatory force" (256 n. 13). Bender's "new historicism," like Stephen Greenblatt's, is open to the charge that it preserves the very sort of objective and neutral critical stance it seems to be exposing as fallacious. To some extent, Bender is himself as analytic and uncommitted an observer as the all-seeing Benthamite warden whose development he traces.

One should take good ideas where one finds them, of course, but Bender's eclecticism has its own sort of spin that in the end tends to weaken his case but, paradoxically at least for me, to enrich his book. His systematic approach is convincing precisely because it is loose and ready-made, liable as McKeon's is not to admit partial failure in the face of the reality and multifariousness of particular texts and thereby to disarm skepticism about the validity of his system. Here's a paragraph on Defoe's *A Journal of the Plague Year* whose excellence is a function of its refusal of systematic simplicity:

Defoe adopts the conceit that fully deployed legal authority in the city turns houses into prisons and its citizens into criminals. From the specific case the *Journal* proposes, a generalized version of the reformist penitentiary follows by converse inference: "total" authority represented through physically enforced mental solitude—through a narratively ordered, sequential control of the particulars of daily life—will make citizens of criminals. Of course the bluntness of these propositions is a function of their exposition here. Defoe naturalizes their shading in a thousand ways by embedding them in the historically specific and highly unusual events of his journal, and by personifying them psychologically through his casuistic narrator's exposition of the debate over the shutting up of houses. The viability of the narrative depends upon a certain density of factual and emotional texture, upon the ebb and flow of multiple reports and competing interpretations. (77)

Compare this paragraph, as a piece of analytic prose, with a few lines from *The Rise of the Novel* on *Clarissa*:

Richardson's very slowness communicates a sense of continual tension held lightly in check: the poised, almost processional, tempo of the narrative with its sudden lapses into brutality or hysteria is itself the perfect formal enactment of the universe which *Clarissa* portrays, a universe where the calm surface of repressive convention and ingrown hypocrisy is momentarily—but only momentarily—threatened by the irruption of the secret violences which it provokes but conceals. (211)

Both of these analyses beautifully attend to the specific effects of textual totality, suspending for the moment but without canceling an interest in the socio-economic totality in which these works exist. What Bender calls the "bluntness" of abstract positions is in both passages balanced by the refinement of particularized observation of the workings of narrative process as it becomes something that has distinctive form. Both passages pay tribute to the power of authorial intelligence and control; both critics define aesthetic power as residing in particular textual moments with profound but necessarily elusive cultural resonance. It seems to me that the current ambition of literary critics to reach for cultural synthesis has to be restrained, like John Bender's, by Watt's example in order to remain true to complex and particularized textual workings like these. Otherwise, we run the danger of becoming mere adjuncts to intellectual history and losing our distinctive and defining status as readers of texts and preservers of their special, irreducibly particular qualities as texts. *The Rise of the Novel* is one of the few works of the last thirty years that can provide a model for such balanced distinctiveness.

Notes

1 Robert D. Hume, "Recent Studies in the Restoration and Eighteenth Century," *SEL*, 28 (1988), 528.

2 Ibid. 528.

3 In a recent review essay about McKeon's book and Nancy Armstrong's *Desire and Domestic Fiction* (1987), Homer Obed Brown notes that *The Rise of the Novel* has been "subjected to devastating criticism ever since it was published." But he then observes very shrewdly that other critics have since then aspired to write *the* replacement of Watt's book, "rather a marvelous tribute to its continued importance, however battle scarred." "Of the Title to Things Real: Conflicting Stories," *ELH*, 55 (1988), 917.

4 Ian Watt, "Serious Reflections on *The Rise of the Novel*," *Novel*, 1 (1968), 206.

5 Ian Watt, *The Rise of the Novel: Studies in Defoe, Richardson and Fielding* (Berkeley and Los Angeles: University of California Press, 1957), 31. All further references in the text are to this edition.

6 Daniel R. Schwarz, "The Importance of Ian Watt's *The Rise of the Novel*," *Journal of Narrative Technique*, 13 (1983), 60. This is a valuable, fair-minded assessment of Watt's achievement that surveys various objections to his work and points out its theoretical shortcomings. Homer Obed Brown echoes this estimate of Watt's importance when he says that he "may have been the first to

suggest detailed links between the early novel's formal characteristics, recognizably novelistic in the more modern sense, and these social and philosophical ideas." "Of the Title to Things Real: Conflicting Stories" 917. On *The Rise of the Novel*'s shortcomings, see a quibbling and literal-minded essay by David H. Hirsch, "The Reality of Ian Watt," *Critical Quarterly*, 11 (Summer 1969), 164–79.

7 Schwarz, "The Importance of Ian Watt's *The Rise of the Novel*" 62.

8 Watt, "Serious Reflections on *The Rise of the Novel*" 213.

9 Homer Obed Brown traces very clearly Watt's modification and adaptation of Leavisite and New Critical techniques to a historical understanding of the eighteenth-century novel. He notes that *The Rise of the Novel* thus formed part of the effort of those critical movements to apply techniques of close reading, formed by reading modern writers like Flaubert and James especially, to fiction from earlier periods. "Of the Title to Things Real: Conflicting Stories" 920.

10 A. D. McKillop, *The Early Masters of English Fiction* (Lawrence, KS, and London: University Press of Kansas, 1956), 75. All further references in the text are to this edition.

11 Looking back to objections from reviewers that his basic thesis was not original, Watt remarks that "originality would have been completely contrary to my chosen procedure." "Serious Reflections on *The Rise of the Novel*" 206.

12 Bram Dijkstra, *Defoe and Economics: The Fortunes of Roxana in the History of Interpretation* (London: Macmillan, 1987), 140. All further references in the text are to this edition.

13 Maximillian Novak, *Realism, Myth, and History in Defoe's Fiction* (Lincoln: University of Nebraska Press, 1983), 3. All further references in the text are to this edition.

14 For a descriptive survey of a good deal of this material and proof of the pain involved for a modern reader in actually reading it, see my *Popular Fiction before Richardson: Narrative Patterns, 1700–1739* (Oxford: Clarendon Press, 1969). For a briefer summary of the issues and some second thoughts on "popular fiction" and its link to the rise of the novel, see my essay "Popular Narrative in the Eighteenth Century: Formats and Formulas," in *The First English Novelists: Essays in Understanding*, ed. J. M. Armistead (Knoxville: University of Tennessee Press, 1985).

15 Michael McKeon, *The Origins of the English Novel, 1600–1740* (Baltimore and London: Johns Hopkins University Press, 1987), 18–19. All further references in the text are to this edition.

16 I recently recommended to a feminist friend that she read McKeon's and Bender's books. When I ran into her a few months later, she said she was disappointed: "These guys talk about the same old authors, the same men we've been reading about for years."

17 Hume remarks that he both admires McKeon's book and disbelieves it: "Pondering this book, I feel like a nineteenth-century atheist regarding a major theological treatise with bemused wonder" ("Recent Studies in the Restoration and Eighteenth Century" 529). Given Novak's skepticism about Watt's "ho-

mologies," one can only wonder what he makes of McKeon's finely calibrated dialectic.

18 John Guillory, "Canonical and Non-Canonical: A Critique of the Current Debate," *ELH*, 54 (1987), 486, 493.

19 Brown, "Of the Title to Things Real: Conflicting Stories" 941–42.

20 John Bender, *Imagining the Penitentiary: Fiction and the Architecture of Mind in Eighteenth-Century England* (Chicago: University of Chicago Press, 1987), 36. All further references in the text are to this edition.

21 Defoe, Watt writes, had grown up while London was still a walled city, but he lived to see all that change: "he lived in the hurly-burly where the foundations of the new way of life were being laid: and he was at one with it." Richardson's works, on the other hand, "express, not the life of the whole community, but a deep personal distrust and even fear of the urban environment" (181).

22 D. A. Miller, *The Novel and the Police* (Berkeley and Los Angeles: University of California Press, 1988), x.

Carole Fabricant

Swift in His Own Time and Ours:
Some Reflections on Theory and Practice
in the Profession

This essay grew out of a paper I was asked to write for a session entitled "Swift: Modernist/Postmodernist Contexts," for the 1990 ASECS Meeting in Minneapolis.[1] Delighted to have an excuse to return (once again) to Swift, and welcoming the opportunity to rethink his significance in light of contemporary concerns, as well as to conceptualize his writings in a way that would have been looked askance upon a mere handful of years ago, I was nevertheless surprised to encounter in myself a certain degree of ambivalence to the project in the course of developing and completing it. Later, after delivering the paper, I began thinking in a more sustained way about the contradictory sentiments it had evoked (and was continuing to evoke) in me, which gave rise to a number of related reflections—on the nature and implications of the new methodological approaches to eighteenth-century literature which have been gaining currency in the past few years and my own relationship to them, especially (though not exclusively) as that relationship has been mediated through my ongoing engagement with Swift, as well as on the institutional and supra-institutional roles played by contemporary literary and cultural critics. In this essay, I would like to explore some of my thoughts on these issues in the hope that such reflections will prove useful and relevant to others in the field who are struggling with similar issues in their scholarship—as well as in their personal and professional lives.

For my ASECS paper what interested me in a consideration of Swift from a modernist/postmodernist perspective were not so much particular formal or stylistic techniques constitutive of his writings as the way in which his texts seem to me to address themselves to a (peculiarly though not exclusively) leftist problematic dealing with issues of relative versus absolute values, linguistic constructions versus historical "reality," totalizing versus local and heterogeneous structures, and unified versus multiple or fragmented selfhood. Concentrating in the paper on one strand of this problematic, that dealing with the relationship of discourse and history (though with side glances at the others as well), I explored some of the ways in which Swiftian texts at one and the same time foreground their radical implication in the vagaries of language *and* insist on their inextricable ties to a world beyond text, on their existence within particular constellations of power and institutional frameworks. Examining his Irish tracts of the 1720s, I discussed how Swift dramatizes the vulnerability of texts once they enter the world, their frequent encounters with a fate (tragically) different from that intended by their authors, not so much because of "textual indeterminacy" or "verbal slippage"—though Swift was certainly acutely conscious of these "dangers"—as because of the wrath or repressive policies of those in power. My conclusion was that Swift's simultaneous suspicion of and reliance on the printed word, his often delighted indulgence in linguistic free play coupled with his stern insistence that words retain their connection to (clearly identifiable referential) meaning, can be seen to lend support to Cornel West's argument, in his ongoing engagement with the intersections of poststructuralist theory, postmodernist culture, and activist politics, that, notwithstanding "the ways in which forms of textualization mediate all our claims about the world. . . . The multilevel operations of power within social practices—of which language is one— are more important [than the linguistic model itself]."[2]

When I got to the last sentence of my paper, it sounded to me more like a beginning than a conclusion, opening out as it does to a myriad of questions both about a Swift who makes claims upon us as our contemporary and about my own purpose in (re)presenting him in this way. The specific topic of the ASECS session for which I wrote my paper obviously demanded consideration of Swift's "contemporaneity"—though in truth I felt more comfortable justifying my project to myself in terms of E. P. Thompson's urging that as students of the seventeenth and eighteenth centuries "we give our vote for Winstanley and Swift" against Walpole and Sir Edwin Chadwick, since by doing so "we are saying that these values, and not those other values, are the ones which make this history meaningful *to us,* and that these are the values which we intend to enlarge and sustain in our present. If we succeed, then we reach back into history and endow it with our own meanings: we shake Swift by the hand."[3]

However theoretically naive this statement may sound to us today, I concur with Thompson's proposition that what we say about the past (whether we label ourselves "old" or "new" historians, or prefer to eschew labels altogether) morally defines and ideologically situates us in the present. Moreover, having written my book on Swift before the idea of the obsolescence of the "author" as traditionally understood had achieved the widespread acceptance it enjoys today in critical circles, I can attest to the fact that I have often felt close enough to Swift over the past years to "shake [him] by the hand" (not to mention to converse and occasionally dispute with him). I must even confess to certain lingering retrograde tendencies in this regard (note my continued eschewal of quotation marks around his name), for, although I agree we should rethink traditional, inescapably metaphysical and implicitly theological, notions of selfhood and subjectivity which produce uncritical models of an essentialist, unified, permanent ego identity—even in Swift's time, after all, such notions were being challenged, first by Locke and later by Hume[4]—and can readily appreciate the potentially liberating implications of Félix Guattari's argument that the insistence on sticking together the subject and the ego to affirm the status of the individual constitutes "a myth of totality—a totalitarian myth,"[5] I'm skeptical about what is gained, and can see much that might be lost, in exchanging the peculiar mode of "being in the world" that I've come to know as Swift (admittedly accessible only through linguistic and ideological mediations) for an amalgam of different "subject positions" or a "signifying machine" or a "multiplicity of centers of intensity."

Swift's autobiographical verses and prose pieces themselves, in their fragmentary structure, formal disjunctions, incessant role-playing, and rich array of occasional selves jostling one another for center stage, attest to the illusoriness of a fixed, monolithic self capable of egoistic assertion and confident mastery of its environment. Moreover, his terse, strangely detached self-portrayal in "The Family of Swift" presents not an essentialist but a phenomenological self, acquiring its definition and continuity through its consciousness of a series of separate but recurring worldly experiences (mainly of rejection and betrayal). But at the same time these writings reveal that Swift, as do most of us (even, I daresay, poststructuralists) kept bumping into himself in the dark and recognizing—not infrequently with a shudder of horror reminiscent of Gulliver's when he looks closely at the Yahoo and discerns a human shape—exactly who it was he was coming face to face with.

Over the past few years, the gradual tempering of the heretofore deep-seated resistance to "new" theoretical approaches to eighteenth-century literature within the field itself has opened up the period to a number of important and exciting investigations along Marxist, feminist, semiotic, and new-historicist lines. An added benefit of these investigations has been their role in encouraging the expansion and re-formation of the eighteenth-century canon, until a decade or so ago arguably consisting of the most white, male, and upper-class body of writings of any period in British literature as taught in the universities. (In this regard I think Paul Lauter is wrong to posit a clear-cut opposition between canon criticism and theoretical studies within the academy, thereby in effect denying their potential for being mutually supportive.)[6] I've personally found this new atmosphere stimulating and nurturing for my own recent explorations of the interconnections between ideology, class, and gender as expressed through various of the period's cultural ("nonliterary" as well as "literary") texts.[7] Along with these journeys into previously uncharted waters, however, I've been feeling equally impelled of late to go back to writers and literary canons I studied earlier, in order to re-(en)vision them from a new perspective and rethink their significance in light of the critical and theoretical questions being raised today. What I've discovered when returning to Swift this time is that the results are *mutually* revelatory: i.e., if contemporary theories or conceptual frameworks shed new light on the subject, the converse holds equally true.

Thus it seems to me that studying Swift points up the need for theory while at the same time it points up the limits of theory in and of itself, fetishized and divorced from practice. If Swift's life and writings teach us anything it is precisely that one's ideological and theoretical allegiances mean nothing unless their connections to the arena of worldly action are concretely articulated—and this message remains consistent whether we look at his ostensibly "conservative," hegemonic writings before 1714 or his more obviously "radical," counterhegemonic writings after 1719. Swift's texts abundantly testify to the absurd sterility of theories spun out of the brain with no consideration given to their practical application or their consequences for daily existence—just as they expose the "madness" of abstract system-builders whose structures continually threaten to topple from their airy heights onto their own heads. What both his didactic and his satiric utterances suggest is that we can ill afford to make do with *either* "pure" theoretical espousals *or* unexamined, merely pragmatic behavior, but must instead think through a position embodying some form of what we might call "theoretical practice," a position fusing general principles, critical analysis of specific situations, and empirical action.

Swift's ambivalent and problematic relationship to institutions—even those to which he belonged or whose interests he technically served, such as the Church of Ireland and (briefly) the Tory government in England—as well as his activities on behalf of a nascent Irish nationalism, which (necessarily) took place outside of an institutional framework altogether, can offer additional food for self-reflection among current eighteenth-century scholars and critics, who (with few exceptions) think, write, teach, and (if they are so disposed) theorize within academic institutions upon which they depend for their livelihood and professional status. Swift's often profound frustrations in having to deal with the official organs of government, and his recognition of the inevitable price one must pay to be affiliated with them, are recorded throughout his personal correspondence and his *Journal to Stella*. Similarly registered are his dissatisfactions with the Anglican church in Ireland, which compromised him (as one of its albeit lowly officials) through its blatantly politicized and anglophilic (hence inescapably colonialist) policies; one need only recall some of his scathingly satiric verses to gauge the extent of his discomfort at belonging to an institution represented by the likes of a Dean Sawbridge ("The True English Dean to be hanged for a Rape") and the Irish bishops ("Our B[ishop]s puft up with Wealth and with Pride. / To Hell on the Backs of the Clergy wou'd ride"). His utter indifference to his sermons and depreciation of them in personal comments to friends contrast revealingly with the care he took with his political pamphlets, suggesting perhaps that he felt able to express his thoughts as "King of the Mob, and Monarch of the Liberties" in a way not possible when he was constrained to speak in his official capacity as dean of St. Patrick's. One might speculate that texts like *The Drapier's Letters*, for all their vulnerability to the wrath of those in power, represented occasions where Swift could exercise both a freedom (albeit momentarily snatched from the jaws of necessity) and a power of his own as a freelance agitator (so to speak) operating outside the rules and expectations of established institutional practices.

Obviously the institutional mechanisms and constraints of the eighteenth century differed vastly from those existing in today's perhaps postmodern but in any case certainly highly bureaucratized and technological world of late industrial monopoly capitalism, a far cry from the world of London bankers, creditors, and stockjobbers that Swift attacked so vehemently in the *Examiner* essays and elsewhere. Nevertheless, I want to suggest that despite the differences, there are certain levels on which we (as critical thinkers and academics) can relate to Swift's situation, and learn from it. Edward Said has argued that Swift can fruitfully be viewed in Gramscian terms, as variously fulfilling the roles of both a traditional and an organic intellectual in his society.[8] I believe we can also think of him in terms of Foucault's conception of the "specific" as opposed to the "universal" intellectual, with Swift again acting in both capacities, never actually relinquishing his role as a "bearer of universal values," but devoting much of his career to involvement in local insurgencies and acts of resistance, and working "at the precise points where [his] own conditions of life or work situate[d him]."[9]

Swift's conflicting roles as specific and universal intellectual may be understood in light of his aspiration, on the one hand, to occupy the position of Royal Historiographer and preserve an official record of British History (with a capital *H*), and on the other, his assumption of the roles of journalist and pamphleteer, recording, commenting on, and actively helping to shape particular historical events, his writings on these occasions adding up to a number of individual, often discontinuous (and, after his return to Ireland in 1714, regional) histories. As the Drapier he envisions his *Letters* as a form of history writing in the latter sense: different from one Signior Lati's *History of England* precisely because they have been written for urgent, partisan, and activist reasons (*PW* 10:110) by one "employ[ing] his Pen upon so transitory a Subject, and in so obscure a Corner of the World" (114), and allied not with noble Augustan genres like epic but with local, popular literary forms ("I begin to grow weary of my Office of Writer; and could heartily wish it were devolved upon my *Brethren*, the Makers of *Songs* and *Ballads*" [93]).

What, one might ask, does all this have to do with those of us who teach and write in the academy today? We too are potentially intellectuals engaged in hegemonic and counterhegemonic struggles on a cultural battlefield and capable of carrying out acts of insurgency (however localized) against the dominant ideologies in society. However, this potential can never be realized by merely exchanging one set of critical approaches or interpretive methodologies for another, nor by hailing the emergence of Theory and its application to eighteenth-century literature as some form of revolutionary salvation. I think we need to be much more careful about the claims we make for our academic endeavors, if only because the claims themselves are so important and not to be taken lightly. Being able, indeed encouraged, to study Swift (or any other eighteenth-century writer or topic) from theoretical perspectives previously frowned upon does indeed signify a welcome change in our field, a derigidifying of critical orthodoxies that have held sway in it for too long, but such study is not, in and of itself, a "radical" act—or even, in all instances, a significantly "progressive" one.

For one thing, we shouldn't minimize the ability of established institutions, in this case academia, to appropriate and "domesticate" what seem (or purport) to be even the most subversive of methodologies. Almost twenty years ago Guattari observed that Marxism and Freudianism had become "so painstakingly neutralized" by institutional forces such as the psychoanalytic movement and the universities that "not only do they upset nobody, but they have even become guarantors of the established order, thus showing by a *reductio ad absurdum* that that order cannot be seriously shaken." [10] He was commenting, of course, upon the European scene, but two decades later we are increasingly having to face a similar situation in this country, with regard not only to Freudianism and Marxism but to other "oppositional" theories as well. The problem is not simply what Gerald Graff sees as "the cycle of routinization" afflicting critical discourses in the academy as a result of certain institutionalized pedagogical practices.[11] For beyond the methodological conflicts whose absence from the classroom Graff (rightly) laments are the more persistent and urgent conflicts in society at large, conflicts whose chronic vulnerability to suppression and mystification reflects a hegemonic control over ideological production: one which functions through the active encouragement of certain kinds of (nonthreatening) disagreement on the one hand, and the silencing of genuine dissent on the other.

The issues being raised here are not unrelated to the ones Swift had to wrestle with throughout much of his life: the fate of intellectual and textual labor in a world of power and institutions. The kind of blatant censorship and repression repeatedly confronting Swift has, however, given way for the most part to subtler, more insidious (and more pervasive) forms of control; in our case, institutional cooptation, professionalization, and the commodification of theory in particular. The production of "new" theories and the active promotion of their use, while offering opportunities for enlightening reevaluations of the past and for the development of a critical (and self-critical) consciousness with genuinely oppositional implications, can at the same time wind up merely replicating the kinds of "production" and "promotion" characteristic of consumer capitalism, creating a supermarket of theories with an endless proliferation of (supposedly) different brands fueled by the pressures of built-in obsolescence and the artifically stimulated demand for a novelty that tends to represent a change in packaging and marketing techniques only. This situation creates strange bedfellows; hence in recent months I've had the experience of being put on the defensive by both a conservative male colleague and a feminist one for continuing to write about Swift: the former, expressing surprise that I haven't moved on to "new territory" (why is it I always think of the Doctrine of Manifest Destiny whenever I hear these words?); the latter, wondering why I was still working on a canonical male writer.

My own feeling is that as long as we view ourselves simply as academics, rather than as intellectuals in a broader (and less institutionally defined) context, most of what we say or do can have little political import beyond narrow professional (re)alignments and careerist maneuvers. That being the case, labeling our colleagues as "left" or "right," "reactionary" or "radical," solely on the basis of which critical or theoretical camp they are perceived to belong to doesn't in itself accomplish much. Such polarization is at once an overpoliticizing of the situation and an example of not being genuinely political enough. Fighting over turf within the bounds of academia is not, after all, the same thing as battling for cultural space within the larger society. Jim Merod speaks to the issue when, noting that "the professional study of texts has become increasingly open to a variety of methodological and critical assumptions while simultaneously becoming more and more an institution closed by insular professional disputes," he laments the fact that "almost everything called 'theory' in higher intellectual circles contributes to the small, well-marked, and politically extrinsic growth of criticism as an industry rather than to efforts to define the contexts and conditions in which intellectual production actually takes place." [12] In a related context Russell Jacoby has bemoaned what he sees as the disappearance of the public intellectual (admittedly to some extent a romanticized ideal as he conceives of it) as a result of an academic absorption and professionalization inseparable from privatization; according to his assessment, "The influx of left scholars [into the universities] has not changed the picture. . . . The slogan that was borrowed from the German left to justify a professional career—'the long march through the institutions'—has had an unexpected outcome: at least so far, the institutions are winning." [13]

Regardless of who is "winning" or "losing" (and I'm not convinced that these are the best terms in which to view the situation), the fact remains that our intellectual growth and development as eighteenth-century scholars have invariably been mediated through—and profoundly affected by—our institutional histories: most obviously, our relationship to academic institutions, but also our involvement with criticism, what Merod calls "an institution within an institution." [14] In my own case, these mediations intersected in a peculiar way when I was hired by the University of California, Riverside, in 1975 to fill a vacancy created by the death of Kathleen Williams. At the time I was already working on my Swift book and was of course familiar with Williams' study, *Jonathan Swift and the Age of Compromise*; even more than knowing it well, however, I thought of it as belonging in the "enemy camp"—as one of the interpretations my book had to counter, although I deemed it politic to pursue my attack furtively given Williams' long association with and considerable stature in a department I desired to do well in, and into which I hoped to be tenured.

Aside from presenting a Swift—moderate and sober in temperament, conservative in outlook—inimical to the one I was coming to know through my own study, Williams' book in many ways represented what I most disliked about traditional eighteenth-century scholarship: sweeping generalizations about "the age" based on assumptions of absolute coherence; the assertion of "universal" values that ignored differences of class, nationality, and gender; the adherence to an idealized vision of order and harmony; the invocation of "historical" contexts and backgrounds which always seemed maddeningly abstract and inert, having little to do with what I took to be the actual stuff of history (i.e., its struggles and contradictions); and a tacit denial of the ideological nature both of its subjects' thought and writings, and of its own interpretations. I saw my opposition to Williams' approach in (among other things) explicitly political terms. After all, in my own mind I was attempting to rescue the lived reality of a human life and the specific textures of a history long buried (as I saw it) under layers of reactionary mystifications and idealizations, following Marx's own method in "rising from the abstract to the concrete," and taking a cue from J.-P. Sartre's synthesis of existentialism and Marxism, which he described as the former's "intend[ing], without being unfaithful to Marxist principles, to find mediations which allow the individual concrete—the particular life, the real and dated conflict, the person—to emerge from the background of the *general* contradictions of productive forces and relations of production." [15]

Rereading Williams' book recently, I was surprised to find that, although my view of its treatment of literary history remained largely unchanged, there were actually aspects of it more like than unlike my own approach to Swift (e.g., its insistence on the importance of considering individual Swiftian texts within the context of his entire canon, including his "non-literary" works, and its assumption that access to Swift the writer depends to at least some degree on an understanding of Swift the man). This led me to reflect upon the pressures that had influenced me to view her book in an immediately adversarial and competitive, rather than (at least partially) collaborative, way, which in turn made me think more critically about the academic model informing our conception of intellectual attainment and scholarly (not to mention career) advancement. Moreover, although still noting the ideological implications of our methodological differences, I felt less inclined to define these differences in terms of polarized political labels, perhaps because I was suddenly struck by the extent of our mutual implication in an endeavor which was, in both our cases, carried out within a similar set of institutional imperatives and constraints, and defined by the same professional rules and modus operandi. Though our books belonged to very different intellectual and ideological worlds, they were part of the same world of academic discipline (and disciplinarity). Both used similar rhetorical gestures and strategic maneuvers to clear a space for themselves within the institution of Swift criticism by defining themselves in opposition to earlier critics; both had to establish their raison d'être by making claims for their ability to dispel previous interpretive distortions and misreadings of their subject. Certain of our arguments (I suspect) had less to do with Swift himself than with our role as professional critics in the academy, each writing at a particular (and different) moment in the development of eighteenth-century studies as a field.

I don't mean to suggest any kind of determinism at work here, but I do think it's important for us to historicize our own positions as academic thinkers and critics along with historicizing the eighteenth century—to try to understand what forces helped shape intellectual decisions which we tend to represent, to ourselves and others, as independent and autonomous choices. In this light I found myself thinking about the implications of Williams' and my common institutional membership—about (for example) what must have been our similar struggles and experiences as women in a male-dominated institution (a good deal more so when I first entered the profession than it is today, and far more so even than that when she entered it), working on a major male canonical writer around whom had been constructed (by men in virtually all cases) a veritable fortress of critical, scholarly, and textual apparatus: a male terrain and sphere of "authority" necessarily intimidating to even the most intrepid female interloper.

I also found myself musing over the fact that my own work on Swift, however "subversive" I might have liked to think it, was in fact supported and underwritten by the same institution that underwrote Williams', winning me security of employment in a university system that has for many years managed the nuclear laboratories at Los Alamos and Livermore, profited from investments in South Africa, et cetera. I think back also to my days as a graduate student at Johns Hopkins University, which, along with generously supporting my graduate career and funding international structuralist conferences and humanities seminars, was being headed by a man who formerly, as ambassador to Brazil, helped carry out bloody U.S. interventionist policies in Latin America, and which was running the Applied Physics Lab, a major producer of napalm during the Vietnam War. True, I periodically emerged from the bowels of the Milton Eisenhower Library (its English literature section was located five floors below the ground, in a symbolic topography perhaps more appropriate than we cared to dwell upon), where I was deeply immersed in a dissertation on John Wilmot, earl of Rochester, to demonstrate against the war and the university's complicity in it, but this (it must be admitted) did not prevent me from accepting the financial benefits, as well as the academic credentials and status, that Johns Hopkins afforded me.

The situation has not changed very much in the years since (if anything, it has gotten worse). Dramatic (not to mention chillingly grotesque) testimony to this fact occurred on June 6, 1991, when Harvard University's John F. Kennedy School of Government bestowed its prestigious degree in Public Policy and Management on General Hector Gramajo Morales, former defense minister of Guatemala and the architect of a military internal security program that (according to six separate international human rights organizations) was exceptionally brutal, responsible for the deaths, disappearance, and exile of tens of thousands of civilians and the extermination of a sizable segment of the indigenous Indian population, as well as for the notorious abduction and torture of Sister Diane Ortiz, who was repeatedly raped, burned over one hundred times with lit cigarettes, and thrown into a pit filled with dead bodies and rats. Gramajo, who boasts of his role in masterminding a "more humanitarian" 1982 strategy to provide development for seventy per cent of the Guatemalan population while killing thirty per cent, was photographed beaming with pride in his graduation cap and gown while waiting to receive his new academic credentials, presumably his passport to high office in future Guatemalan elections. In his own only-too-sobering words, "I consider myself first of all a product of the American Education system. . . ." One can only wonder how many Harvard-sponsored conferences on Postcolonial Theory and Subaltern Literature it would take to counterbalance the Kennedy School's "education" and legitimation of one of the worst mass murderers in recent history.[16]

Today institutions such as Johns Hopkins and the University of California are recipients of larger-than-ever U.S. Defense Department contracts, a reflection of the increasingly close ties between the academic and the military sectors of society, and throughout the recent past I've continued to emerge periodically from underneath stacks of books, research notes, and papers to join protests in downtown Los Angeles directed against U.S. support of death-squad "democracy" in Central America and to demonstrate at the Westwood Federal Building against the war in the Persian Gulf. Now as in 1968 I am painfully aware of the inadequacy of my response given the magnitude of the destruction taking place, but at the same time thankful that I managed to liberate a few hours from a schedule so filled with career demands and professional busy work that it leaves insufficient time for even carrying on a normal personal life, let alone for engaging in any sustained way in political acts of conscience.

It is circumstances such as these—and my assumption is they are hardly unique to me—which force us to confront the inherent limitations of being (merely) "oppositional" critics within the academy, and to try to identify, with a view toward overcoming, the common obstacles impeding our ability to function in a meaningful way *both* as academics *and* as public intellectuals. I hasten to add that by the latter term I mean to signify not the elite group of white male thinkers Jacoby has in mind, whose "free-floating," wholly independent status we need to view skeptically, as something of a nostalgic myth, but a much larger, more heterogeneous group of thinkers whose very eschewal of any claims to "free-floating," heroically detached status may be seen as a source of strength rather than a shortcoming: a sign of their willingness to validate their perceptions not through what Donna Haraway calls the "conquering gaze from nowhere" (i.e., the criterion of objectivity as traditionally conceived), but rather on the basis of "situated knowledges" and "the embodied nature of all vision."[17] For an academic to become a public intellectual in this sense requires, not "transcending" the material and institutional conditions of her professional existence, but, on the contrary, *using* these in order to develop perspectives and to articulate connections that might otherwise remain invisible to those situated differently in the world. I refer in particular to those perspectives and connections capable of illuminating the links between what we, both individually and collectively, do in the university and the public policies which help to determine who among the nation's youth will wind up in our classrooms (ultimately, in positions of power in the professional-managerial class) and who will wind up instead on our inner-city streets or on some foreign battlefield, having been sent to kill or be killed in the next regional "mission possible" or high-tech extravaza staged on behalf of the New World Order.

Functioning as a public intellectual means being critical of our own involvement, *as academics,* in this very process of discrimination; for as Richard Ohmann (among others) has observed, our profession contributes in significant ways to the hegemonic operations of society, training the kinds of workers most needed by the system and confirming the class origins of our students by helping to determine who will advance in their school careers and who will not (hence who will succeed or fail in later life).[18] A concern with the theoretical and methodological differences among us must needs take into account issues such as these if it is not to lapse into professional insularity and parochialism. I don't believe, in any case, that these differences should blind us to the necessity to spend more time reflecting upon our *shared* institutional histories, not in order to affirm a specious sense of community but in an effort to understand the ways in which intellectual labor, of whatever critical or ideological orientation, can become reified and alienated—severed from the world of political atrocities which it often indirectly helps to sustain (or at least allows to continue, in most cases without even token intervention) as well as distortedly polarized by an aggressively competitive model of intellectual "progress"—within the academic system: a subset of the larger capitalist system in which we live.

But there is more to the story (I am arguing) than just ideological mystifications and institutional appropriations. Reading Williams' book again I was struck by its insistence (both explicit and implied) upon "setting the record straight"—a goal I could readily relate to in connection with my own work on Swift. I think there are important levels on which we need to take this goal seriously, as a genuine, deeply felt impulse that can't satisfactorily be explained (away) by rhetorical strategies or self-concerned professional ambitions, even though it inevitably partakes of both. It is possible to take such a view of this goal without having recourse to the myth of some disinterested public realm in which "absolute" truths can be attained by scholars objectively pursuing knowledge for its own sake, and while continuing to recognize that the very belief that methods of literary scholarship and criticism can be used for such an epistemological purpose is itself an ideology. These necessary qualifications granted, the project to set the record straight, to correct misconceptions about the past (not to mention the present), must be understood as more than a wholly subjective, invariably deluded endeavor generating only ideological fictions, linguistic aporias, or self-subverting textual production if we are not to reduce all critical pursuits to a vacuous, masturbatory game that is as inherently anti-intellectual as it is politically untenable (because it denies any grounds on which we can make judgments and act upon them). Without taking this project of clarification and rectification seriously, we may be quite capable of functioning as academic technicians or "experts" of one sort or another, but we will never truly be able to act in the capacity of intellectuals: of individuals whose responsibility is, as Noam Chomsky puts it, "to speak the truth and expose lies" (not least "the lies of governments"), as well as "to see events in their historical perspective" by weighing the present through analogies with the past.[19]

Once again Swift can help to clarify and illuminate the issues in this regard. Much of his life was devoted to the project of setting matters straight, dispelling delusions, and correcting wrongs (as he understood them), in terms both of affecting the historical course of events and of representing these events in writing. I use the word "project" here in a (loosely) Sartrean sense, as an endeavor determined by its social and material conditions but at the same time surpassing them; as a class-based act that is nevertheless a free invention on the part of the individual, directed toward "a certain object, still to come, which it is trying to bring into being";[20] as a dialectical act that negotiates the interaction between subjective identity and objective worldly manifestation. Swift's project continually acknowledged the impossibility of its own fulfillment but nevertheless insisted on the necessity of the repeated attempt. Throughout his Irish tracts, for example, he reveals his profound frustration at "all the Warnings I have in vain given the Publick, at my own Peril, for several Years past" (*PW* 12:22), yet continues to communicate such warnings and to devise new strategies for undeluding his readers and clarifying the issues at hand.

Especially relevant for our purposes here is Swift's historical project—his endeavors to set the record straight (and, over the course of a long career, straighter and straighter) about the past, in the present, for the future. We see this most clearly in the drama (and ultimately the tragedy) of Swift's struggle, over a span of years, to dispel what he saw as hardening misconceptions about the events that had occurred under the Tory ministry, and in particular his fierce determination, bordering at times on obsession, to write—and publish—a true account of the circumstances surrounding the peace ending the War of the Spanish Succession, which he personally, as author of *The Conduct of the Allies*, helped bring about. Although he (obviously) never succeeded in conveying an "objective" picture of this period, his repeated efforts and revisions served to foreground the importance of striving to produce a record of what actually happened in the past so that these events wouldn't fade from the collective national memory, and so that their interpretation could be held accountable to an external standard of verification.

Through a variety of forms and (sub)genres—political tracts, periodical essays, commentaries on treaties, "memoirs," "enquiries," "free thoughts," "considerations," etc.—all leading up to the posthumous publication of a self-proclaimed "history," Swift kept dealing with the same general materials from somewhat different perspectives, often with different immediate purposes in mind. Thus *An Enquiry into the Behaviour of the Queen's Last Ministry* ends with bleak reflections on the vices of men and the corruptions of government, while *The History of the Four Last Years of the Queen* terminates on an optimistic note, with the ratification of the peace treaty and the rejoicing of the people. On one level, the effect of these multiple accounts is to problematize history by calling into question the possibility of a single, totalizing, "closed" historical narrative, and certainly Swift's output in the combined roles of historian, pamphleteer, and journalist (not to mention balladeer) contributed to an acknowledgment of this impossibility. However, the point of these varied and fragmented accounts was not to relativize history by suggesting its susceptibility to different viewpoints and interpretations, all equally valid (or invalid, as the case may be), but, on the contrary, to *fix* its meaning by showing how a particular course of events remains basically the same in the face of continual retellings, and despite the changing reflections we might make about these events and the varying political lessons we draw from them, thereby vindicating the endeavor "to set future ages right in their judgment" about aspects of their past (*PW* 7:xxxiv).

Swift's lifelong struggle trying to connect language and history in a way that did justice to both, and that didn't allow words (even his own often rambunctious, anarchically rebellious ones) to subsume, by overwhelming and textualizing, the things to which they were testifying, took on an added sense of urgency in the final decade of his life when, beset with recurring physical pain and illness, and sensing death to be near, he insisted upon trying to publish a record of events which would ensure that what he deemed a particularly significant moment in English history would not die with him. Never did the order of words and the order of things (whether present or past) seem so far apart for Swift, and never did he try so desperately to bring them together and vindicate language's referential capacity, its power to preserve important truths for posterity. As he put it in his "Preface" to the *History*: ". . . I pretend to write with the utmost impartiality, the following History of the four last years of her Majesty's reign, in order to undeceive prejudiced persons at present, as well as posterity; . . . as a faithful historian, I cannot suffer falsehoods to run on any longer . . ." (*PW* 7:xxxiv).

It is easy enough to dismiss Swift's claim of "utmost impartiality" as an expression of either absurd naivete and self-delusion (at best), or rhetorical manipulation and calculated deceit (at worst); and indeed, Swift's *History* has not met with a happy fate among recent commentators.[21] I think a more balanced assessment can be achieved, however, if we consider the *History*, not as an isolated historical document to be weighed in light of (some mythic standard of) absolute factual accuracy or objectivity, but as an expression of Swift's ongoing engagement, and final struggle, with capturing history's meaning within a verbal construct that both partakes of, and stands apart from, the biases and conflicts it describes. Swift, a political animal if there ever was one, knew very well that an "impartiality" based on a stance of Olympian detachment from worldly events and on a claim of total disinterestedness was an empty fiction, although he also knew that to abjure the role of impartial analyst altogether meant rendering oneself powerless to counter the deliberate misrepresentations of those who would manipulate the truth in order to perpetuate their own power: meant giving up the weapons necessary to combat a situation in which "the whole Body of the People are drawn in by their own supposed Consent, to be their own Enslavers" (*PW* 8:180).

Thus, in a letter to the earl of Orrery written in his later years, Swift freely acknowledges the role of "Zeal" and personal advocacy ("to defend the Proceedings of that blessed Queen and her Ministry, as well as my self . . .") in writing the *History*, and admits to having had "some Regard to increase my own Reputation" (as well as his income) by publishing the work. Yet in the same breath he asserts unequivocally, "I did through the whole Treatise impartially adhere to Truth" (*C* 5:89). I think we can fairly conclude that Swift perceived no *necessary* contradiction between certain types of partisan actions, especially if informed by (the right kind of) committed engagement in worldly affairs, and the "impartial" adherence to truth. Indeed, it would no doubt have seemed clear to him that such involvement is more likely to enrich than to compromise the latter by helping to anchor "truth" (which can at times show an embarrassing propensity toward airy abstraction) in the realities of a lived, and fully human (hence necessarily but not *merely* subjective), existence.

We might think in this connection of the *Verses on the Death of Dr. Swift*, where one "quite indiff'rent in the Cause" intervenes in the idle "Chat" about Swift at the Rose Tavern and "[Swift's] Character impartial draws" (lines 305–6). Here again it is relatively easy to deconstruct the speaker's allegedly "impartial" stance by pointing out (as a variety of critics have) those aspects of his eulogy which indicate clear (political) partisanship and (personal) advocacy; yet here again, it would be a mistake to dismiss the speaker's words as mere subjective delusion or as part of the poem's ironic structure. For what we see here is another version of Swift's struggle to rescue truth from the distorted prism of petty slander, egocentric interpretation, and the obfuscating effect of mere verbiage that increases in both volume and emptiness as time elapses, that gets caught up in semiotic replication rather than referential assertion.

The *Verses* dramatizes the fact that one can never get outside of language entirely (witness the lengthy "eulogy" ending the poem, which dispels the idle gossip and malicious lies swirling around Swift as object of discourse but which replaces them with its own mode of verbal representation and reconstruction), yet at the same time the poem reveals the possibility of affirming a reality beyond and unsubsumable by text, and impervious to the subversions of verbal irony—in this case, the reality of Swift's worldly engagements on the stage of history, first as would-be reconciler of the Tory ministers in London (lines 369–74); later, as Drapier, fighting " 'To save that helpless Land [Ireland] from Ruin' " (416), and as Dean, bequeathing " 'the little Wealth he had, / To build a House for Fools and Mad' " (lines 483–84). The *Verses*, like Swift's historical pieces, demonstrates that partisan investments and principled advocacy need not negate the role of "faithful historian."

My mind returns again and again to thoughts of Swift in the late 1730s, feeling increasingly removed from the world of the living, as well as from his former self—he lamented to correspondents that he had "grown an entire Ghost of a Ghost of what I was" and become "the Shadow of the Shadow of the Shadow, of &c &c &c of Dr. Sw——" (C 5:77, 89)— struggling with fierce determination to reconnect himself to the flow of worldly events (and perhaps also to his earlier selves, thereby recapturing his sense of a wholeness and fullness of being, and asserting his claim to a unified identity) by publishing his *History*, in the face of persistent discouragement and outright opposition on the part of the 2d earl of Oxford,

Erasmus Lewis, William King, and others, who urged extensive revisions and deletions from the manuscript, and who kept warning of the dangers (real, but often exaggerated for their own self-interested purposes) of publication (see, e.g., C 5:105, 107). In the end, the opposition prevailed and the work was never published in Swift's lifetime, becoming one more casualty of the censorship and textual suppression that plagued his entire career as writer.

It won't do to dismiss Swift's efforts to get his *History* into print as merely an exercise in nostalgia, as the self-indulgent act of an old man desirous of idealizing the past. After all, the man who could compare Irish exiles resettled by the English in America to those "whom the *Romans* placed in their Armies, for no other Service than to blunt their Enemies Swords, and afterwards to fill up Trenches with their dead Bodies" (*PW* 12:60), and who could describe the founding of a colony in terms of "the Natives [being] driven out or destroyed, their Princes tortured to discover their Gold; a free Licence given to all Acts of Inhumanity and Lust; [and] the Earth reeking with the Blood of its Inhabitants" (11:294), was hardly a romanticizer or mythifier of history—was, on the contrary, someone who knew that history is what hurts, what results from the bruising encounters between oppressors and oppressed, what causes suffering to physical (not textual) bodies. He was someone who would have appreciated the force of Fredric Jameson's observation that "we may be sure that [history's] alienating necessities will not forget us, however much we might prefer to ignore them." [22] If the *History* conveys a highly positive view of certain events during Queen Anne's reign and presents a celebratory account of the negotiations culminating in the Treaty of Utrecht, its optimism is anything but facile. In other pamphlets written during the same period Swift made no bones about exposing the destructive conflicts and dissensions within the Tory ministry; in the *History*, however, he had other aims in mind, and both his narrative focus and his tone shifted accordingly.

Swift, who never had a good thing to say about war and had numerous scathing things to say about it, beginning with his early *Ode to Sir William Temple*, which extols Temple as a peacemaker and castigates "War! that mad Game, the World so loves to play, / And for it does so dearly pay" (lines 76–77), no doubt saw in the publication of his *History* an opportunity to deliver a final stinging obituary on the war policies of the Whigs and to commemorate, for the benefit of both the generation coming of age in the mid-1730s and subsequent generations, a fleeting moment in English history when the forces of peace triumphed over militaristic ambition and adventurism. Again and again Swift's imagination (and pen) returned to that moment in renewed attempts to capture its essential meaning and to commemorate it in the most appropriate and enduring way. His fragmentary *Modest Enquiry*, for example, concludes with the following proposed epitaph for Queen Anne's tomb:

That in Compassion to the Miseries of Europe, *and the Sufferings of Her Own Subjects, after a bloody and expensive War which had lasted 20 Years, She concluded a Peace: And that She might transmit the Liberties of Her People Safe to Posterity, She Disbanded the Army: By which Glorious Atchievements She acquired the Hatred of a Faction, who were fond of War, that they might plunder their Fellow-Subjects at Pleasure: And of an Army, that they might do this with Impunity. (PW* 8:197)

However cynically we might want to interpret the Treaty of Utrecht (it was, after all, hardly a nobly disinterested document from England's point of view, given its Asiento clause and related trade concessions), there can be little doubt that the peace it officially proclaimed impressed itself deeply on Swift's consciousness and retained an important symbolic value for him throughout the subsequent decades of his life, giving a special meaning to his efforts as an old man to publish his account of the events that had made it possible.

Through the essays and pamphlets he wrote between 1710 and 1713, Swift personally helped ensure that a generation which he lamented "can[not] remember any thing but war and taxes, and . . . think it is as it should be" (*PW* 16:397) became one that enjoyed the fruits of peace for an extended period. But by the time Swift turned his attention to preparing his *History* for print, the engines of war were once again revving up in England; patriotic cant and anti-Spanish sentiment (fanned into hysteria by the Jenkins' ear episode) were becoming increasingly pervasive, Walpole's peace policies were attracting growing criticism, and the nation was moving inexorably toward involvement in the War of the Polish Succession. As a recent historian puts it, "by the mid-1730s another generation had risen which had not known the strains of a major war, and which regarded warfare as glorious and even beneficial."[23] To whatever extent Swift had in mind the specific circumstances in England during his efforts to publish the *History* (he was far more preoccupied at the time with local Irish affairs), it is probable he would have been concerned in a general way to present fresh lessons of peace to a generation that was likely to have forgotten (or never to have known) the horrors of war, especially given his sense of the precariousness of any peace no matter how popular or beneficial; as he reflects in *The Conduct of the Allies*, " 'Tis easy to entail Debts on succeeding Ages, and to hope they will be able and willing to pay them; but how to insure Peace for any Term of Years, is difficult enough to apprehend" (*PW* 6:55).

As I see it, Swift was acting in the combined roles of specific and universal, traditional and organic intellectual in his attempts to publish his *History* over twenty years after its composition. Without actually going beyond his own local involvement in the circumstances of a particular historical moment, he strove to commemorate for posterity a body of more general and abiding values embodied in the past: values that in fact remain consistent throughout his writings, despite his shifts in political position over the years. As a writer of "utmost impartiality" about events long since passed, Swift hoped to replace his role as public propagandist with that of public intellectual: to speak with the authority of one no longer beholden to any established (political) institutions of power—though continuing to speak with the force of situated and embodied, rather than "transcendent," knowledge—about issues of truth and deception, war and peace, that were as relevant in 1737 as they had been in 1713, and that would be equally germane to future generations, including our own today. Through his publication of the *History*, I think Swift wanted to leave a special legacy for posterity, of a kind very different from his "House for Fools and Mad": a memorial to a popular peace, "Proclaimed in the usual Manner; but with louder Acclamations, and more Extraordinary Rejoicings of the People, than had ever been Remembered on like Occasion" (*PW* 7:167), achieved over the opposition of those for whom "the bleeding Condition of their Fellow-Subjects, was a Feather in the Balance with their private Ends" (6:59).

I would argue that in undertaking this task Swift was indeed performing in the office of "a faithful historian": combining principled conviction and impassioned ideological engagement with a scrupulous attempt to "set the record straight" about former events, and along with Thompson saying, through his interpretation of the past, "that these values, and not those other values, are the ones which make this history meaningful to [him], and that these are the values which [he] intend[s] to enlarge and sustain in [the] present" (not to mention to bequeath to the future). As I write this I am conscious of the fact that in my reflections here I too have been situating myself in relation to particular values, and have been constructing an interpretation based on a similar combination of ideological engagement and a striving for both commemoration and clarification of the past, not only for its own sake but also for what it can tell us about the present.

Swift, of all the so-called Augustan writers, was the one most haunted by the relativity and flux of human existence, the one readiest to acknowledge the inescapable partialness of his perspective as well as the one most willing to reveal his complicity in the ambiguities of language and the indeterminacies of textual production. It is in these areas that we find the clearest evidence of Swift's appeal to modernist and postmodernist sensibilities.

Yet, at the same time, as I've been suggesting throughout these reflections, Swift was the one most successful in clearing a space for himself in which he could write and act forcefully from grounds that were other than merely relative and indeterminate. I submit that the paradox informing his success in this regard has something to teach all eighteenth-century scholars, of whatever ideological stripe, and has a particular resonance for those of us who wish to speak in the academy, and act in the world, as committed leftist intellectuals.

Notes

References to Swift's poetry are to *Swift: Poetical Works*, ed. Herbert Davis (London: Oxford University Press, 1967). The following abbreviations appear in the text following quotations of Swift's prose:
PW: The Prose Works of Jonathan Swift, 16 vols., ed. Herbert Davis and (for Vols. 15 and 16) Harold Williams (Oxford: Basil Blackwell, 1939–74).
C: The Correspondence of Jonathan Swift, 5 vols., ed. Harold Williams (Oxford: Clarendon Press, 1963–65).

1 A somewhat revised version of my ASECS paper is included in a Special Issue, "What's Left of the Left?" edited by James Thompson, of *The Eighteenth Century: Theory and Interpretation* 32, no. 3 (Fall 1991).

2 Anders Stephanson, "Interview with Cornel West," in *Universal Abandon? The Politics of Postmodernism*, ed. Andrew Ross (Minneapolis: University of Minnesota Press, 1988), 271.

3 E. P. Thompson, *The Poverty of Theory and Other Essays* (London: Merlin Press, 1978), 234.

4 For a useful discussion of the changing and conflicting attitudes concerning identity in Swift's time see Christopher Fox, *Locke and the Scriblerians: Identity and Consciousness in Early Eighteenth-Century Britain* (Berkeley and Los Angeles: University of California Press, 1988).

5 Félix Guattari, *Molecular Revolution: Psychiatry and Politics*, trans. Rosemary Sheed (New York: Penguin, 1984), 183.

6 See Paul Lauter, "The Two Criticisms," in *Literature, Language and Politics*, ed. Betty Jean Craige (Athens: University of Georgia Press, 1988), 1–19; and "Canon Theory and Emergent Practice," in *Left Politics and the Literary Profession*, ed. Lennard J. Davis and M. Bella Mirabella (New York: Columbia University Press, 1990), 127–46. In many ways I'm sympathetic to Lauter's criticism of the elitist and insular character of academic(ized) theory and its aloofness from the concretely political struggles both within and outside of the university, but I feel he overstates his case, ignores those interconnections between theory and pedagogical practice that do exist, and winds up promoting a stance of "theory bashing" that to me has disturbingly conservative (even reactionary) resonances.

7 See, for example, my essay, "The Literature of Domestic Tourism and the Public Consumption of Private Property," in *The New Eighteenth Century*, ed. Felicity Nussbaum and Laura Brown (New York and London: Methuen, 1987), 254–75. The editors of this volume make a strong case for the expanded application of contemporary theory to eighteenth-century studies in their introduction (1–22).

8 Edward Said, "Swift as Intellectual," *The World, the Text, and the Critic* (Cambridge, MA: Harvard University Press, 1983), 82–83.

9 Michel Foucault, *Power/Knowledge: Selected Interviews and Other Writings, 1972–1977*, ed. and trans. Colin Gordon (New York: Pantheon, 1980), 126. For a provocative discussion of the relationship between, and the relative efficacy of, Gramsci's and Foucault's respective conceptions of the intellectual's role in society see R. Radhakrishnan, "Toward an Effective Intellectual: Foucault or Gramsci?" in *Intellectuals: Aesthetics, Politics, Academics*, ed. Bruce Robbins, Cultural Politics 2 (Minneapolis: University of Minnesota Press, 1990), 57–99.

10 Guattari, *Molecular Revolution* 253.

11 See Gerald Graff, *Professing Literature: An Institutional History* (Chicago: University of Chicago Press, 1989), chaps. 14 and 15, et passim.

12 Jim Merod, *The Political Responsibility of the Critic* (Ithaca and London: Cornell University Press, 1987), 7, 80.

13 Russell Jacoby, *The Last Intellectuals: American Culture in the Age of Academe* (New York: Basic Books, 1987), 190. For a critique of Jacoby's argument based on what is viewed as his idealized and parochial conception of what a "public" and "independent" intellectual is, see Bruce Robbins' Introduction to *Intellectuals: Aesthetics, Politics, Academics* xii–xv. As my own discussion makes clear, I agree with at least a couple of the critical points made by Robbins.

14 Merod, *The Political Responsibility of the Critic* 4.

15 Jean-Paul Sartre, *Search for a Method*, trans. Hazel E. Barnes (New York: Vintage Books, 1968), 57.

16 See Dennis Bernstein and Larry Everest, "Hector at Harvard," *Z Magazine* (July/August 1991), 25–29.

17 See Donna Haraway, *Simians, Cyborgs, and Women: The Reinvention of Nature* (New York: Routledge, 1991), chap. 9 passim. (The quotations appear on 188.)

18 See, e.g., Richard Ohmann, "The Function of English at the Present Time," in *Left Politics and the Literary Profession* 42–46.

19 See Noam Chomsky, "The Responsibility of Intellectuals," *The Chomsky Reader*, ed. James Peck (New York: Pantheon, 1987), 59–82 passim. (The quotations appear on 60, 78.)

20 Sartre, *Search for a Method* 91.

21 See, for example, Irvin Ehrenpreis' comments about the unreliability and bias of the *History*, which supports his conclusion that "the work fails as history," in *Swift: The Man, His Works, and the Age*, 3 vols. (Cambridge, MA: Harvard University Press, 1962–83), 2:597–604 (601).

22 Fredric Jameson, *The Political Unconscious: Narrative as a Socially Symbolic Act* (Ithaca, NY: Cornell University Press, 1981), 102.
23 W. A. Speck, *Stability and Strife: England, 1714–1760*, The New History of England no. 6 (London: Edward Arnold, 1977), 234.

8 *William C. Dowling*

Ideology and the Flight from History in Eighteenth-Century Poetry

A number of essays in the present volume register the extraordinary impact the new historicism is currently having on eighteenth-century studies, and in a general way my own argument concerning poetry and ideology is meant as a contribution to the enterprise. Yet in thinking through that argument I have been conscious of a certain impatience that one encounters more and more frequently nowadays, a sense that the new historicism, for all its early promise as a theoretical movement, is presently in danger of dwindling into little more than a routine academic exercise, a recycling of drearily predictable formulas about gender and class and marginalization and "the construction of the subject" and the like. No matter where one stands in relation to recent theory, I think, one has to grant a modicum of justice to the claim. To read the current issue of almost any journal in literary studies is too often to have a vision of new historicist interpretation as a ponderous machine into which texts are fed at one end while, after a certain shuddering and heaving and clanking of gears, foreordained results emerge prepackaged at the other.

In what follows, I'd like to suggest that one way out of this impasse, if that is what it is, may lie not in more theorizing but in a deeper consideration of certain issues at once raised by the new historicism and then, for whatever reason, ignored or neglected by most of its practitioners. One such issue is my subject now: the manner in which "history" may be conceived as a domain of reality projected by literary texts as their own exteriority—not just "the world outside the work," but that world as in some sense created or projected by the work as a reality lying immediately beyond its own boundaries as discourse. My argument in turn assumes a point I have recently had occasion to make elsewhere, which is that the new historicism has been decisive for the study of Augustan writing precisely because it has permitted us to grasp "history" in the way it really did and does exist for works like *Absalom and Achitophel* and the *Epistle to Arbuthnot* and *Gulliver's Travels*, as an already-constituted field of symbolic meaning or significance, an abstract battleground of antagonistic forces in whose combat poetry has a power to intervene (see Dowling, "Pocockian Moment").

In the present essay, I want to consider the related question of what happens when this conception of history implodes or collapses. The focus of my inquiry is the mid-century poetic revival, as it is now commonly called by students of eighteenth-century literature: the renunciation of Augustan ethical purpose by the Wartons and others in the name of a "pure poetry" of more intense personal experience, with which is associated a certain movement toward twilight and melancholy, gloomy groves and graveside musings and the sober contemplation of Gothic cathedrals and medieval ruins. The idea of this revival as a "flight from history" was given currency several years ago by John Sitter's *Literary Loneliness in Mid-Eighteenth-Century England*, as an alternative to the notion of poets like the Wartons and Gray and Collins as pre-Romantics, harbingers of a Romanticism for which, in the older literary histories, they had been made to serve as voices crying in the poetic wilderness. One great virtue of Sitter's account is precisely that it directed attention not forward to literary developments still lying in the comparatively distant future but backward to that Augustanism against which the mid-century revival was demonstrably a reaction: "By the midcentury, retirement has hardened into retreat. The poet characteristically longs to be not only far from the madding crowd, which Pope had wanted as much as Gray, but far from everybody. . . . The melancholy poems seem merely to be part of a larger turning-away from the socio-historical world to which poetry traditionally belonged" (85–86).

At the same time, it is not altogether clear how this is supposed to move us closer to any genuine understanding of the mid-century revival. For it is not that the truth of any such account is in question—to the contrary, a bright undergraduate, given an eighteenth-century anthology and a few hours to read, might be depended upon to notice a radical shift between the crowded urban scene of Pope and Swift and the solitary landscape of Gray and the Wartons—but that its truth appears to be merely inductive, less an explanation than a hopeful gesture in the direction of something needing to be explained. The reason that the notion of a "flight from history" nonetheless gained a certain currency, I think, is that the ideas both of flight and of history imply a sense of ideological crisis that, though Sitter himself left its nature wholly unexplored, does indeed underlie the mid-century revival. Thus, for instance, something like Sneyd Davies' deliberate rejection of public affairs in an epistle to a neighbor—"French pow'r, and weak allies, and war, and want— / No more of that, my friend" (CA 1:144)— is in some obvious sense presupposed when Thomas Warton focuses on a characteristic poetic scene:

> Beneath yon ruin'd abbey's moss-grown piles
> Oft let me sit, at twilight hour of eve,
> Where thro' some western window the pale Moon
> Pours her long-levell'd rule of streaming light;
> While sullen sacred silence reigns around,
> Save the lone screech-owl's note, who builds his bow'r
> Amid the mould'ring caverns dark and damp,
> Or the calm breeze, that rustles in the leaves
> Of flaunting ivy, that with mantle green
> Invests some wasted tow'r.
>
> (CF 7:509)

To gaze inward upon the interior landscape of a poem like Warton's *The Pleasures of Melancholy* is immediately to see why the notion of a mid-century flight from history makes a certain sort of sense, for the twilight scene of Warton's solitary musings could scarcely be at a greater distance from the tea tables and jostling streets of Pope and Swift and Gay, or from the clamor of their bitter ideological battle against Walpole and corruption and modernity. Yet there is at the same time something altogether curious about thinking of this as a flight or escape from history, for the moss-grown towers of the ruined abbey that Warton seeks out in his evening solitude are a troubling reminder of a national past filled with religious and civil strife, a visible memorial of the long historical process that has brought England from being a remote corner of medieval Christendom to its present status as an independent modern state. To speak of a flight from history in such poems is, quite obviously, to speak of a past that has somehow got dissociated from history, real events that have somehow gained the status of the imaginary without ceasing to be real.[1]

This is the eighteenth-century Gothic revival, in short, not simply as the medievalism of the Wartons or Gray's fascination with a remote and primitive Scandinavian past, but also in the more extreme guise of Ossian's *Fingal* or Chatterton's Rowley poems, a past almost wholly imaginary but nonetheless unwilling, even to the point of outright imposture, to give up its claims to historical actuality. This is precisely the feature of mid-

century medievalism that directs us to look for its origins in ideology, and
in particular in that English tradition, its own roots going back as far as
the notion of common law precedent, in which the attempt to resolve a
present crisis in the realm most often takes the form of a story about the
national past—a story about Magna Carta or the rights of freeholders or
the immunities of Commons that, in the usual way of ideology, attempts
to resolve in imaginary or symbolic terms a contradiction at the level of
the real. In the immediate background of the mid-century poetic revival, in
turn, lies a particular and important episode in this tradition, what J. G. A.
Pocock has called the ideology of the Ancient Constitution (340).

The central figure in Pocock's account is Harrington, whose *Oceana*
constitutes a break with what Harrington himself called the "Gothic" ar-
rangements of the English constitution—an idea of order and degree and
descending authority never questioned in its essentials by the Jacobean
antiquaries—in favor of a "Venetian" balance of powers the idea of which
traces back through Florentine political theory to Polybius and ultimately
to Aristotle's *Politics*. Yet the paradox of Harrington's impact on English
political thought is that *Oceana* itself was to have little direct influence
on constitutional debate: it was not Harrington's own elaborate scheme
of rotating elective powers that would determine the course of subsequent
political discussion, but his introduction of the categories of classical republican theory into a historical context in which, especially during the
period immediately after 1660, they would acquire a new and extraordinary ideological potency. This is also the context in which Harrington's
most famous contribution to post-Restoration political debate, his exalta-
tion of the gentry or landowning class as embodying the political virtue of
the English nation, was also, on Pocock's account, to assume a burden of
implication never intended by Harrington.

The Harringtonian revolution in English political thought, accordingly,
was the work less of *Oceana* than of what Pocock calls the Harringtonian
revival of 1675, the landmarks of which are the anonymous *Letter from a
Person of Quality to His Friend in the Country* and the famous speech in
the House of Lords in which the earl of Shaftesbury may be said to have
invented Country ideology in a single protracted moment of rhetorical
incandescence. Along with Harrington's own vision of the gentry and freeholders of the shires and county boroughs as the "community of virtue"
central to civic humanism (Pocock 408), the cardinal principles of Country ideology after 1675 would be a notion of the aristocracy as friend and
protector of the *populus* against tyranny—pictured in the altered political circumstances of post-1660 England as the monarch with a standing
professional army at his back—a notion of the Court and its machinery of
patronage as the agency of corruption, change, and modernity, and, finally,
a notion of the Ancient Constitution as always having been implicitly the

mixed and balanced constitution through which, in classical republican theory, the state is preserved from inward decay and historical decline.

This gives us the immediate intellectual background of the revisionary account of literary Augustanism that has been emerging in recent years under the aegis of the new historicism: Augustanism as a critique of early or emergent capitalism, and in particular as a defense of a passing organic or traditional society against a new money society in which all human bonds are in danger of dissolving in favor of crude economic relations and the cash nexus. This is the context in which Bolingbroke's idealization of the Elizabethan age, for instance, and of Elizabeth herself as a monarch who "united the great body of the people in her and their *common interest*," [2] must be seen as part of his more general idealization of organic society, and in which his constant appeals to the Ancient Constitution, and in particular to what he calls England's Gothic institutions of government, must similarly be viewed in light of his more general mythologizing of the traditional past:

A spirit of liberty, transmitted down from our Saxon ancestors, and the unknown ages of our government, preserved itself through the almost continual struggle, against the usurpation of our princes, and the vices of our people: and they, whom neither the Plantagenets nor the Tudors could enslave, were incapable of suffering their rights and privileges to be ravished from them by the Stuarts. Let us justify this conduct by persisting in it and continue to ourselves the peculiar honor of maintaining the freedom of our gothic institutions of government, when so many other nations, who enjoyed the same, have lost theirs. (Quoted in Meehan 13)

The Bolingbroke who spent a political lifetime trying to pull England back from the brink of a dark and chaotic modernity, in turn, is a spokesman for literary Augustanism in the sense Isaac Kramnick taught us to see twenty years ago, the sense in which Swift's satires and Pope's Horatian poems were a direct response to the new world of money and speculation—Pope's "blest paper credit"—ushered in by William of Orange and his Dutch advisors, the world of the National Debt and the South Sea Bubble and Walpole's Robinocracy and modern Whigs like Davenant's Tom Double, penniless before the Glorious Revolution but now grown obscenely rich through a system of unreal speculative wealth even as the ancient landed families of the kingdom decline. This is Augustanism as, in Raymond Williams' phrase, a "retrospective radicalism" whose political opposition to Walpole represents an urgent plea for the moral regeneration of English society in the civic humanist mode, the Machiavellian *ricorso* or *ritorno ai principii* that, through a return to moral origins, is able to rescue a society from the downward cycle of history that carried Greece and Rome into decline.

As a myth of endangered civic virtue, and in particular of an imperiled agrarian England yet preserving the simplicity of Rome during the early republic, Country ideology as invoked by Bolingbroke or the Augustan poets is ideological in just the sense enshrined in pre-Althusserian Marxist theory, a system of ideas and beliefs very obviously engendered by underlying material conditions—in this case, the drastically altering property relations brought about by an emergent capitalism—and to that degree an unreal emanation of what Marx himself was wont to call the material production forces of a society. Yet the great virtue of Althusser's alternative account is that it allows us to grasp the sense in which Country ideology even at this stage is *relatively* autonomous: not, as once imagined by an idealist intellectual history, a disembodied system of ideas somehow floating along independent of real or material existence, but also not the mere unreal or passive reflection of underlying economic circumstances.[3] Nothing makes this clearer, perhaps, than the relation of Country ideology to another cultural myth of the same period, the myth of northern liberty.

This is the myth of cultural origins taken as the subject of Kliger's researches forty years ago, and given in summary form by McKillop in his still-classic Rice Institute pamphlet on the backgrounds of Thomson's poem *Liberty*. It is, in very brief terms, the idea, tracing ultimately to a crucial passage in Lucan's *Pharsalia* but given more immediate currency by Viscount Molesworth's *Account of Denmark* (1694), that the hardy races of the frozen north were the source not only of the heroic virtue that had renewed European society after its descent into Graeco-Roman sloth and servitude,[4] but also of the mixed government, guaranteeing to freemen a democratic voice in the management of public affairs, out of which had developed the Ancient Constitution glorified by Country ideology. On this account, the indomitable spirit of liberty exhibited by Englishmen through the centuries, and even now subjected to a new threat by the forces of Walpole and modern corruption, was something that had arrived in England with the Anglo-Saxons, whose manner of self-governance is what Bolingbroke has in mind when he speaks of "the freedom of our gothic institutions of government."

Beyond its immediate significance for the Ancient Constitution, however, the great importance of the notion of northern liberty is that it permitted a reimagining of the English past in essentially mythic or literary terms, as a story eighteenth-century Englishmen could tell themselves about their own beginnings that at once set England outside the historical cycle of Graeco-roman decline and yet connected its history with that of the Mediterranean world on which the conquering hordes of the North had descended when luxury and internal corruption had done their work. The logic of the myth of northern liberty, in short, as it bears on Country ideology and literary Augustanism and then subsequently on the medieval or Gothic revival of mid-century, is the logic of a single embracing protonarrative that gives sudden and unexpected coherence to the scattered fragments of story and myth and ideology, the piecemeal bits of classical and modern history and native tradition, floating in suspension in the cultural memory of an English society in the midst of ideological transformation.

To take the myth of northern liberty as a story or cultural narrative, by the same token, is to see that its "plot" is the notion of *translatio,* the migration of political liberty and civic virtue west and northward from the moribund civilizations of the Mediterranean to northern Europe and now to eighteenth-century England. This is the context in which the theme of northern liberty becomes, in effect, a single great mythic cycle into which whole blocks of eighteenth-century writing fit as separate episodes: the idea of southern sloth and servitude taken over from Burnet's *Travels* and introduced into eighteenth-century poetry in Addison's *Letter from Italy,* the meditation on vanished greatness that is the subject of poems like Dyer's *The Ruins of Rome* or Mickle's *Almada Hill,* the "progress" motif celebrated in direct terms in Glover's *London, or the Progress of Commerce* and indirectly in Thomson's *Seasons* or Dyer's *The Fleece,* and, lastly, the whole tradition of "Whig panegyric" that, beginning with the Hanoverian apologetics of Ambrose Philips at the beginning of the century, will throughout the period celebrate England's arrival at the apogee of her own epicycle of historical development, her growth in wealth and power and consequence and her prospective greatness as a world civilization.

This is a logic, once again, belonging more to narrative or story than to "ideology" as such, and its power to subsume ideological distinctions has long been the despair of historians trying to make sense of eighteenth-century English politics. Yet the paradoxes of eighteenth-century politics begin to resolve themselves, it seems to me, the moment we think of Country ideology not as a compromise reached under the pressure of political expediency but as what Fredric Jameson has called a shared code, the common symbolic language within which antagonisms are fought out by all parties to a historical conflict. The strength of Jameson's point is that some such code *must* exist for conflict to work itself out within a culture, as you and I must be able to make ourselves understood to each other in English or some other common language before we can disagree about politics or religion or the automobile you sold me day before yesterday. Jameson's own example of this is the manner in which Christianity operated as a shared code in the English Civil War, such that all parties to the conflict, even the most radical of the splinter sects that emerged in the moment of the Cromwellian ascendancy, were compelled to portray themselves in opposition to the others in terms of a more "pure" Christianity rather than political disagreement as such. This is precisely the manner in which Country ideology, as a myth of civic virtue imperiled by corruption, would operate in eighteenth-century England.

One great virtue of Thomson's *Liberty* in this context is that it epitomizes the cultural myth from which Country ideology drew its strength as a shared or common code, gathering into itself the dispersed themes of Opposition thought—the language of civic humanism and Machiavellian regeneration-through-*ricorso*, the myth of nothern liberty, the *translatio* or progress-of-empire motif—and giving them back as a single narrative of rise and fall, progress and decay, ending with the gigantic question mark of England's own destiny as a world civilization. Thus, for instance, Thomson is able to move from a general picture of the heroic tribes of the frozen North—"Hard like their soil, and like their climate fierce / The nursery of nations!" (3.532–33)—to a compelling picture of ancient Britain as home of a similarly heroic virtue: "Bold were those Britons, who, the careless sons / Of nature, roam'd the forest-bounds, at once / Their verdant city, high-embowering fane, / And the gay circle of their woodland wars" (4.626–29). And thus, in the same way, he is able in *The Seasons* to see in the very landscape of those early Britons a spirit favorable to virtue and liberty: "These are the haunts of meditation, these / The scenes where ancient bards th'inspiring breath, / Ecstatic, felt" (*Summer* 521–23).

The other great virtue of *Liberty* is that it keeps so insistently in view the question mark suspended over the end of the story, alerting us to the sense in which even Thomson's famous celebrations of England in *The Seasons*—"Rich is thy soil, and merciful thy skies . . . / Unmatched thy guardian-oaks; thy vallies float / With golden waves, and on thy mountains flocks / Bleat numberless" (*Summer* 1446–50)—demand to be read not as straightforward Whig panegyric but as praise in the conditional mood: what England *might* be, might even yet become, should there be victory after all in the war against Walpole and corruption and modernity. The darkening background against which *Liberty* itself was written is caught, in turn, in a letter from Aaron Hill to Thomson in 1735: "I look upon this mighty work, as the last stretched blaze of our expiring genius. It is the dying effort of despairing and indignant virtue" (quoted in McKillop 100). This is the mood of longer-term pessimism that makes *Liberty*, as much as Pope's last satires, emblematic of Augustanism in the bleak final phase when it has begun to understand that the triumph of what Yeats would later call the "filthy modern tide" is inevitable.

This is then the background of the Augustan collapse, which may in the present context be taken as the crisis of ideology grasping itself as "mere ideology": a grim recognition that, when pitted against blind economic or

material forces carrying a society relentlessly toward some alternative cultural dispensation, moral utterance in general and poetry in particular are
powerless to alter, or even much to retard, the process of historical change.
The precise moment of the Augustan collapse is usually taken to be marked
by Pope's famous endnote to the *Epilogue to the Satires*—"This was the
last poem of the kind printed by our author, with a resolution to publish
no more," etc.—but a truer sense of its meaning as an event symbolic for
eighteenth-century literary culture may be gotten from a poem like John
Brown's *Essay on Satire*, written soon after Pope's death, in which the
passing of Augustanism and its greatest poet is already looked back on as
an actual alteration of the world: "Exulting Dulness ey'd the setting light, /
And flapp'd her wing, impatient for the night: / Rous'd at the signal, Guilt
collects her train, / And counts the triumphs of her growing reign" (CA
5:1).

    This is the triumph of modernity, in short, as grasped by those still dwell-
ing mentally inside Augustan moral categories, the world as it looks when
the apocalyptic conclusion of the 1743 *Dunciad* is taken as an accurate
picture of English society after the death of traditional values. Acceptance
of the same cultural verdict then gives us the strain of elegiac Augustanism
in poets like Goldsmith and Cowper, where, as in *The Deserted Village* or
The Task, the new money society is seen as having permanently triumphed
and all that remains is to mourn the loss of that organic or traditional order
in whose name Augustanism had fought its long rearguard action against
modernity. The story of *translatio* left momentarily suspended in Thomson's *Liberty* is thus seen as completing itself, after the death of Pope, in
England's slow descent into luxury and corruption, brought about by the
inexorable workings of that cyclical history—what Dyer, in *The Fleece*,
calls "the revolving course of mighty Time"—that throws up and tears
down civilizations as blindly as the forces of geology and climate throw up
and tear down the mountains of the earth.

    Yet this same Augustan cry of despair could at the same time be heard
as "mere ideology" in quite another sense—that is, as the high-sounding
cant of an interest group which, having been unaccountably excluded from
power, is bending all its energies toward getting back in. This is "ideology"
as it was understood by an older Marxism, and in the study of eighteenth-
century politics by the writers of Namierite history. During the Augustan
period proper it underlies the charge most often leveled against Pope and
his circle by writers on the Walpole side. "If their representation of things is
true," sniffed Walpole's *Gazetteer* in May 1738, "there never was a people
sunk so low in vileness and infamy as we; for I think, according to their
account of the matter, there are not above ten or a dozen wise and hon-

est men in the nation, and those all within the circle of their own friends
and acquaintance" (quoted in Goldgar 167). Extraordinarly enough, the
Gazetteer's is just the view that will be taken by Joseph Warton over forty
years later in his Essay on Pope, observing about the Horatian poems that
they testify to little more than Pope's "petulance, party-spirit, and self-
importance" (2:438) in portraying so gloomily an England that had been
rising in prosperity and consequence all the while.

The temptation is perhaps to see Warton at such moments as spokesman for a doctrine of unembarrassed progressivism that in the wake of
the Augustan collapse has won the day simply through a lack of ideological competition. There is, certainly, much in the concluding volume
of the Essay on Pope—published, it will be recalled, over two decades
after the first volume—to encourage such a notion. "Our country is represented," says Warton, again speaking about Pope's Horatian poems, and
more generally about Country ideology in the 1730s, "as totally ruined,
and overwhelmed with dissipation, depravity, and corruption. Yet this
very country, so emasculated and debased by every species of folly and
wickedness, in about twenty years afterwards, carried its triumphs over all
its enemies, through all the quarters of the world, and astonished the most
distant nations with a display of uncommon efforts, abilities, and virtues.
So vain are the prognostications of poets, as well as politicians" (2:426).
Yet Warton's perception of a certain hollowness or emptiness in Country
ideology does not add up, any more than does the conviction of the older
Samuel Johnson that the Opposition rhetoric of his youth had been mostly
grandiose cant, to Whiggism. What has occurred to put a chasm between
Pope's last satires or Thomson's Liberty and the Warton who writes this
way in 1782 is immensely more complicated.

In Warton's impatience with Country ideology, that is to say, we are
dealing not with a mere political shift but with something much closer to
what Althusser, following Bachelard, has called an epistemological rupture—a break, as Mary Tiles says in her splendid study of Bachelard as a
philosopher of science, "with what is given as intuitively self-evident, or
obvious, whether this be at the level of ordinary sense perception, everyday experience, or abstract principles."[5] The epistemological rupture in
this case is the sudden sense, occurring in England at about the middle of
the eighteenth century, that Graeco-Roman theories of cyclical history are
utterly irrelevant to the modern world. The alternative notion of history,
what we normally call bourgeois progressivism, is at this point for writers
like Warton something largely vague and undefined, amounting to little
more than a general sense that material progress, as a widespread and irreversible historical tendency, is leading to a general amelioration of social

conditions. In its Augustinian or "Tory" form, as with Dr. Johnson, this is a notion wholly compatible with the more traditional conviction that human nature is something permanent and unchanging; in its "progressive" form, as with certain of the philosophes or, later, Condorcet, it will become the conviction that human nature too is produced by history and is therefore amenable to historical improvement.

In either case, what matters is that the notion of cyclical history, the story of rise and fall that human societies had been telling themselves for two thousand years, is suddenly seen as an exploded theory. To mid- and later-eighteenth-century writers, however, still too close to the point of epistemological rupture to grasp it as such, this registers simply as a sense that there is now something strange or unfathomable about Country ideology and literary Augustanism, as though the vocabulary of Pope and Bolingbroke had suddenly been rendered opaque to those living just a few years afterward. This is the spirit in which Joseph Warton writes about Pope as a poet of party spirit and petulance, and in which Johnson will treat poets like Akenside and Thomson as enthusiasts of a misguided patriotism. The poet of *The Seasons* and *Liberty*, Johnson would famously say in his "Life of Thomson," was composing at a time when "a long course of opposition to Sir Robert Walpole had filled the nation with clamours for liberty, of which no man felt the want, and with care for liberty, which was not in danger." Such is the language of civic humanism and Machiavellian *ricorso* as it appears when the cyclical theory of history that sustained it has suddenly lost meaning, as though someone living after Newton's *Principia* were to persist in offering Ptolemaic explanations of heavenly motion, or someone living in eighteenth-century Europe were to demand that the Greek and Roman myths be taken seriously as religion.

The vantage point from which Augustanism appears in this light is the emergent paradigm of what P. A. Sorokin has called progressive linearism, which as it governs Johnson's later thinking gives us the writer who consistently celebrates material progress, the conversationalist who always hates hearing ancient times praised at the expense of the present, and preeminently the Johnson of Boswell's *Life*, the London-dweller whose love of urban life is so exuberant that he at times comes to seem, for all his Toryism and religious orthodoxy, the very type of modern man. In the writing of Joseph Warton, it gives us not only the commentator who sees Pope as a mere creature of party, but a celebration of England as a "rich and commercial" nation, an expanding imperial power destined to ride the wave of material progress to dominance as a world civilization. In the poetry, especially, of Thomas Warton, whose role as moving spirit of the mid-century poetic revival was even more significant than that of his brother, it gives us "Whig panegyric" taken out of Thomson's conditional mood and put into the simple declarative, as in Warton's ode to Queen Charlotte on her marriage in 1761:

> Lo! the fam'd isle, which hails thy chosen sway,
> What fertile fields her temperate suns display!
> Where Property secures the conscious swain,
> And guards, while Plenty gives, the golden grain:
> Hence with ripe stores her villages abound,
> Her airy downs with scatter'd sheep resound;
> Fresh are her pastures with unceasing rills,
> And future navies crown her darksome hills.
> To bear her formidable glory far,
> Behold her opulence of hoarded war!
>   (CF 5:506–7)

The voice is that of the Thomas Warton who will subsequently assume the title of poet laureate, and who will do so, moreover, in a context involving none of the embarrassment attending the laureateship in the days of Dryden and Pope. For what made the Shadwells and the Cibbers of the preceding age figures at once comic and mildly repellant was the notion that poetry in their hands had been debased from its high public function, delivered over to pygmy rhymsters by a court determined to neutralize the poet's power to enunciate the values of genuine civilization in a time of venality and corruption. For Warton, on the other hand, it can be assumed that such public utterances as his ode to Queen Charlotte simply register an emerging popular sense of England as a nation in the vanguard of material progress, preserved by a mixed constitution and native tradition of liberty from the tyranny that has kept nations like France out of the mainstream of a progressive history. This is the context, with prosperity and national consequence now something that can be safely left to the impersonal forces of historical development, in which poetry-as-such—what Warton himself would call "pure poetry"—will be reoriented toward an interior world of private or personal experience.

This is the mid-century poetic revival, in short, as it would emerge from the demise of Country ideology as a shared code of cultural conflict, not a "flight from history" so much as a sudden and abrupt alteration in the meaning of "history" for eighteenth-century English culture. For what had made the age of Pope and Swift "Augustan" had been a sense of poetry as having a power to work change upon the world, and in specific terms as having this power because of its preservation of an idea of the virtuous republic in a time of cultural crisis and moral disarray. This had been the meaning of their own poetry for Virgil and Horace, haunted by memories of civil war and general social dissolution even in the moment when

Augustus had managed to restore an uneasy peace to the Roman world, and it is what had allowed Dryden and Pope to see in the situation of the Augustan poets a mirror of their own situation in the age of William of Orange and Sir Robert Walpole. The ultimate significance of Country ideology was thus that it had for the Augustans sustained a sense of "history" as a field of symbolic action, of poems as events with enormous consequences in the domain of the real. This is the idea of history that had vanished in the Augustan collapse.

2

In the poetry of the mid-century revival, one has recurrently the sense of a legendary past that, with the demise of Country ideology, has somehow floated free of its moorings in "patriot" or Opposition polemic to become an object of contemplation in its own right. Thus, for instance, even a ceremonial utterance like Warton's ode to Queen Charlotte will very often betray, along with its celebration of England's present prosperity, a growing fascination with the English past as the realm, in Bishop Hurd's phrase, of chivalry and romance. To be sure, there are ritual gestures in the direction of the Ancient Constitution and northern liberty—"Lo! this the land, where Freedom's sacred rage / Has glow'd untam'd through many a martial age" (CF 7:506)—but the overwhelming attraction is toward a past existing in the poetic imagination: "Here Poesy, . . . / Mid oaken bowers, with holy verdure wreath'd, / In Druid-songs her solemn spirit breath'd: . . . / Here Spenser tun'd his mystic minstrelsy, / And dress'd in fairy robes a queen like thee" (CF 7:507). In the same way, one encounters in *Newmarket*, a satire written when Warton was still feeling his way out of the Augustan mode, a sudden enraptured sense of an English country seat as the very scene of romance:

> And see the good old seat, whose Gothic tow'rs
> Awful emerge from yonder tufted bow'rs;
> Whose rafter'd hall the crowding tenants fed,
> And dealt to Age and Want their daily bread;
> Where crested knights with peerless damsels join'd,
> At high and solemn festivals have din'd;
> Presenting oft fair Virtue's shining task,
> In mystic pageantries, and moral mask.
>
> (CF 7:534)

Newmarket is one of the comparatively rare poems in which the moral vocabulary of Augustanism may be seen to have lingered on, in this or that isolated instance, until mid-century, and in fact its picture of the English

gentry as a class that has dwindled into a mere tribe of jockeys and race-
course touts is meant as a requiem for Country ideology.[6] Yet beyond its
dire warnings about Luxury and Corruption, beyond, even, its satiric exploitation of the Augustan metaphor of gambling as the very symbol of
the new speculative society of stockjobbers and credit managers, there
is a sense of an excluded or suppressed poetic landscape trying to press
its way into the foreground. Thus, for instance, though Warton after the
lines just quoted immediately catches himself and turns back to satire with
a contemptuous portrait of Hilario, owner of the "good old seat" just
described—"Hilario bets,—park, house, dissolve in air; / With antique
armor hung, his trophied rooms / Descend to gamesters, prostitutes, and
grooms" (CF 7:534)—the memory of crested knights and peerless dam-
sels, the mystic pageantries of a bygone age, persists as something anoma-
lous in this literary context, a momentary and almost inadvertent glimpse
of a world lying outside satire.

   In the free-floating or disembodied past that thus asserts itself more and
more as a privileged scene in mid-century poetry, we are dealing with
something implied by Althusser's concept of ideological overdetermination and such extensions of it as Poulantzas' theory of social formations
or Jameson's treatment of *Ungleichzeitigkeit*, and yet seldom mentioned in
discussions of ideology and literature. This is the principle that anything
once entering into culture considered as an ideological formation then inevitably assumes an autonomous existence there, outliving the underlying
material conditions to which it had arisen as an imaginary response and
assuming, as often as not, a wholly new burden of symbolic implication.
Thus it is that the myth of the Gothic past elaborated by Country ideology—northern liberty and primitive virtue, bold Britons and the Ancient
Constitution, the Elizabethan age as a golden moment of national unity—
does not vanish with the demise of Country ideology, but lives on instead
as a depoliticized imaginative ideal, the scene of Gothic towers and crested
knights that draws Warton's fascinated gaze away from the ostensible
concerns of *Newmarket* as a contemporary satire.

   The role of the Gothic past in the mid-century revival thus becomes, as
modern criticism has long understood, to offer a refuge from that desacral-
ization of the world that presented itself to poets like the Wartons and
Gray as the one lamentable consequence of an otherwise progressive history, the one great loss to human existence, in a world increasingly blessed
with advances in knowledge and material progress, which it then becomes
the object of poetry to repair. It is the unsentimental voice of progressive
history personified as "severer Reason" that we hear, for instance, at the
very end of Thomas Warton's ode on Vale-Royal abbey, reminding the
poet and his audience that it is out of the dissolution of the feudal order

that the "new glories" of modern civilization are even now arising, "More useful institutes, adorning man, / Manners enlarg'd, and new civilities" (CF 7:515). Yet this comes late in a poem which until this instant has been about a speaker who, contemplating the ruins of a twelfth-century abbey, has journeyed in his own mind into a magical past in which belief in the supernatural was universal, in which "Learning, guarded from a barbarous age," took refuge in the silent cloisters of the monastery, and in which heroic men returned from far crusades to lay down their arms and pray out their lives in peaceful sanctity.

The great virtue of the old romances from this point of view is that they serve so powerfully, as Warton puts it in his essay on Spenser, "to rouse and invigorate all the powers of imagination" (1:268), which is testimony to the ideological function now being assumed by this primitive past of mystery and magic in the mid-century context, a pitting of poetry and the poetic imagination against the wholly instrumental rationality that has brought about England's prosperity as a "rich and commercial" nation and, beyond that, an age of material progress. "The Wartons," says Wallace Jackson, "went rummaging through history to find hypothetical identities into which the self could move, habitations for the imagination that were to be exploited as a source of power" (181), and the same is true in varying degrees of Collins and Shenstone and Gray: the point is always that the primitive or medieval past becomes an alternative sphere of mind or imagination, a sanctuary from which the spirit may return roused and reinvigorated to a world undergoing a relentless disenchantment. This is the Gothic past that earlier floated free of its ideological moorings at the demise of Country ideology, in short, now assuming a new role within the ideology of bourgeois progressivism, a myth no longer disembodied but being drawn into an alternative relation to the real.

The terminal point of the mid-century revival as a poetic movement is the inward turn occurring in the instant the poet understands that, in any gaze at ruined cloisters or moss-grown towers, it is the imagination itself that is supplying the sense of mystery or magic, and that it is the imagination itself, and not, after all, the primitive or Gothic past, that provides the ultimate sanctuary in a disenchanted world. The immediate result will be the visionary odes of a mid-century poet like Collins, preoccupied not with anything external to the mind but with an interior scene in which the imagination, drawing on that primordial level of consciousness from which magic and mystery may be presumed to have derived in more primitive ages, provides the objects of its own contemplation. "By the vigorous effort of a creative imagination," declared William Duff in his *Essay on Original Genius*, the poet "calls shadowy substances and unreal objects into existence. They are present to his view and glide, like spectres, in silent, sullen majesty, before his astonished and entranced sight" (177). Such theories ultimately concern, as Jackson points out, not simply poetry but reality itself: "the protected place becomes the self, building its defenses against the world and generating through the treasured instrumentality of the imagination a world within that can be set against the outer world" (187–88).

In Collins' visionary odes or Duff's theory of original genius, then, ends the story that began when, in the first stirrings of Country ideology in response to early or emergent capitalism, the primitive past of northern Europe and the "gothic institutions" of the English nation took on mythic shape in an appeal against the new money society of Walpole and the Robinocracy. For from the Augustan perspective what Duff is describing would be not genius but derangement ("Is there, who lock'd from ink and paper, scrawls / With desp'rate Charcoal round his darken'd walls?"), precisely that state of alienation and fragmentation that must occur when the bonds of traditional society are dissolved by invisible market forces transforming human beings into mere economic integers or individual units. From the perspective of progressive ideology, however, what is being celebrated is not alienation but the autonomy of a separate bourgeois consciousness, a new world in which people will learn to congratulate themselves on their self-containedness or "individuality" or personal freedom. This is the context in which the mid-century revival demands to be understood less as a flight from history than as a radical transformation of what "history" would subsequently mean for poetry. To have seen this is, I think, to encounter an object lesson in the way history, reconceived as a reality created or projected by literary works themselves, today proposes itself as a domain remaining to be investigated by the new historicism.

Notes

1 The process of dissociation can be traced in a poem like Dyer's *The Ruins of Rome*, where the cyclical theory of history that was at the center of the Augustan appeal for a Machiavellian *ricorso* visibly begins to produce a past that is becoming an object of contemplation in its own right, and thus a source of the "pleasing melancholy" that defines the midcentury mood:

> Behold that heap
> Of mouldering urns (their ashes blown away,
> Dust of the mighty) the same story tell; . . .
> The solitary, silent, solemn scene,
> Where Caesars, heroes, peasants, hermits lie,
> Blended in dust together. . . .
>   There is a mood, . . .
> There is a kindly mood of melancholy,

That wings the soul, and points her to the skies;
When tribulation clothes the child of man, . . .
A gently-wakening call to health and ease.
How musical! when all-devouring Time,
Here sitting on his throne of ruins hoar,
While winds and tempests sweep his various lyre,
How sweet thy diapason, Melancholy!

(CF 4:287)

2 Quoted from *The Idea of a Patriot King* by Goldgar (139), on whose account of the literary Opposition to Walpole I am drawing in this paragraph. Cf. Thomson in *Liberty*, describing the defeat of the Spanish Armada:

Matchless in all the spirit of her days!
With confidence unbounded fearless love
Elate, her fervent people waited gay,
Cheerful demanded the long threaten'd fleet,
And dash'd the pride of Spain around their isle. . . .
The trembling foe even to the centre shook
Of their new-conquer'd world, and skulking stole
By veering winds their Indian treasure home.
Mean-time, Peace, Plenty, Justice, Science, Arts,
With softer laurels crown'd her happy reign.

(5.934–46)

3 I discuss the Althusserian issue of relative autonomy at length in *Jameson, Althusser, Marx*, chap. 3.

4 Thomson, *Liberty* (the speaker is Liberty personified):

And there a race of men prolific swarms,
To various pain, to little pleasure us'd;
On whom, keen-parching, beat Riphaean winds;
Hard like their soil, and like their climate fierce;
The Nursery of Nations!—These I rous'd,
Drove land on land, on people people pour'd;
Till from almost perpetual night they broke,
As if in search of day; and o'er the banks
Of yielding empire, only slave-sustain'd,
Resistless rage'd, in vengeance urg'd by ME.

(3.529–38)

5 Tiles 56. Bachelard's theory of the *coupure epistémologique* is meant to apply purely and rigorously to the internal development of the respective natural or physical sciences, Althusser's version of the same idea to the distinction between ideology and "science" in Marx's theoretical writings. My claim in the present argument is that something precisely analogous must be posited as occurring in the cultural field at certain crucial moments in history—that one cannot adequately explain a phenomenon like the mid-century poetic revival without having seen the importance of the cyclical theory of history's having suddenly "gone dead" *as* a theory at the same cultural moment. I hope to de-

velop this claim more substantially in a work on the logic of the new historicism now in progress.

6 The transition to elegiac Augustanism occurs when, in the work of poets like Goldsmith and Cowper, the satiric voice gives way altogether to lament or recrimination. Cf., for instance, *The Task*:

> we yet retain
> Some small pre-eminence; we justly boast
> At least superior jockeyship, and claim
> The honours of the turf as all our own!
> Go, then, well worthy of the praise ye seek,
> And show the shame ye might conceal at home
> In foreign eyes!—be grooms, and win the plate
> Where once your nobler fathers won a crown!—
> 'Tis gen'rous to communicate your skill
> To those that need it.
>   (2.274–83)

Works Cited

CA. *Fugitive Poetry: A Classical Arrangement of Fugitive Poetry*. Compiled by John Bell. 18 vols. London, 1789–1810.

CF. *English Poets: Minor English Poets, 1660–1780: A Selection from Alexander Chalmers' The English Poets*. Compiled by David P. French. 10 vols. New York: Benjamin Blom 1967.

Cowper, William. *Poetical Works*. Ed. H. S. Milford. 4th ed. London: Oxford University Press, 1971.

Dowling, William C. "Teaching Eighteenth-Century Literature in the Pocockian Moment." *College English*, 49 (1987), 523–32.

Dowling, William C. *Jameson, Althusser, Marx*. Ithaca: Cornell University Press, 1984.

Duff, William. *An Essay on Original Genius*. London, 1767.

Goldgar, Bertrand A. *Walpole and the Wits*. Lincoln: University of Nebraska Press, 1976.

Jackson, Wallace. *Vision and Re-Vision in Alexander Pope*. Detroit: Wayne State University Press, 1983.

Jameson, Fredric. *The Political Unconscious*. Ithaca: Cornell University Press, 1981.

McKillop, Alan D. *The Background of Thomson's "Liberty."* Rice Institute Pamphlet 38, no. 2. Houston: Rice Institute Press, 1951.

Meehan, Michael. *Liberty and Poetics in Eighteenth-Century England*. Dover, NH: Croom Helm, 1986.

Pocock, John Greville Agard. *The Machiavellian Moment: Florentine Political Thought and the Atlantic Republican Tradition*. Princeton: Princeton University Press, 1975.

Sitter, John E. *Literary Loneliness in Mid-Eighteenth-Century England*. Ithaca: Cornell University Press, 1982.

Thomson, James. *The Complete Poetical Works of James Thomson.* Ed. J. Logie Robertson. London: Oxford University Press, 1963.

Tiles, Mary. *Bachelard: Science and Objectivity.* Cambridge: Cambridge University Press, 1984.

Warton, Joseph. *Essay on the Genius and Writings of Pope.* 2 vols. London, 1782.

Warton, Thomas. *Observations on the Faerie Queene of Spenser.* 2d ed. 2 vols. London, 1762.

Williams, Raymond. *The Country and the City.* London: Chatto and Windus, 1973.

9 *Donna Landry*

Commodity Feminism

"Commodity feminism?" Yes, feminism is being fetishized as a marketable commodity within eighteenth-century studies. And, like other forms of critical theory, feminism has been commodified before it could become fully institutionalized[1] or realize its most radical effects. In this historical moment, the moment of what Donna Haraway has described as "the stripped down atomism of Star Wars, hypermarket, postmodern, media-simulated, citizenship,"[2] why should we have expected any other turn of events? Of course feminism would be commodified, as has happened to all currently "new" critical approaches. Even giving feminism a singular name is evidence of that tendency to reify and label in order to market more efficiently, for there are many feminisms, many strategies for "undoing" ideologies of gender and disassembling patriarchal relations. Yet the market inexorably homogenizes and consolidates them into a unitary "feminism" in which the trading remains active, despite a recessionary economy.

To speak of feminism's commodification in relation to eighteenth-century studies, however, is to mark a particularly sharp contradiction, and to convey a peculiar sense of belatedness. Feminism is already well established in nineteenth- and twentieth-century studies, through historical connections between literary movements and women's suffrage, and through the already canonical status of writers like Jane Austen, George Eliot, and Virginia Woolf. (Where are the U.S. and other Anglophone women writers on this list?) Less predictably, the investigation of gender is well on its way to being a central focus for students of the Renaissance. But like other forms of critical theory, feminism has only just arrived on the professional and scholarly agendas of eighteenth-century specialists.[3] In that case, why bemoan the terms or the means of its arrival? Is it not better that feminism be represented? In this collection of essays reflecting on the current state of the field, for example, there are only two essays by women, and only two that address feminism, so that women and feminism represent one another, simultaneously included and marginalized.

Given certain disciplinary resistances, then, is it not churlish to find fault with the token acceptance, even the fetishization of feminism when ignorance, neglect, hostility, and condescension are the likely alternatives? Perhaps, because I remain skeptical about relations between feminism and eighteenth-century studies at the moment, my title should be "Churlish Feminism." The recent, sometimes genial, sometimes patronizing, accommodation of feminism within the institution needs to be scrutinized. Such accommodations always cost something. I would like to examine some of those costs here.

I

We would do well to begin by remembering what Marx described as the effects of commodification generally:

The necessary physical properties of the particular commodity . . . —in so far as they directly follow from the nature of exchange-value—are: unlimited divisibility, homogeneity of its parts and uniform quality of all units of the commodity. As the materialisation of universal labour-time it must be homogeneous and capable of expressing only quantitative differences. Another necessary property is durability of its use-value since it must endure through the exchange process.[4]

Commodity fetishism[5] designates a double movement within ideology and everyday practice, the simultaneous reification of social relations, which become things in themselves, and the personification of the products of our labor, which acquire a life of their own. Marx draws attention to the "peculiar social character" of the labor necessary for commodity production as the key to this precise historical development. Only "private individuals who work independently of each other" will produce commodities: "Since the producers do not come into social contact until they exchange the products of their labour, the specific social characteristics of their private labours appear only within this exchange."[6] And it is in this exchange that value is constituted, and that a certain abstract equality between exchangeable goods is necessarily presupposed.

We should not forget that commodities have a use- as well as an exchange-value, though as Marx makes clear, it becomes increasingly difficult to specify the use-value of commodities within capitalist societies apart from their exchange-value. Feminism's use-value for women lies in its emancipatory potential, its usefulness as an instrument of social transformation. Academic feminism's use-value in this sense is partly legible in the material changes within social and political institutions, including universities and publishing houses, that the women's movements of the last twenty years have brought about. That use-value is also partly legible in the continuing social innovations and counterhegemonic practices which particular groups of women continue to produce around the globe. When we focus on feminism within the academic marketplace, however, as I shall do in this essay, we are concentrating on feminism primarily in the light of its exchange-value. Its use-value remains, but within the overdeterminations of the market, such use-value in any pure sense is impossible to locate. The implications of Marx's theory of the commodity for analyzing the construction of subjectivity within modern capitalist societies are multiple,[7] but what price a feminism constructed thus?

Marx goes so far as to put in play a putative subjectivity for commodities themselves, in a passage that has particular resonances for feminism:

> If commodities could speak, they would say this: our use-value may interest men, but it does not belong to us as objects. What does belong to us as objects, however, is our value. Our own intercourse as commodities proves it. We relate to each other merely as exchange-values.[8]

Once we have refused to grant "men" the status of an unmarked category by exposing its gender specificity, the history of women as commodities, as objects of exchange between men within forms of indigenous patriarchy within a capitalist world-system, can be made to "speak" from between the lines of Marx's text. Between them, Gayle Rubin and Luce Irigaray have said just about everything important there is to say regarding the status of women as commodities, though nothing about feminism in the marketplace.[9] The exchange of women shores up a homosocial as well as patriarchal social and symbolic order. Women have value only in so far as they can be exchanged, and they can be exchanged only in so far as they are valued comparatively and interchangeably. Female commodities mirror back to the men who exchange them "the cult of the father," representations of phallocratic authority; female commodities cannot by definition mirror each other. Replying to Marx's hypothesis "If commodities could speak," Irigaray retorts: "*So commodities speak. To be sure, mostly dialects and patois, languages hard for 'subjects' to understand.* The important thing is that they be preoccupied with their respective values, that their remarks confirm the exchangers' plans for them." [10] As we might expect, Irigaray recommends that women rebel by not going on the market, by not complying with the exchangers' plans, and, instead, initiating forms of commerce—social, sexual, linguistic, and economic—amongst themselves.

Feminist movements constitute one form of strategic resistance to the exchange of women, though the exchange of women itself is a reductive model that does not account for differences of, for example, class, race, or sexuality among women. Nor does the exchange of women explain away women's agency and complicity in oppression, again along the axes of race, class, or (hetero)sexuality. It is, however, within feminism's emancipatory potential as a social and political movement, working against patriarchal exchange, that the use-value, rather than the exchange-value, of feminism as a commodity is to be found. But to the extent that feminists happen to be or identify as women, the exchange of feminisms in the academic marketplace is overdetermined by the traffic in women, or capitalist-patriarchal business-as-usual. "Unlimited divisibility," "homogeneity of its parts," "uniform quality," "durability" within the wear-and-tear of exchange, the absence of social contact among the "private individual" producers except at the moment of exchange, indeed the absence of any sense of value except in exchange, as exchange-value: How does feminism conform or fail to conform to these modelings?

II

Having written these paragraphs about feminism and commodification in the usual analytical style, acknowledging one's interests but remaining disembodied, unsituated in any concretely historical or autobiographical way, I would now like to turn to an interested history of the relation of feminism to eighteenth-century studies: My own institutional history in relation to both, and the place of commodification in each.

At the University of Virginia, where I was a graduate student in the late 1970s, the eighteenth century was strongly represented by a number of famous male faculty, theoretical reflection and methodological self-consciousness were much encouraged, and feminism was not a theory. Feminism was a political movement in which some of us had sometimes been active, as high school or college students, forming women's groups, working in women's housing and radio collectives, and at rape crisis centers. Needless to say, we had no official feminist mentors, and the only

female faculty, who were few and far between, held untenured or temporary appointments. How were we to connect feminism with our scholarly
research, beyond working on women writers? Austen, Eliot, and Woolf
were acceptable interests, and Anne Finch, countess of Winchilsea, turned
up in Ralph Cohen's eighteenth-century poetry syllabus; American women
writers fared rather worse. Clearly, there wasn't much to go on, either
theoretically or empirically, in the construction of a feminist scholarly
paradigm.

Elaine Showalter's *A Literature of Their Own* (1977) and Sandra Gilbert
and Susan Gubar's *The Madwoman in the Attic* (1979) had to face
some pretty stiff competition in the theory stakes.[11] Arguably, despite
their ground-breaking contributions to feminist scholarship and criticism,
neither book was politically or theoretically sophisticated enough to persuade an audience brought up on Marxism, reception theory, psychoanalysis, Foucault, and Derrida, on *New Literary History* as well as the old
literary history, that this was it, the feminist model we had been awaiting.
And neither book was sufficiently compelling to override deeply ingrained
misogynist anxieties, including our own, about the theoretical or political
rigor of this new liberal-individualist feminist scholarship.

Some of us interested in feminism and the eighteenth century pursued
Marxist criticism, which could be employed in at least two ways as a recognizably rigorous analytical method. Ralph Cohen, for one, recognized the
Marxism of a Raymond Williams or a Terry Eagleton as Theory, and Irvin
Ehrenpreis was prepared to accept an interest in "the social and political"
dimensions of literary works as History. His concept of the social extended
to sexual relations, provided one also paid attention to partisan rivalries,
to the ways in which, for instance, Lady Mary Wortley Montagu's quarrel
with Pope and Swift could be said to have had something to do with her
friendship with Walpole and their friendship with Bolingbroke. However
vexed those friendships might have been, certain Whig and Tory, Hanoverian and Stuart (perhaps Jacobite) sympathies overdetermined such
a literary (and class-specific and gendered) quarrel. Leo Damrosch and
James Turner, younger, underappreciated by their senior colleagues, offering different, in some ways contradictory styles of dissent, positively encouraged new kinds of work that engaged questions of ideology, gender,
and sexuality. They might not do feminist work themselves, but they were
sympathetic to it.

Circumstances were ripe for the formation of reading groups and other
alternative forms of education, especially those with a theoretical edge.
Throughout these years there was a graduate-student-run "Theory Group"
which various faculty sometimes attended; other reading groups kept
forming and dissolving. The "Marxist-Feminist" reading group, in which

I first read the work of U.S. feminists in other disciplines (Heidi Hart-mann, Zillah Eisenstein) and argued over *The German Ideology* and *The Origin of the Family, Private Property, and the State*, gave way to the "Charlottesville Socialist-Feminist Alliance," in which Michael Ryan was the sole English department faculty participant.

It seemed symptomatic that the two faculty members most interested in Marxist and feminist work, Turner and Ryan, were denied tenure, and that the most stimulating feminist interventions in town came from Gayatri Spivak, who was not a faculty member at Virginia but a full professor at the University of Iowa and then at the University of Texas. Known to us as the translator of Derrida's *Of Grammatology* and the author of difficult theoretical essays, she commuted between Iowa City, Austin, Paris, and Charlottesville to see Michael Ryan, establishing that there could be other networks of affect, intellectual exchange, and knowledge/power than the predominantly male homosocial continuum at Virginia. Hers seemed to be a pedagogy at least momentarily "without constraint": as an officially absent presence, she had the effect of teaching and politicizing us *without* doing so, without any local institutional apparatus and without any of the particular pieties characteristic of that institution.

These were exciting times in which to be entering the discipline of lit-erary studies. It was intensely pleasurable to recognize that what we were reading and preparing to write about might be perceived as "oppositional" by the institution, at least oppositional in the sense that it was not part of the official curriculum. In fact, as my former colleague Leo Braudy has been quick to point out, the institution probably thought what we were up to was "trivial" or "irrelevant." "Political criticism" was more clearly oppositional than feminist critical and canonical revisionism, in that it led to political action, as in the formation of a graduate students' union and public discussions of teaching assistants' wages and student representation on committees within the English department.

Feminism was slower to achieve institutional acceptance than this labor-ite or trades-unionist, usually male-identified, version of left politics, but by the time I departed from Virginia, an interdisciplinary women's studies program was under way, and a "Feminist Theory Group" was forming to challenge the by-now venerable, still largely gender-blind "Theory" group. The founding of *Iris*, a women's studies journal, was soon to follow. And in the 1980s Virginia was little different from other English departments in its decision to hire more female and minority faculty and to encourage certain kinds of interdisciplinary work. It is now, I am glad to say, much easier to "do" feminism at Virginia than it was, but that in itself is not enough.

One of the effects of feminism's institutional success within the university has been to academicize for subsequent generations of students what we had the illusion of engaging in, however naively, as an "authentically" oppositional, political practice. Those of us who didn't train officially as feminist critics, but as period specialists with a strong interest in critical theory, especially Marxism and poststructuralism, and who went on reading and doing feminism unofficially until we had sufficient institutional independence or support to allow it to transform our work, have certain investments in our "authentic," because unsanctioned, relation to our feminism as a critical practice. Those of us who didn't have official feminist mentors, but who fought to make our work both as politically challenging as we could get away with, and as impeccably scholarly as we could make it, in order to persuade a suspicious male mentor of our critical worth, value our struggle as symptomatic of how difficult it is for feminism to change the world. It still unnerves me slightly to encounter young feminist critics whose introduction to feminism has been a course in graduate school, usually one in "French Feminist Theory."

Such developments are not, of course, to be regretted, since they do signify institutional change, but the presence of feminist courses within English departments is not "feminist" or "political" enough to represent a feminist politics in its entirety. That there is still an active women's movement, despite media minimizing and the premature announcement of our arrival at a "postfeminist" era, has been demonstrated both quietly in the continuing stream of returning women students in educational institutions around the globe and spectacularly in abortion, reproductive, and gay rights campaigns such as the march on Washington in April 1989. I would like to suggest that we can resist commodification partly by making connections to feminist activism outside the university as well as inside, but we can also do it by historicizing the place of feminism within our discipline.

III

And here we confront within current feminism some of the signs of commodification specified by Marx: Feminism's unlimited divisibility, the homogeneity of its parts, and its durability. To take the last of these first, feminism has endured long enough within the academy already to be divided generationally as well as politically. In a recent essay Alice Jardine has proposed a four-way generational split among academic feminists in the United States: Those who received their Ph.D.'s before 1968, those who got them between 1968 and 1978, those with degrees from 1978–88, and the newest generation, Ph.D.'s 1988–98.[12] Only the last two generations had any chance at all of training under explicitly feminist mentors, many important developments in feminism seem to have happened "around 1981," as Jane Gallop has observed, and between 1978 and 1988 many English departments changed their minds dramatically regarding whether or not feminism constituted a theory or acceptable critical approach, so that the penultimate generation is very divided in its experience. Jardine's model is in some ways too neat, since some feminists have been in graduate programs for a very long time, or in and out of them, their studies interrupted by other demands—filial, familial, affectional— so often made upon women in our society. But the divisions to which she points hold true for many if not all cases.

Recent Ph.D. candidates who "do" feminism are likely to have been introduced to it in a course in graduate school and to have had little experience of women's groups, activist organizing around women's issues, or the bad old days of massive institutional silence regarding feminism. As a result, they are likely to think about feminism as one field among others, one particularly marketable theoretical approach. In this sense, even the presence of feminist courses in the university curriculum is a sign of feminism's commodification as institutional containment as well as evidence of its gradual transformation of institutions.

Feminism's durability, its unfolding history as a social and political as well as intellectual movement, assures that there will be historically significant differences between feminists and feminisms. And paradoxically, those differences, the unlimited divisibility of positions within the movement, can become invisible from the perspective of academic institutions. Unlimited divisibility and an increasing homogeneity of the parts: While political, racial, sexual, class, ethnic, and national differences proliferate within feminism, a spurious substitutability may well govern the institutional agenda, particularly with regard to hiring, the academic market in its most nakedly political-economic form, when feminists and feminisms may seem inextricable and interchangeable commodities.

Differences within feminism can take on a peculiarly agonistic quality because they contravene the concept of sisterhood. How can "we" be united against "patriarchy" and "capital" if each of these terms is subject to problematization and to respecification in different concrete situations, different material contexts? How can nonsynchronous, sometimes intersecting, sometimes contradictory forms of oppression and self-representation be articulated? Hence the language of multiple and mobile subject positions, and of situated discourses or knowledges within a postcolonial and global context.

Here the interpenetration of feminism and poststructuralism becomes apparent, signifying a great divide between "pre-" and "post-" poststructuralist feminisms. It sometimes takes the form of a perceived split between "theory" and "experience" in feminist discourse. Sometimes, not always, this split lines up with a generational division identified by Jardine, the late 1970s and afterward as opposed to what went before. We could call these later, more self-consciously theoretical versions of feminism anti-essentialist in that they problematize categories founded on philosophical essences by showing them to be constructed relationally, discursively. But even such an anti-essentialist feminist language sensitive to differences within the category "women" may prove inadequate to disarm completely attacks on the tendency of Western or "Imperial Feminism" [13] toward pre-mature totalization. And the older feminisms resistant to "unlimited divisibility" have come to be seen as not even adequate, according to younger feminist critics like Biddy Martin and Chandra Mohanty, "to the task of articulating the situation of white women in the West," let alone other women, elsewhere. [14]

This valorization of feminist critique as limitlessly divisible, potentially untotalizable narratives responsive to the concrete specificities of particular historical and cultural contexts is by no means a hegemonic position within feminism. Indeed, many of our most eminent feminist critics continue to define their positions in relation to the category of "women," relatively unspecified and uncrosshatched by other axes of difference. [15] One of the consequences of the unlimited divisibility model most feared by feminists who continue to employ "women" as an undifferentiated category is that under all this pressure from other axes of difference, women will once again disappear. Unlimited divisibility might in the end produce ultimate invisibility. But this caution, I think, depends upon unnecessarily clinging to an either/or: Either we keep "women versus men" as our governing binary, unmuddied by other differences, or we succumb to patriarchal silencing once more.

I don't think it is as simple as that, nor as simple as the slogans I am about to propose: No feminism without materialism. No feminism without anti-essentialism. If anything, we "anti-essentialist" feminist critics have not yet gone far enough in our insistence on the necessity for rigorous accounts of unlimited divisibility as constitutive of subject positions, including feminist subject positions, globally today. And if anti-essentialism is not to freeze into an orthodoxy, strategically we need to take seriously in certain contexts what Stephen Heath, Gayatri Spivak, and others have termed "the risk of essentialism." [16] But as a risk, to be sure; not as a comfortable settling back into the category of "women." As Denise Riley has recently reminded us:

the risky elements to the processes of alignment in sexed ranks are never far away, and the very collectivity which distinguishes you may also be wielded, even unintentionally, against you. Not just against you as an individual, that is, but against you as a social being with needs and attributions. The dangerous intimacy between subjectification and subjection needs careful calibration.[17]

That careful calibration requires a recognition of the materiality of discourses within which the shifting category of "women" has its being. As Riley suggests, quoting Marx on the concept of labor, "even the most abstract categories . . . are nevertheless, in the specific character of this abstraction, themselves likewise a product of historical relations, and possess their full validity only for and within those relations."[18] Difficult as this sounds, the tension that Riley proposes between "women" as a foundation of and "women" as an irritant to feminism is a necessary and productive tension that populist appeals for a return to "real women" ignore at their peril.

To take the academic institution as representative of other institutions once again: When academic institutions mediate some of these real, material differences between women, political differences become professional rivalries, and intellectual differences become counters in the competition for academic status and material rewards. Rather than political debate, and the possibility of working through differences collectively, boundaries are established, positions are consolidated and replicated defensively, and gatekeeping and policing are institutionalized. Since policing has its origins in the defense of private property, the policing of feminism frequently takes the form of claims to ownership of the purest feminist praxis.

The unlimited divisibility of feminism, therefore, works in at least two ways. Politically and intellectually, the public working through of differences can be productive if intensely difficult. But under the hot lights in the arena of professional competition, the staging of differences tends to devolve into the repressive tactics of the purity police, on the one hand, and the embattled defense of turf on the other.

An example of this collective mindset occurred at a panel at the 1989 MLA meeting in Washington, D.C. Entitled "Where Have We Been? Where Are We Going? III: Is There an Anglo-American Feminist Criticism?," the panel was apparently organized to stage a dialogue between U.S. and British feminists, perhaps in the interests of problematizing the usefulness of strictly nationalist distinctions in a taxonomy of feminisms. But the panel became an occasion for U.S. feminist defensiveness and breast-beating. Toril Moi's materialist, though not necessarily "British," feminist critique of the essentialist, antitheoretical tendencies of "Anglo-American" feminism emerged as the threatening Other to a U.S. feminism so obsessed with defense against all criticism from outside as to be largely oblivious to the British women on the panel, or at least largely incapable of addressing them. Almost all the audience's questions were directed toward

Jane Marcus, ironically disavowing her status as a "representative" American feminist, but leading the attack on Moi's misrepresentation of recent U.S. feminist history. Most of the questions involved a plea for seeing U.S. feminism in its richness and complexity, contrary to Moi's highly critical simplifications.

Does such a plea mean that "our" feminism is by definition beyond reproach, or not in need of continual critical transformations, simply because it has been attacked too monolithically as antitheoretical? How much of the U.S. defense of turf, of "our" feminism as Feminism, with a capital F, repeats the same tendency toward what many feminist critics have challenged as totalizing, straight white women's, "imperial" or colonialist feminism?[19] So the defense of American pluralism within feminism can in fact smuggle back in a spurious homogeneity as a defense against the false appearance of homogeneity. Thus Feminism turns out to be, after all is said and done by these Other women, "our"—straight, white, Anglo professional women's—feminism, and we're supposed to be proud of it. America—love it or leave it. The land of the free (market) and the home of the brave (bourgeois subject).

IV

Feminism looks more homogeneous or heterogeneous depending on where one stands. And as with other commodities, only a committed user can fully experience the fiercer forms of brand loyalty which can make other positions, other brands just disappear. And it is not simply that to a nonfeminist male academic, one feminism looks very much like another. Sometimes one feminism *is* very much like another, and their name might well be "French feminist theory," signified by the Holy Trinity, or is it a firm, of Cixous, Irigaray, and Kristeva—the law according to "French feminism" (F. F.). Those of us who have been involved in departmental searches for junior feminists in the past year or so have amassed a considerable dossier on "F. F. Law." "Feminist theory" in a job application letter is almost certain to mean "French feminism," though other varieties like postcolonial, lesbian, materialist, new historicist, psychoanalytical, deconstructive or poststructuralist, and black or African-American feminism do surface from time to time.

The overdeterminations of the marketplace could well be responsible for this particularly concentrated form of commodification. First there is the continuing romance between U.S. intellectuals and French culture, in which French ideas figure prominently. In this sense U.S. feminism might be said to have absorbed rather uncritically some of the hierarchies of the wider, nonfeminist academy. Then, too, "French feminist theory" has been made more available than any other feminist theory in summary and book form: Moi, Alice Jardine's *Gynesis*, Jane Gallop's *The Daughter's Seduction*, articles by Ann Rosalind Jones and Gayatri Spivak, new books by Judith Butler and Diana Fuss taking on the essentialism versus anti-essentialism debates.[20] I've even made the inevitable reference to Irigaray myself in this essay. And "French feminist theory" sells because, being French, it sounds like Theory, another commodity whose future seems remarkably academically secure at the moment. Thus a particular charge of being (prematurely) commodified can be brought against the position that labels itself "French feminism" in the academy, especially when only "F. F. Law," Cixous, Irigaray, and Kristeva, are called upon to represent it and even other forms of French feminist theory, most notably the "materialists," including Simone de Beauvoir, Christine Delphy, Catherine Clément, and Monique Wittig, are ignored.

This is the sense in which a spurious homogeneity or substitutability in the marketplace, feminism's commodification emerging through what Marx calls its "uniform quality," can also signify academic feminists impeccably dressed in business suits, in uniform and looking uniformly as if they're hoping to do as much business as possible on the market, rather than preparing for the crash. Now clothes are not trivial, except when men are making invidious comparisons between important things like sports and trivial things like fashion, as Virginia Woolf observed. But the number of references one hears to feminist theory, or theories, as fashion statements might give us pause, since seeing feminism thus unproblematically could be all too easily conformable with the demands of that other market in which women and not feminisms are exchanged.[21]

V

Leaving Virginia with a dissertation on "new theoretical" readings of Pope's more explicitly "political" later career proved a marketable option. I was hired by Princeton, as part of an exchange of women between Princeton and Virginia: One black woman and one white woman for one black woman and one white woman over a couple of years. Coincidentally, Valerie Smith, who has written so well about commodification and the marketability of work on race and gender that she was bound to figure in my discussion of "commodity feminism," also figures in this personal and institutional history, this history of marketability. The exchange of women that brought us both to Princeton from Charlottesville was also overdetermined by the practices through which such institutions perpetuate and reproduce themselves. Princeton had tried to hire Irvin Ehrenpreis, my dissertation director, several years before; an Ehrenpreis student was already a desirable commodity, and a woman would also help boost the number of women in the department.

Marketability leads to mobility. Those affective and intellectual networks established at Virginia continued to do their work, and Gerald MacLean, who is Canadian and British, and I, who am American, found ourselves forming a "Dink" household (Dual Income, No Kids) in order to satisfy the immigration men so that we could continue to live together, if possible. Since both of us were early-modern English specialists from the same graduate school, with the same dissertation director, we kept moving, trying to get two jobs somewhere in the same part of the country. Commodified labor in academic life is what takes place thousands of feet above the clouds in airplanes, shuttling between apartments and conference hotels, commuting in order to have a "personal life," living on credit. Such a scene of writing lends new meaning to Marx's description of the private labors of individuals who have no sense of their fellow workers except at the point of exchange—airports, conferences, MLA conventions. These are the conditions of possibility for new forms of social identity that Raymond Williams called "mobile privatization," identities based on unlimited mobility and consumable resources, mobile shells composed of our relationships with lovers, friends, and relatives. As Williams puts it, "this small-unit entity is the only really significant social entity. . . . It is a shell which you can take with you, which you can fly with to places that previous generations could never imagine visiting." [22] When lovers and friends are also professional colleagues, the professional and the personal are conflated; one's professional life *is* one's personal life and vice versa. Unalienated labor or total commodification: Which is the result?

The effect of all this exchange-value on feminist writing has meant taking up a discursive position grounded in community and political commitment, but one that manifests itself in highly privatized, marketable forms of professionalism, from the job interview and the MLA talk to competition for grants, salary raises, and time off—in which to raise one's market value through publication, and preferably publication of a labor-intensive kind. The connection between exchange-value and the labor-intensive production of feminism for the marketplace can be discerned in the kinds of feminist work that seem most readily assimilated by academic institutions. It seems important to try at least to account for the readiness of some of my fellow eighteenth-century scholars to endorse, in principle if not in more tangible ways, my research on laboring-class women poets, when other kinds of feminist work in the eighteenth century were being savaged.[23]

VI

How often do we ask of a new critical approach or a new book, "But is this really new?" How often has this question been answered affirmatively within literary studies if the new work offered new historical research, "new facts," rather than "merely" new strategies of reading? The recent apparent triumph of "new historicism" over "deconstruction" within the field seems a case in point, especially when the new historicism looks remarkably like the old, and the deconstruction is radical and political rather than formalist by another name. To some extent feminist foraging outside the canon for increasingly obscure, marginalized, and so theoretically or politically or even antiquarianly interesting figures or contexts is a response to culturally imperative desires for the new, the fashionably novel, the previously unexploited. This cultural imperative often takes the particular name of the clearing of new professional space, but the space of the profession is not free from larger cultural contingencies.

I came to work on eighteenth-century laboring-class women poets as a direct result of mobile privatization. One way of coping with commuting as a way of life is to stay on the move perpetually, and to spend summers somewhere other than where either commuter lives or teaches. For us that third home-away-from-home was England, not surprisingly. The North Library of the British Museum teems every summer with North Americans. It has sometimes seemed as if the entire English departments of the University of Virginia and UCLA were in residence there. Eighteenth-century scholars are, of course, particularly well represented. While ostensibly revising my dissertation on Pope in the hope of making it into a book, I found the archival resources of the B. L. irresistible. I began by tracking down Mary Collier, whose poem *The Woman's Labour* I had found excerpted in Sheila Rowbotham's *Hidden from History* back in Charlottesville.[24]

The recovery of women's texts from the past still tends to be ideologically slanted toward aristocratic and upper-middle-class women; class, race, and national or ethnic differences between women are subsumed under this rubric of the exceptional woman of privilege, the aristocratic foremother. Since I was working from certain problematics generated by Marxist or materialist feminism and by reading social and women's history alongside literary texts, problematics perhaps best articulated by Michèle Barrett and by Gayatri Spivak,[25] strategically I wanted to find out as much as possible about eighteenth-century women of the laboring classes. How do class and gender represent or figure one another? How can we best account for the specific forms of oppression experienced by working-class women during the capitalization of agriculture in England that marked a

moment in the long transition to capitalism? What might the relations between gender ideology and the history of capitalism be, since indigenous
forms of patriarchy clearly predate both imperialism and capitalism in the
colonial arena? What happens when we consider the eighteenth century
as the century of slavery, rather than as the century of "Augustan values,"
whether conceived ironically or not? [26]

What had begun as a chapter in a projected second book on eighteenth-
century women writers became a book in itself, as several summers spent
in various British libraries and a move to California, the Clark Library,
and the Huntington added the names of Ann Yearsley, Mary Leapor, Janet
Little, Elizabeth Hands, Mary Masters, Elizabeth Bentley, Susannah Har-
rison, and Ann Candler to the project. I decided that Phillis Wheatley
ought to be included because her *Poems On Various Subjects, Religious
and Moral* was first published in London, not in Boston; there was a sense
in which an already existing discourse of poetry by plebeian female "prodi-
gies" in Britain had paved the way for Wheatley's contribution to the new
debates about African writing and the slave trade. Laboring-class women
poets were already an established commodity in the literary marketplace
by 1773, when Wheatley's *Poems* appeared. I thought it was important
that revisionist literary history take this poetic discourse into account, and
that feminist revisionists in particular not fall into the petit-bourgeois-
intellectual trap of identifying our own professional upward mobility with
an exclusive admiration for aristocratic foremothers, whose texts and histories were so much more plentiful and accessible than Collier's, or Yearsley's, or Hands's. So there I was, contributing to the commodification of
these working-class women writers, making my own career by recovering
their exploited labor.

The figure of the solitary scholar burrowing in the archives is perhaps
less representative for feminists than for many other academics; there is
much more exchange of information about sources and arguments than I
am accustomed to observing outside these networks. There is some evidence that feminists collaborate more than other scholars in the humanities, and that they consciously work at maintaining a sense of research
as collective rather than strictly privatized labor, in spite of the demands
of the marketplace. Laura Brown and Felicity Nussbaum in particular encouraged me to publish some of my work in progress at a crucial stage,
and they gave that essay rigorous and careful readings. When they speak in
their own work of political criticism or materialist feminism, those terms
signal a collective project to transform our discipline.[27] In this sense of
collectivity lies a trace of feminism's emancipatory value, its use-value.

When *The New Eighteenth Century* came out, Mary Collier's poetry,
her complex subjectivity, her protofeminist protest coupled with a certain

resignation to unchanging social hierarchies in a moment when revolution was largely inconceivable, were once again accessible to students of the period. But they had also become a tidy package of text/context/method within a disciplinary paradigm and an institutional field of power. *The Muses of Resistance* will, I hope, establish the plebeian female discourse that Collier helped to formulate, *as* a discourse, as an important, interesting, and politically useful strain within eighteenth-century English poetry. But it will also reify that discourse intellectually. As an expensive Cambridge book, elegantly produced, dressed for success in the literary marketplace, it will transform these poets into a consumable commodity. That is, of course, how they were initially offered to the public, but the marketplace itself has changed in several ways.

Like every other artifact in consumerist culture, the plebeian aesthetic object, the proletarian text, the figure of the laboring woman writer, or the woman of color, can and will be fetishized. What the laboring-class woman poet represents for eighteenth-century studies, the African-American or third world woman does for the contemporary U.S. and postcolonial scenes. Valerie Smith has argued that, all too frequently in contemporary criticism, when the time comes to materialize or historicize the discourse, a black woman is invoked.[28] Summoned within the context of the material, of intractable historical reality, the black woman functions as a sign of the engaged nature of the discourse through its sensitivity to race, and as a sign of the critic's mastery of the new critical language of historicity. Thus is the black woman both fetishized and theoretically silenced at the very moment of her appropriation by theory. Gayatri Spivak and Chandra Mohanty have made comparable arguments regarding the fetishization of the third world or subaltern woman within the critique of colonial discourse.[29] And we should recognize that this specific form of commodity fetishism will occur both despite and because of our institutional complicities with the history of the construction of the international division of labor.[30] I hope that *The Muses of Resistance* will contribute to our understanding of a few specifics of that history, and that such understanding will not be beside the point.

These are some of the costs of feminism's commodification. They seem to me to constitute new sites of resistance rather than reasons for nostalgia or despair. We should remember that one of the signs of commodification is an ever-increasing "homogeneity of the parts." Such homogenization leads to greater interchangeability. If we wish to resist commodification, we need to eschew certain gestures toward homogenizing feminism: putting forward one school as definitive, letting a commodified version of, say, "F. F. Law" stand for feminism in all its complex historical variety, employing charged categories like race and colonialism without engaging with contemporary debates in those fields, capitulating to institutional pressures to tokenize feminism by rendering it "a special interest" while male business-as-usual continues to hold sway.

The peculiar energy with which commodities are charged in the process of their circulation is a libidinal energy. Feminists would do well not to underestimate the power of that economy, of those libidinal/political-economic desires, as they overdetermine both the exchange of women and the exchange of their theories in the academic marketplace. To know desire is to be in circulation, and to *desire* to be in circulation.

The very marketability of academic feminism in the 1990s can provide evidence to support our nonfeminist colleagues' suspicions that we are simply playing our own heady, new status as desirable commodities for all it is worth, left pieties notwithstanding. As Irigaray observes, there is nothing new about the commodification of women, or even about female commodities speaking for themselves: "The important thing is that they be preoccupied with their respective values, that their remarks confirm the exchangers' plans for them." We had better remember that the exchange of women is an old, old story, and that competition amongst ourselves as women, in a market of gender quotas and fiercely contested professional status, is the most "natural" form of complicity in the world. Feminist critique as political criticism, however, can be our means of resisting that complicity, though no critique can hope to escape in a totalizing way some complicity with its structural context.

As feminists and political critics, we should recognize the degree to which some critical reflection upon our self-representations in the marketplace may help us resist the commodification we cannot elude. If we don't make academic feminism's uneven histories visible and accessible, no one else will. There can be no going back to a time before commodification, and it is up to us to articulate the historical differences between us, and their institutional effects, productively and not sancti- or acrimoniously. Valerie Smith is right to suggest that "When we consider our relation to the institutions within which we work and by means of which our ideas are circulated, we will be able to resist the conditions that commodify and threaten to divide us."[31]

As feminists and political critics, we can disrupt business-as-usual by situating our differences within and against the institutions that would like to contain us, to mute our potentially disruptive presence, once they have conceded the need to have us there at all.

Notes

A version of this essay was presented at the "Ends of Theory" conference at Wayne State University in March 1990. I would like to thank many of the participants and members of the audience there as well as Leo Braudy, Julia Emberley, Caroline Gebhard, Elaine Hobby, Peter Kulchyski, Gerald MacLean, Felicity Nussbaum, Hilary Schor, and Rajani Sudan for their specific comments and suggestions.

1 It must first be said that "institutionalized" here is a double-edged weapon and a fighting word. As Nancy Armstrong has shown, if the institution we have most immediately in mind is the university, especially its humanities departments, then we need to confront the ways in which the contemporary liberal arts program reproduces "in more sophisticated dress" the "female curriculum," the knowledges which the late eighteenth and nineteenth centuries considered "safe" for middle-class women to consume and transmit within the domestic sphere. See Armstrong, "The Gender Bind," *Genders*, 3 (November 1988), 1–23, but esp. 15–16.

2 Donna Haraway, "Situated Knowledges: The Science Question in Feminism and the Privilege of Partial Perspective," *Feminist Studies*, 14, no. 3 (1988), 575–99; this passage on 575.

3 See Felicity Nussbaum and Laura Brown's introductory essay, "Revising Critical Practices," in *The New Eighteenth Century: Theory, Politics, English Literature* (New York and London: Methuen, 1987), 1–22, for an analysis of the resistance to theory and political criticism specific to the field.

4 Karl Marx, *A Contribution to the Critique of Political Economy*, trans. S. W. Ryazanskaya, ed. Maurice Dobb (Moscow: Progress Publishers, 1970), 49.

5 "It is nothing but the definite social relation between men themselves which assumes here, for them, the fantastic form of a relation between things. In order, therefore, to find an analogy we must take flight into the misty realm of religion. There the products of the human brain appear as autonomous figures endowed with a life of their own, which enter into relations both with each other and with the human race. So it is in the world of commodities with the products of men's hands. I call this the fetishism which attaches itself to the products of labour as soon as they are produced as commodities, and is therefore inseparable from the production of commodities." Marx, *Capital: A Critique of Political Economy*, trans. Ben Fowkes (New York: Vintage Books, 1977), 1: 165.

6 Marx, *Capital* 1: 165.

7 See, for example, Jack Amariglio and Antonio Callari, "Marxian Value Theory and the Problem of the Subject: The Role of Commodity Fetishism," *Rethinking Marxism*, 2, no. 3 (Fall 1989), 31–60, who argue from a "nondeterminist" position that Marx "depicts the social constitution of the individual as much a 'precondition' for commodity trade as an effect of this trade," and that "Commodity fetishism, therefore, allows Marxist discourse to conceptualize the political and cultural, as well as economic, constitution of individuality as a form of social agency" (34, 49).

8 Marx, *Capital* 1: 176–77.

9 See Gayle Rubin, "The Traffic in Women: Notes on the 'Political Economy' of Sex," in *Toward an Anthropology of Women*, ed. Rayna R. Reiter (New York and London: Monthly Review Press, 1975), 157–210, and Luce Irigaray, *This Sex Which Is Not One*, trans. Catherine Porter with Carolyn Burke (Ithaca:

172   DONNA LANDRY

Cornell University Press, 1985), 170–97.

10 Irigaray, *This Sex* 178, 179.

11 Elaine Showalter, *A Literature of Their Own: British Women Novelists from Bronte to Lessing* (Princeton: Princeton University Press, 1977), and Sandra M. Gilbert and Susan Gubar, *The Madwoman in the Attic: The Woman Writer and the Nineteenth-Century Literary Imagination* (New Haven and London: Yale University Press, 1979).

12 Alice Jardine, "Notes for an Analysis," in *Between Feminism and Psychoanalysis*, ed. Teresa Brennan (London and New York: Routledge, 1989), 73–85, esp. 85 n. 38.

13 Valerie Amos and Pratibha Parmar, "Challenging Imperial Feminism," *Feminist Review*, 17 (Autumn 1984), 3–19.

14 Biddy Martin and Chandra Talpade Mohanty, "Feminist Politics: What's Home Got to Do with It?" in *Feminist Studies/Critical Studies*, ed. Teresa de Lauretis (Bloomington: Indiana University Press, 1986), 191–212; this passage on 193.

15 In the same 1986 volume in which Martin and Mohanty's essay appears, for instance, Tania Modleski criticizes Jonathan Culler's would-be deconstructive male-feminist framing of the question of "reading like a woman." She challenges Culler's formula of the "hypothetical woman reader" by arguing for the importance of feminist criticism's empowering of "real women," represented by, or rather, "actual-"ized in, the "female feminist critic." See "Feminism and the Power of Interpretation: Some Critical Readings," in *Feminist Studies/Critical Studies* 121–38; see esp. 133–34, 136. For an anti-essentialist critique of Modleski's notion of "female empowerment," see Diana Fuss, *Essentially Speaking: Feminism, Nature & Difference* (New York and London: Routledge, 1989), 27–28.

16 See Fuss, *Essentially Speaking* xi–xiv, 1–21 for a summary of this debate.

17 Denise Riley, *"Am I That Name?" Feminism and the Category of "Women" in History* (Minneapolis: University of Minnesota Press, 1988), 17.

18 Riley, "Am I That Name?" 15–16, quoting Marx, *Grundrisse* (Harmondsworth: Penguin, 1973), 104, 105.

19 See, for example, bell hooks, *Feminist Theory: From Margin to Center* (Boston: South End Press, 1984); Cherríe Moraga and Gloria Anzaldúa, eds., *This Bridge Called My Back: Writings by Radical Women of Color* (New York: Kitchen Table: Women of Color Press, 1981, 1983); Gayatri Chakravorty Spivak, "Three Women's Texts and a Critique of Imperialism," in *"Race," Writing, and Difference*, ed. Henry Louis Gates, Jr. (Chicago and London: University of Chicago Press, 1986), 262–80; Hazel Carby, "White Woman Listen! Black Feminism and the Boundaries of Sisterhood," in *The Empire Strikes Back: Race and Racism in 70s Britain* (London: Hutchinson, 1982), 212–35; Chandra Mohanty, "Under Western Eyes: Feminist Scholarship and Colonial Discourses," *Feminist Review*, 30 (Autumn 1988), 61–88.

20 Toril Moi, *Sexual/Textual Politics: Feminist Literary Theory* (London and New York: Methuen, 1985); Jane Gallop, *The Daughter's Seduction: Feminism and Psychoanalysis* (Ithaca: Cornell University Press, 1982); Alice A. Jardine, *Gynesis: Configurations of Woman and Modernity* (Ithaca and Lon-

don: Cornell University Press, 1985); Ann Rosalind Jones, "Inscribing Femininity: French Theories of the Feminine," in *Making a Difference: Feminist Literary Criticism*, ed. Gayle Greene and Coppelia Kahn (London and New York: Methuen, 1985), 80–112, and "Julia Kristeva on Femininity: The Limits of a Semiotic Politics," *Feminist Review*, 18 (November 1984), 56–73; Gayatri Chakravorty Spivak, "French Feminism in an International Frame," *In Other Worlds: Essays in Cultural Politics* (New York and London: Methuen, 1987), 134–53; Fuss, *Essentially Speaking* (1989); and Judith Butler, *Gender Trouble: Feminism and the Subversion of Identity* (New York and London: Routledge, 1990).

21 See the by now classic exchange between Nancy K. Miller and Peggy Kamuf in the Summer 1982 issue of *Diacritics*, reprinted with an "update" in *Conflicts in Feminism*, ed. Marianne Hirsch and Evelyn Fox Keller (New York and London: Routledge, 1990), 105–33. Miller counters Kamuf's "high-heeled" Parisian feminism with a "common-sensical" return to "sensible shoes"—the feminism of good old bourgeois American empiricism?

22 Raymond Williams, "Problems of the Coming Period," *New Left Review*, 140 (July/August 1983), 7–18; this passage on 16.

23 See Donna Landry, "The Resignation of Mary Collier: Some Problems in Feminist Literary History," in *The New Eighteenth Century* 99–120, and *The Muses of Resistance: Laboring-Class Women's Poetry in Britain, 1739–1796* (Cambridge: Cambridge University Press, 1990).

24 Sheila Rowbotham, *Hidden from History: Rediscovering Women in History From the Seventeenth Century to the Present* (New York: Pantheon, 1974), 24–26.

25 See Michèle Barrett, *Women's Oppression Today: Problems in Marxist Feminist Analysis* (London: Verso, 1980), and Spivak, *In Other Worlds* 197–221, 241–68; "Can the Subaltern Speak?" in *Marxism and the Interpretation of Culture*, ed. Cary Nelson and Lawrence Grossberg (Urbana and Chicago: University of Illinois Press, 1988), 271–313; and "The Rani of Sirmur," in *Europe and Its Others: Proceedings of the Essex Conference on the Sociology of Literature, 1984*, ed. Francis Barker, Peter Hulme, Margaret Iversen, and Diana Loxley, 2 vols. (Colchester: University of Essex, 1985), 1: 128–51.

26 See, for example, Irvin Ehrenpreis, *Literary Meaning and Augustan Values* (Charlottesville: University of Virginia Press, 1974), and Howard D. Weinbrot, *Augustus Caesar in "Augustan" England: The Decline of a Classical Norm* (Princeton: Princeton University Press, 1978).

27 See Laura Brown, *Alexander Pope* (Oxford: Basil Blackwell, 1985), 1–5, 13–23, and Felicity A. Nussbaum, *The Autobiographical Subject: Gender and Ideology in Eighteenth-Century England* (Baltimore and London: Johns Hopkins University Press, 1989), xi–xxii.

28 Valerie Smith, "Black Feminist Theory and the Representation of the 'Other,' " in *Changing Our Own Words: Essays on Criticism, Theory, and Writing by Black Women*, ed. Cheryl A. Wall (New Brunswick and London: Rutgers University Press, 1989), 38–57.

29 See Mohanty, "Under Western Eyes," and Spivak, "Feminism and Deconstruc-

tion, Again: Negotiating with Unacknowledged Masculinism," in *Between Feminism and Psychoanalysis* 206–23.

30 The microelectronic revolution, for example, upon which so much professional production depends, is inextricable from third world proletarianization in the export-processing zones (EPZs) of the capitalist periphery. See June Nash and María Patricia Fernández-Kelly, eds., Introduction, *Women, Men, and the International Division of Labor* (Albany: State University of New York Press, 1983), vii–xv. As Gayatri Spivak observes, "even such innocent triumphs as the hiring of more tenured women or adding feminist sessions at a Convention might lead, since most U.S. universities have dubious investments and most Convention hotels use Third World female labor in a most oppressive way, to the increasing proletarianization of the women of the less developed countries," *In Other Worlds* 291 n. 44.

31 Smith, "Gender and Afro-Americanist Literary Theory and Criticism," in *Speaking of Gender*, ed. Elaine Showalter (New York and London: Routledge, 1989), 56–70; this passage on 57.

10 *David B. Morris*

Samuel H. Monk and a Scholar's Life: Humanism as Praxis

Camerado, this is no book,
Who touches this touches a man.
—Walt Whitman, "So Long!"

Samuel Monk was thirty-three when the book appeared that would soon establish him as a major figure in the modern history of eighteenth-century studies. *The Sublime: A Study of Critical Theories in XVIII-Century England* (1935) in effect rediscovered or created its subject for subsequent readers. Everyone who writes on the sublime today—even though it is now permissible to avoid reference to such ancient authorities as Monk and Longinus—writes within a tradition of scholarly discourse that did not exist before 1935. Indeed, the sublime is mysterious less for its untraceable origins (where it surely lies enfolded with tragedy and epic) than for its series of perfectly explicit new beginnings. Thus sometime in the first century A.D. the otherwise unknown rhetorician named Longinus superseded conventional discussions of the high or great style with his truly seminal treatise entitled *Peri Hupsous*. In the postclassical and medieval worlds, strangely, this remarkable text became almost invisible, but at length the underground tradition of the sublime reemerged when Boileau in 1674 published his prestigious translation of Longinus with the fateful title *Traité du Sublime*. Thereafter, especially dating in England from the 1730s, Monk describes how eighteenth-century criticism and aesthetics reorganized themselves to accommodate the new enthusiasm for whatever in nature or in art might be designated most lofty, heroic, wild, ennobling, awesome, vast, terrifying, irregular, horrid, exotic, passionate, dazzling,

175

painful, gloomy, spectacular, transcendent or, in a word, sublime. *The Sublime* not only created a coherent history from a welter of forgotten or disregarded texts. Among its great contributions was to encourage the writing of other new literary histories about a period that—as Monk showed—contained within the sturdy walls of neoclassicism a concept antithetical to all boundaries.

Some ten years after publication of *The Sublime*, Sam (as everyone who knew him well soon called him) was hitching a ride on a DC-3 cargo plane back from the European theater where the culture he loved so deeply—the culture of Mozart and Racine, of Piranesi and Dr. Johnson—lay buried in rubble. His classic essay on European aesthetic theory ("A Grace Beyond the Reach of Art" [1944]) had appeared a few months earlier while its author served in France, Holland, and Germany as an intelligence officer with the 559th Bomber Squadron of the Ninth Air Force. As an officer, he was entitled at war's end to catch a ride on a military plane rather than wait for slower repatriation. The only space for passengers consisted of crude bucket seats installed along the sides of the fuselage. Over the Atlantic the plane hit very rough weather. Its instruments failed. Accurate navigation was impossible and fuel was rapidly running out.

The irony of an accidental death as he returned from the fields of death-by-design was not lost upon an exhausted scholar who knew in their original languages the literature of France, Spain, Germany, Italy, as well as ancient Greece and Rome. The irony that may tell most about him is that at the moment of the sublime—when death might seem almost palpable in the roaring, pitching machinery that engulfed him—Sam fell asleep. Like his great favorite John Bunyan in *The Pilgrim's Progress*, he not only slept amid "the wilderness of this world" but also dreamed a dream. In the violently tossing plane he dreamt that on either side of him, each holding a hand, were his wife, Wanda, and his mother. When he awoke, the plane was just touching down in Iceland.

This episode—of which an historian might truly say that nothing happened—seems significant to me for several reasons. For modern scholars who (after the perils of tenure) now inhabit a thoroughly codified world of institutions, retirement programs, conferences, sabbaticals, and fellowships, it is useful to recall that ten years after publishing his first book Samuel Monk was not busily reading proof for his second or third (or fourth) book. Further, the war that interrupted his scholarship was not simply an unforeseen catastrophe, like an earthquake or illness. It represented a massive clash between opposing systems of value. Thus in the experience of war the most intimate details of private life were bound up with public events and public themes. The defense of Europe implied (at least for those of Sam's persuasion) a struggle to preserve values absolutely central to Western civilization. The intimate intermingling of public and of private experience, of course, assured that the most noble public motives and sentiments could not subdue a stubbornly personal interest in disaster. Sam's motives for enlisting—in Memphis, on May 1, 1942, at the age of forty—were deeply personal. One year earlier his wife, Wanda, a talented painter whom he had only recently married, drowned before his eyes in a terrible accident. He enlisted, he said, in order to die.

The dreams of returning veterans are likely to be sentimental, full of nostalgia for the peacetime world they left behind, but the important fact about the dream of Captain Samuel Monk was its imagery of absence. The two people he loved most were both dead. Wanda had died in 1941. His mother had died in 1925—some three years after the death of his father—so that he was returning to a new world indelibly marked by loss and returning from an old world far more vividly devastated. The pain of Wanda's death was so intense (as he wrote to a friend) that it kept him alive. Thereafter he credited a constitutional toughness—a certain coarseness of fiber, as he put it—for allowing him to pass through life's fires more or less untouched. Yet there was something beyond inertia or toughness that kept him going in a postwar world that for him sometimes resembled a landscape of tragedy. Sam, that is, felt himself profoundly connected with an enduring tradition of values that can be summarized in the term Christian humanism. This humanist tradition cannot be reduced to a uniform set of explicit doctrines, as so often happens in contemporary critiques determined to explode the last traces of what they consider simply a placid, moribund, and retrograde ideology. Humanism, in the instance of Samuel Monk, was a way of life, a social practice, a means of doing things, a reason to keep going on.

I

"Excessively refined persons have a communion with the abyss," wrote the poet Allen Tate in his novel *The Fathers* (1938), adding, "but is not civilization the agreement, slowly arrived at, to let the abyss alone?" Sam was in an especially good position to appreciate this reflection. Like Tate, he was a Southerner, bred to refinement, someone for whom manners did not mean etiquette but rather a courtesy interfused with the deepest sources of personal identity. Refinement, as Tate understood, can constitute an act of creation: it opposes or holds off a nothingness from which it never fully breaks free. Expressed as politeness, the agreement to let the abyss alone gives an edge even to moments of private gaiety or pleasure. Sam told of an occasion when the two Southerners Monk and Tate drank late into the night (was it in London?) reciting together the poetry of A. E. Housman, especially the poem that ends "Take my hand quick and tell me, / What have you in your heart. . . . Ere to the wind's twelve quarters / I take my endless way." Friendship, in such a view, is more than like-mindedness. It is intimate self-revelation acted out against a backdrop of inevitable loss. Poetry, as part of friendship, as part of the self, could not be reduced (or elevated) solely to an object of scholarly analysis. Indeed, scholarship for Sam never transformed literary works into objects. His objectivity was tempered by a personal sense about the ways in which literature functions within individual human lives.

The crucial importance of the human reader and human writer is doubtless somewhere near the heart of Sam Monk's version of humanism. "You see how naturally one comes to the humanistic principle," wrote William James in his lecture "Pragmatism and Humanism": "you can't weed out the human contribution." (James continues: "Human motives sharpen all our questions, human satisfactions lurk in all our answers, all our formulas have a human twist.") For Sam the crucial human contribution expressed itself in his teaching as well as in his writing. He was, in his prime, a remarkable teacher. Although a Princeton mentor had informed him that because of a persistent stammer Sam of course would never teach at a major university, one account tells of students and colleagues overflowing into hallways when he gave a public lecture. Berkeley, Columbia, and NYU all sought him for visiting professorships. Yet what he offered his listeners in the Age of New Criticism was something very different from the detailed analysis of form. Joseph Butwin, a student in Sam's undergraduate eighteenth-century course, remembers him this way:

Sam in class—seated at a desk, never, he said, in forty years (even in Memphis) without jacket and tie, turning the pages of a book, explaining it, explaining its references, not so much analyzing it as putting us in a position to do so, and then gluing everything into place with the emotion latent in his reading, particularly those passages of stoicism and sorrow in Swift and Johnson. I say stoicism, but I don't think Sam was himself a stoic. He was an epicure with a relish for endurance and decline—Swift from the top down, Pope's long disease, the melancholy Johnson. What a man to undermine the smugness of neoclassicism. . . .

It is certainly true that Sam's classicism embraced a deep reverence for the baroque, dissenting, and gothic masterpieces spurned by most neoclassical theorists. In addition, one particularly crucial feature of Joe Butwin's recollection is the emotion that clearly infused Sam's reading and interpretation of eighteenth-century texts.

Feeling, even with the advent of reader-response criticism, has rarely found a secure and respected place in modern scholarship. For instance, the New Criticism at its most facile threatened to become all technique,

Samuel Monk, circa 1935

ingenuity set free to work its sterile contrivances, in which sense it curiously resembled the dry-as-dust historical and philological scholarship it
overthrew. Without ever compromising the demands of intellect, Sam (this
proper, seated figure in coat and tie, who spoke with a knowledge deeper
than any of his students would command) nonetheless somehow communicated an understanding that knowledge lived and moved in a realm of
human feeling. A method was not what he taught but rather, by example,
a particular relationship with books. Its emotion was something the war
years had deepened and intensified, as if to discuss a text rather than to
route a bomber were a daily return to a form of life both infinitely precious
and fragile.

The relationship with books that gave life to Sam's teaching also underlies his writing. *The Sublime* began as a dissertation at Princeton: "Ideas of
the Sublime from Boileau to Burke" (1929). Yet well before Lovejoy made
the history of ideas into an academic discipline as revolutionary as the New
Criticism it seems clear that Sam was working out his own relationship
to ideas. In fact, we may now find his work more useful than Lovejoy's
precisely because he avoids describing ideas as if they were semidetached
units amenable to a rather schematic (almost positivist) method of analysis.
The Sublime instead describes the central idea it treats as firmly rooted in
human culture—shaped by and shaping a particular historical moment—
amenable mainly to a broad narrative treatment that describes specific
writers and their relation to literary change. Although R. S. Crane proposed a different reading of the sublime, distinguishing between what he
termed "natural" and "rhetorical" versions of sublimity, he seems exactly
right in the insight that what Monk offered students of the sublime was
essentially a "story." No undergraduate, of course, would mistake those
closely printed and formidable pages of *The Sublime* for ordinary fiction.
Yet Monk's narrative of a century-long engagement with the sublime creates a work that differs substantially from Lovejoy's history of ideas, which
was finally less a form of history than a new way of doing philosophy. The
sublime suited Sam's approach because it never was simply an idea: it was
the passion of an age.

Method was something Sam never much liked. In 1969 he sent to a
worried student working on her dissertation in London the following autobiographical advice: "I have, as you must know, the least theoretical mind
in the profession. I therefore simply can't suggest an outline that you could
follow. I don't believe in outlines, though I should. Whatever I've written, worthy or worthless, has been the result of reading and feeling my
way into my subject as I went along. . . . DON'T chart yourself a predetermined road." This strict avoidance of method may sound paradoxically
methodical. The danger of orthodox method, however, was not only that

it predetermined the road one would follow. It also preempted feeling. Sam's hostility to the anesthesia of method owed something to the inter-departmental battles of the 1950s in which method became a code word for the program championed by departments of education. In this aca-demic warfare Sam was likely to hear himself dismissed as an old-fashioned "gentleman scholar" devoted to the quaint idea that understanding lit-erature required a detailed knowledge of particular works and specific periods (often called, in contrast to method, "content"). More important, his opposition to method in part stemmed from a home-grown "radical empiricism"—in the sense employed by William James—that distrusted abstract reason and clung to the irreducible, concrete, pragmatic, affective facts of human experience. When method was discussed in less abstract, less polemical contexts, Sam was more open-minded.

It is his openness that former colleague G. Robert Stange remembers most vividly and ascribes to a triumph of character. He recognized in Sam qualities he also saw in the great American scholar F. O. Matthiessen: an instantly visible probity, a vast pleasure in scholarship, a commitment to the life of the mind that inspired in others a similar sense of commit-ment. Despite marked differences, Stange continues, in both men "there was a deep sense of sadness, an awareness of the limited possibilities of the human enterprise, a pessimism that actually heightened the wonder of the imaginative achievements they celebrated and clarified for us; and in both—very important, I think—a continued openness to new ideas and methods." Sam's friendship with fellow Southerners Allen Tate and Robert Penn Warren kept him close to the sources of the New Criticism, even as he chose wisely in sending his essay "A Grace Beyond the Reach of Art" to the new *Journal of the History of Ideas* established at Johns Hopkins by Arthur O. Lovejoy. Yet it remains very hard to ally Sam's work with a single, specific critical method. His openness was such that what he re-ceived he seemed to convert or to transform into the components of a personal point of view.

A personal point of view—rather than a method—would seem to be what gives strength to his perhaps most famous essay: "The Pride of Lemuel Gulliver" (1955). One might say that Sam subscribes to standard New Critical dogma in rigorously distinguishing between Gulliver and Swift. This distinction between author and character is drawn so sharply that it helped to earn Sam the (somewhat dubious) honor of having created the "soft" school of Swift criticism. Sam spoke with wry indifference on his appointment as the dean of softness. He also wrote seriously—in a let-ter to a friend—that the notorious essay had been written "*con amore* and out of personal feeling." "You won't be surprised," he cannot resist adding, "to hear it has taken a severe beating from the Great Ones." As he understood the dangers of method, he understood the penalty for subordinating method to personal feeling.

II

What emotion is it that animates "The Pride of Lemuel Gulliver"? Where shall we locate its sources? How does it express itself within the refined pages of a scholarly essay? To such questions only indirect and tentative replies are possible. I think we must begin with the Victorian reading of Gulliver's fourth voyage that interprets Swift's portrait of the Yahoos as an insane and obscene blasphemy against mankind: a view Sam utterly rejected. "The legend of Swift as a savage, mad, embittered misanthrope," he writes, "largely rests upon this wrong-headed, sensational reading of the last voyage. In my opinion the work is that of a Christian-humanist and a moralist who no more blasphemes against the dignity of human nature than do St. Paul and some of the angrier prophets of the Old Testament." This opinion certainly sets Monk at odds with contemporary (hard-school) critics who explore and celebrate Swift's complicity in the irrational. For Monk, the clear distinction between author and character permits an almost clinical contrast: "Jonathan Swift was stronger and healthier than Lemuel Gulliver." Gulliver, in this reading, resembles Kurtz in Conrad's *Heart of Darkness*. As Monk writes of Gulliver, he "looks into the obscene abyss of human nature unlighted by the frail light of reason and of morality, and the sight drives him mad." Sam's Swift (Marlow-like) sees what Gulliver sees—yet survives.

Why does Swift survive the vision that drives Gulliver mad? For Monk, the "ultimate danger" that confronted Gulliver in his explorations was that "he would discover something that he was not strong enough to face." Where Swift surpassed Gulliver was in resisting an escape into "a sick and morbid pride" that permits him to believe he is inherently superior to the rest of Yahoo-tainted humankind. This (racist) presumption of an absolute superiority over one's fellow human creatures is for Monk the ultimate madness of Enlightenment rationalism. What preserved Swift from Gulliver's final derangement was not simply a strong constitution or a decision to let the abyss alone. Monk's religious language in his final paragraphs suggests that he understands Swift's strength as implicit in the vision of Christian humanism. The Christian humanist assumes from the start that we are all irremediably damaged. The real question for Monk is not whether we are Yahoos but instead whether we acknowledge our weakness, how we deal with it, what we make of our damaged state.

Perhaps the purest madness would be to assume that we are entirely free from the pride of Lemuel Gulliver. "You put your finger on it several years ago," Sam wrote to a correspondent, "when you said that I am the most arrogant humble man you ever knew." In his essay he notes as well the "arrogant pride" that Swift displayed in his personal conduct. Yet he distinguished sharply between Swift's everyday arrogance (a human failing) and Gulliver's "dehumanizing pride." If it seems fair to question a hint of arrogance in the critic who finds his own vision so firmly reinforced by the vision of the author, such that both Monk and Swift at times appear to share a single worldview, we also should recognize the strengths that flowed from a solidarity between critic and author. "We 'fought' the war together," wrote one veteran from Sam's air force unit, "and he enlivened and uplifted many a depressed, war-weary pilot or gunner. Sam taught the rest of us that despite the personal tragedies in one's life (and *he* certainly had them) that life can continue to be meaningful." The writer adds: "His deep reverence for humanity made all the difference."

The final sentence from "The Pride of Lemuel Gulliver" asserts that until the darkness of his last years Swift "did not abandon his fellow man as hopeless or cease to announce, however indirectly, the dignity and worth of human kind." It is thus not hard to imagine that what strengthened Sam in his darkest hours was precisely the Christian humanist vision that he believed gave strength to Swift. In this sustaining rather than vicious circularity, the study of literature was simultaneously a source of values: a means of fortifying the reader against perils to body and spirit. For the humanist, one seldom-mentioned purpose of reading is that it helps us confront the danger we will discover something—or experience something—we are not strong enough to face.

My aim here is not to defend or to attack the "soft" school of Swift criticism—and certainly not to mount a rearguard argument for turning back the clock—but rather to suggest that Sam's view of Swift as Christian humanist bears an interesting relation to a speech he delivered in 1947 entitled "Colleges and Freedom of Opinion in a Revolutionary Era." The occasion of the speech is inseparable from its significance. Sam had been honorably discharged in San Antonio on December 5, 1945, and spent the next year on a Rockefeller Fellowship. The speech (on June 2, 1947) marked his departure from the small Presbyterian college—Southwestern at Memphis—where he received his undergraduate degree and where he continued to teach upon completing graduate work at Princeton. It was an important moment of transition. He was now forty-five and about to leave for the University of Minnesota, where he had just accepted the professorship he would hold until his retirement.

The speech is full of references to his wartime experience, and yet Sam addresses the future rather than the past, America rather than Europe, social issues rather than literary texts. "We are told," he explained to the assembled alumni, "that this is an era of neo-barbarism, in which the forces that are most active and powerful are hostile or indifferent to the values of Christian humanism, those very values that have sustained Western civilization for the last five hundred years." At stake in the classroom was more than issues of valid interpretation. Sam's sense of solidarity with the great writers whom he transmitted to a new generation drew strength from a belief that their writings articulated the values which had shored up Western civilization since the time of Chaucer.

What might those values be? We should not imagine that Sam had somehow managed to extract a series of explicit propositions supported in every major work of Western literature from Chaucer to T. S. Eliot. His speech, in fact, begins by opposing Samuel Johnson's view of the American colonists as a "race of convicts" who should be "thankful" for anything the British allow them "short of hanging." Sam was opposing not Johnson's colorful denunciation of Americans—Johnson here was no match for Monk—but rather the Johnsonian belief that public expression of subversive opinions (almost an American art form) should be forbidden. Against Johnson, Sam offers his listeners the following anecdote from a correspondence immediately following publication of *The Sublime*:

In 1936 I received a letter from a distinguished German scholar, then in his eightieth year. He had written famous books on English literature and had spent his life in the atmosphere of intellectual freedom that characterized the German universities of the nineteenth century. Suddenly the lights were put out; the windows of the mind were barred. He did not dare to write fully of what was going on, but he did imply his bewilderment and sorrow. And he wrote one sentence that I have never forgotten: *Meanwhile*, he said, *we do what we can for literature, which is rapidly taking the place of church and parliament in this country.* Even in 1936 it was plain from that sentence that the German mind was enslaved, that the universities had declined their responsibilities, that teachers had been driven into their cells and had been told to attend to their business, the past, and to acquiesce in the present, in the rising tide of Nazi tyranny.

Sam's deep affection for German culture gave his indictment of its failures a personal grief.

It is important to recognize that Sam in his speech is less concerned with Nazi tyranny than with the abandonment by colleges and universities of their inherent "responsibilities" for protecting intellectual freedom. Equally significant, he insists that the responsibility of the individual scholar extends beyond an understanding of the past. "Our military might overthrew the Nazi state two years ago," he reminded his conservative, southern audience in a period of nascent McCarthyism, "but the evils of which Hitler was only the agent—racism, intense nationalism, cynical indifference to human worth, spiritual and moral nihilism—those evils are still abroad among all peoples." His humanism insists that scholars must practice their craft within a contemporary social world whose threats and evils and injustices they actively resist. The speech, published in the *Southwestern Bulletin*, was so eloquent and timely in its defense of the university as an institution dedicated to intellectual freedom that the remaining press run was bought up and taught by Dartmouth College.

The speech also helps us to understand certain curious features of "The Pride of Lemuel Gulliver." For example, well before "relevance" became a watchword among student dissidents in the 1960s Sam found ways of situating Swift within a contemporary landscape: "He would have hated the improvisations of the New Deal; he would have deplored the vast powers of our Federal Government; he would have loathed the whole program of the Labor Party in Britain. And were he alive, he would fight the abstract state of this century with every weapon within reach." The intelligence officer of the 559th Bomber Squadron reminds modern readers that the flying island of Laputa oppresses the lands below "by means of what we call today air power; it can withhold sun and rain as a punitive device, or can harass through bombing raids, or even tyrannously crush all opposition by settling its great weight upon the land below." Swift's description of the paranoiac regime of Tribnia leads Monk to reflections that seem engaged in creating their own invisible allegory: "Too great a concentration of power leads to tyranny; tyranny breeds fear; fear breeds the obnoxious race of spies and informers. The abstract state becomes the police state." These words carry a double-voiced inflection. Sam reads an eighteenth-century satire filtered through a contemporary language that inescapably recalls the House Un-American Activities Committee and, ominous in its vagueness, "certain testimony given in late years in Washington."

This surprisingly contemporary and political reading of *Gulliver's Travels* was prompted not by an abiding interest in politics but rather by a conviction that the legacy of Christian humanism includes not only an indictment of human depravity but also an active resistance to every form of social, moral, and political evil. Sam thus emphasizes the paradox that Swift was "a Tory who fought valiantly and at times successfully for the oppressed." "Living in Ireland," he continues, "contemptuous of the Irish, detesting their Catholicism, he none the less became their champion against the oppression and exploitation of his adopted country by the English Court and Parliament." He interrupts the flow of scholarly exegesis to insist that a resistance to social injustice is something that crosses party lines. In words which carry their own autobiographical subtext he reminds readers of *Gulliver's Travels*: "Too many liberals are unaware of the fact that a man may be a non-liberal without being illiberal; that he may distrust the abstract power of government, the theoretical formulae of economists, politicians, and social scientists and the like without ceasing to be actively and effectively concerned for human welfare." Such passages show a literary criticism that refuses to retreat into apolitical formalisms or an isolated absorption in the past.

Sam's humanism expressed itself in an ongoing and principled concern for human welfare. He lived in spare, almost austere, surroundings that— as he enjoyed puns on his name—it no doubt occurred to him to call monastic. While spending little on personal comforts, he generously supported family and friends who needed help. For years he contributed financially to the NAACP. One instance is particularly telling. He and Wanda never returned to church after the violent *Kristallnacht* (November 9, 1938) when the smashed windows of every Jewish shop in Germany— along with torched synagogues and murder—signaled the clear outbreak of what has come to be called "The War against the Jews." Civic conscience and private conscience were one. And both for Sam were inseparable from the humanist's practice of literary criticism.

Christian humanism seems strongly predisposed to ignore or to dominate the non-Christian world. Until the 1950s and 1960s, for example, prominent American universities run by scholars who considered themselves humanists undeniably pursued antisemitic policies designed to keep Jews out. It is thus useful to linger for a moment on Sam's response to *Kristallnacht*. His love of Germany and his friendship with fine exemplars of German humanism had made him particularly sensitive among Americans of his class to the way Germany was going into the abyss. He was responding to the climactic events of *Kristallnacht* with an agonized awareness of what they meant. He and Wanda were in church that morning after the smashed windows, as he perceived it, smashed the last hopes for German society in the era of Hitler. It was because they were so appalled that nothing was said about such an awful event that Sam and Wanda decided never to attend church again. At issue was far more than the failures of a single Memphis clergyman. (The silence of American churches proved interdenominational.) Sam's unfaltering Christian humanism somehow managed to coincide with a personal repudiation of institutional Christianity.

What is perhaps most remarkable about "Colleges and Freedom of Opinion in a Revolutionary Era" is its optimism. Such optimism in a man who held Swiftian views of human nature and who had just returned from a scene of unprecedented brutality is best understood not as a matter of temperament but as an intellectual achievement. As he told the assembled alumni of Southwestern at Memphis:

However pessimistic a thinking and sensitive mind may be today, I do not believe that it is necessary to despair of the survival of either our society or of humanity in general. We have merely reached a crisis in which it is necessary that we make every effort to hold fast to the heritage of humanistic values to which you subscribed, perhaps unthinkingly, when you enrolled as students in this college. It is necessary for us to cease accepting as something given and to be taken for granted the privileges of a free society, and to make them operative once more in the world around us.

We should notice that Sam envisions the values of humanism as automatically implicit in an academic setting—where the great works of world literature are freely taught. A student, by enrolling, endorses even unknowingly the values on which the institution is founded: values that center on the free pursuit of truth in a society that honors, or at least protects, disagreement and dissent.

Those who remember the black pessimism of Sam's final years might think it, in retrospect, not the gloom of someone unable to relish change or conflict but rather a measure of how far he believed colleges and universities in the Vietnam era had failed to hold fast to the humanistic values he saw as the only defense against barbarism. The failure was especially crucial because he saw the university not as an isolated retreat or ivory tower but as a place where knowledge might be preserved, nourished, and ultimately made "operative" in the social world. When in Sam's view the values of humanistic inquiry seemed lost, when the university came to resemble the abstract state or a scene of street violence, when man and humanism were officially pronounced dead by the structuralist revolution, Sam, understandably, felt isolated in his convictions. As always, what sustained him were the great works of the past and (like Swift) his deep love for individuals, a love he shared with a circle of devoted friends, of whom I was one.

III

The important point about Samuel Monk's version of humanism is that he lived it. Humanism was not a set of doctrines but a locus of values, and literature was where the values of humanistic learning might be said to live most intensely. Thus literature was less a subject to be mastered than a form of life one might possibly come to enter, through long study, meditation, and a habit of mind that recognized the intimate connection between literature and the social world in which we read it. As in the ancient mode of scriptural interpretation called midrash, understanding for Sam was always something more than a mental state. "Midrashic understanding," writes Gerald L. Bruns, "is reflexive and reciprocal: we take the text in relation to ourselves, understanding ourselves in its light, even as our situation throws *its* light upon the text, allowing it to disclose itself differently, perhaps in unheard-of ways." Certainly this description captures something of the unusual dialogue between text and history—between past and present—that underlies Sam's engagement with *Gulliver's Travels*.

The humanist dialogue with literature also went on, however, in the absence of classrooms and texts. It took seriously the now unfashionable idea that the knowledge one derived from works of literature might provide a form of personal enlightenment. "Much of what little wisdom I have learned," Sam wrote in a letter, "has been taught me by Samuel Johnson"—a statement he follows, typically, by disputing Johnson's claim that we will cling to life no matter how intense its pains. Indeed, Sam possessed a Johnsonian melancholy that nonetheless proved bracing to visitors educated in a popular culture that relentlessly instructed them how to become their own best friends. Even after his retirement to Charlottesville in 1969, each mail seemed to bring new chapters, essays, offprints, and requests for help. "I always make a point of serving these people promptly," he wrote in a letter, "for that is about all that's left for any justification of my crowding this over-populated 'blighted star,' as Tess called it." It was from Johnson's *Vanity of Human Wishes* that he took another reflection upon the trials of his old age: "Superfluous lags the vet'ran on the stage." Such behavior reveals far more than professorial habits of allusion. Literature for Sam was a vital and indispensable medium for encountering the world, a resource for sharpening his perception of his own place and time, even if the knowledge it sharpened was bitter. The sharpness of the perception at least helped to make its bitterness palatable, since to understand his state through the complex lenses of literary language was very different from blindly suffering or merely enduring it.

If humanism possessed any tools with which to oppose barbarism, surely its most potent instrument was knowledge. We will misunderstand its variety, however, if we think humanism was invariably committed to a view that literary knowledge revealed itself through the possession of classless, genderless, universal truths. One friend wrote in semidespair after a young woman had objected that his Shakespeare course had transformed Shakespeare into an existentialist. Sam's reply came immediately:

Do you really, my dear, dear friend, expect to please 40/60 graduate students every time you mount the podium? You don't believe that in your lectures you are telling *the* truth, but *a* version of Shakespeare that, in that it interests you and has validity of a sort, gives animation to your lectures. GREAT! How many Shakespeares have there been? to name a few owners, and only a few, Jonson, Dryden, Pope, Johnson, STC, Chas. Lamb, Bradley, Knight, the Freudians, Jan Kott—ad infinitum. Send your girl to the library, after telling her that this summer you have decided to examine WS from one modern point of view. Tell her that there are two miles of books she can read and that she can't escape meeting *her* boy somewhere in the stack. And that you'll welcome him when he shows up in her term paper. . . . You mustn't have tender spots except when the tenderness is about *something*.

The advice—really a theory that truth in literary studies is always the truth of versions—has nothing in common with an anything-goes pluralism. Once, as Howard Anderson and John S. Shea recount, Sam stopped during a masterly clarification of the complexities of eighteenth-century critical thought. He shook his head, flung his papers on the desk: "Lies, all lies." His humanism held a firm ethical horror of saying the thing that was not. It was insufficient to hold that humanistic knowledge was always a knowledge of versions. Sam also demanded a version that experts in the field could distinguish from a lie.

IV

Humanism is regularly criticized for a complacently elitist stance—expressed in an imperious preference for high culture over popular culture as codified in a narrow canon of masterpieces that reinforces elitist values. Within an individual life, however, the humanist tradition imposed high responsibilities toward the past it preferred. Sam believed that art was deeply bound up with issues of human worth and social practice, including freedom of choice. Further, he did not regard the great works of the past as somehow universal and timeless but rather as radically contingent: they continue to exist, he believed, only insofar as they are entrusted to our interpretation and care. Although Dante undoubtedly helped to disseminate the discourse of scholasticism, the discourse of scholasticism could not create or preserve Dante's *Commedia* or the *Summa Totius Theologiae* of St. Thomas Aquinas or the exquisite cathedral at Chartres. The humanist thus labors to protect an endowment to which the contemporary world— because of its immersion in popular culture—will usually remain indifferent, and the value that humanism assigns to this endowment gives a solid ethical foundation to immediate and practical decisions about what to do. The following story is supplied by Sam's longtime friend and colleague Jack Levenson, who was among the very few people with whom Sam could be brought to discuss it.

This is Jack Levenson's account. As the intelligence officer of his air force unit, Sam regularly got reports of operations about which he was to brief the pilots going up on bombing missions. One day (in the early summer of 1944) he read that the targets were to include an ammunition dump located only a kilometer at most from the center of Chartres. He understood not only the approximation of accuracy—or rather inaccuracy—that was involved. He also understood that the explosion, even if accurate, was going to be dangerously close to the cathedral. It was ridiculous to believe that a mere captain of intelligence should try to make his way through channels to the commanding general of the Ninth Air Force, explaining to superior officers at every layer of command in between that the target was unthinkable. Unless you've been in the army, there is no way of conveying the combination of *Don Quixote* and *The Castle* and *Catch 22* that was enacted in the matter of just a few hours. And it had a happy ending. The mission was called off, and Sam had the pleasure of being known to a select few as the man who saved *la plus belle église de l'Europe*. How just that his moment of military glory should have been a triumph of nonviolence.

John Clark, another longtime friend and colleague, summarized the episode this way: our postwar world owes the cathedral of Chartres to Samuel Monk. Did saving a cathedral and French civilians perhaps endanger Allied soldiers? All the evidence suggests that Sam knew far better than most the terrible ethical uncertainties of war. Humanism for him meant acting, inevitably, in the absence of certain knowledge. It reflects the importance of absences that the *Directory of American Scholars* (7th edition) in its biographical entry on Samuel Monk—compiled doubtless from information that Sam supplied—omits all mention of his military service. What is left unsaid may be precisely that which allows us to intuit the crucial differences between a career and a life. It also allows us to reflect upon the concrete ways in which humanism helped to create and to preserve a legacy that otherwise might well be missing.

V

Any future sociology of the profession of English will need to deal fairly with the men and women of Samuel Monk's generation who chose to call themselves humanists. Certainly humanism cannot be blamed for all the enduring wrongs of a world whose prejudices it sometimes shared. "I think my feminist credentials are good," writes one woman who knew Sam's sometimes blinkered courtliness, "and I valued his courtesy and felt valued by it, not belittled in any way." If humanism conveniently served the self-interest of white, male, bourgeois, Western reason, it also contained within it the principles of self-criticism and an imperative for opposing every social prejudice and political injustice. Humanism for Sam meant reaching beyond the narrowed discourses of a specific class or region or nation or school of thought. Our justified suspicion of origins thus should not blind us to the significance of small historical facts. Samuel Monk was born on March 25, 1902, in Selma, Alabama. He emerged from a world that is no longer ours.

Monk's house in Selma, Alabama circa 1895

Selma is a small, unexceptional southern town that (according to one elderly resident) survives without anyone's being able to say why. A sign erected by the chamber of commerce in the 1920s proclaimed that by 1930 the population of Selma would reach the euphonious number 30,000—but they never made it. The area is primarily an agricultural community, and in 1902 there were obviously no automobiles, no electric lights, no radios. Yet we may well underestimate the cultural life that a small community created for itself. There was a stately opera house. The Hotel Albert— whose name commemorates its associations with Victorian grandeur— was modeled on the Doge's Palace in Venice. The Monk house (where Sam's father, W. S. Monk, was born and died) stood on a large corner lot on the main street. Close by was the Roman Catholic Convent of Mercy and the Temple Mishkan Israel. W. S. Monk was a deacon in the Broad Street Presbyterian Church and his wife, Lucy Holt Monk, sat on the board of directors of the Orphan's Home of the Presbyterian Church, where she also served as secretary of the presbyterial and secretary of the synodi- cal and held from time to time every office the auxiliary of the church had power to bestow. His father—who died when Sam was twenty—was president of the Central Alabama Dry Goods Co. and served as a director of the City National Bank and of the City Savings Bank. Sam came from a hardworking, prosperous, churchgoing family.

He left Selma in 1920 to attend college and (except for brief visits) never returned. His refinement, which owed much to the manners and tastes of his parents, remained distinct from the behavior of those whom the class structure of the South endowed with claims to "aristocratic" breeding. Indeed, if he did not exactly reject his personal past, he recalled it with something less than affection:

My father was never proud of me until I made good socially and scholastically in the little cow college to which I was sent. I am sure that I am not a moral coward (my war record shows that), but a physical coward I have always been. I was timid about playing rough games with the boys, was scorned for my bookishness, and truly enjoyed "getting my lessons," a routine that was absolutely rigid until Friday night; then I could choose to study that night or Saturday night. Never Sunday night! In high school I broke loose and enjoyed roller skating on week-end nights with the girls and boys, and other such. I gained some popularity by my 17th year.

This unsentimental recollection suggests not only the deep pleasure Sam took in learning but also a determined labor of self-creation. It is significant that in other moods he spoke proudly of Southwestern at Memphis when he considered its transformation from a fragile college struggling in the economic and intellectual distress of the post-Reconstruction South into the strong and vigorous institution (now Rhodes College) where he took top honors in history and in comparative literature. "It is difficult to think of anything more typically Southern," he wrote in an introduction to Waller Raymond Cooper's *Southwestern at Memphis: 1848–1948*, "than this achievement by a small group, not known outside their own community, unaided by funds from Northern foundations, but determined to work as individuals in the rebuilding of the cultural life of their own area." In a sense, Sam built or rebuilt his own cultural life.

Whatever has been constructed, as we know, may be equally deconstructed, but the parallel between lives and texts is not exact. The death of his wife, for which he could not help accusing himself, left an irreversible pain. In his own mind, his work fell short of the stature he granted that of such contemporaries as his learned friend and fellow Princetonian Rensselaer W. Lee. On occasions Sam referred to himself, in a favorite formula, as a "first-rate second-rate scholar." He was childless, never remarried, and felt periods of extreme isolation. In a hard-drinking department at Minnesota, he drank more than any physician would advise. His closest friends sometimes received calls at night threatening suicide. He was notorious for fainting on gala occasions. "I was fond of Sam and I suppose I saw him almost every day," writes a woman who knew him well, "but Oh! he was so neurotic." A young friend, slyly alluding to the (hard-school) claim that Sam's Swift was somewhat too well-adjusted, made the mistake of referring to "the well-adjusted SHM." Sam wrote back:

Have I been so long with you, and have you not known me, Gates? For shame! I am, if self-knowledge is possible I'll say this, the mal-adjusted SHM adjusted to his maladjustment. Hence my eccentricities of mind, life, manner and manners, my rather unabashedly revealed emotions, my curious flight from one aspect—most aspects—of life, and my passionate embracement of those aspects that enrich my odd soul. To be adjusted to this world is to be damned. I may be that anyway, of course, but at least I have the illusion that I'm storing up grace. This may sound like idle banter, but it is not wholly that.

Among the values humanism sets foremost is self-knowledge. It should be clear that Sam did not believe such knowledge was easy to obtain, given what he understood about his own psyche and about its need for illusion. Whatever grace he stored up was required to offset a heavy burden of guilt. The self he encountered within was not the classical Cartesian ego undivided by hidden conflict or free from interior contradiction. Its darkness was exactly what made the luminous values of humanism so crucial.

VI

The major contribution that Samuel Monk made to American culture is probably not *The Sublime*, despite its importance to eighteenth-century scholars, but rather the introductions and notes that he wrote for *The Norton Anthology of English Literature*. When first published in 1935, *The Sublime* had a press run of 528 copies. (Humphrey Milford, Esq., of the Oxford University Press, who was entrusted with foreign distribution of *The Sublime*, received a grand total of 12 copies.) After a total sales of 442 copies, the book was removed from print in 1952. Appetite for the sublime revived with the appearance of the postwar generation of students, when the entire American educational system was rapidly expanding. Thus twenty-five years after its initial publication *The Sublime* was reprinted in 1960 as an Ann Arbor paperback with a run of 5,000 copies. It was also reprinted the following year with another run of 5,000 copies. (In addition, there was a clothbound edition of 500 copies, and the book was simultaneously printed in Toronto by Ambassador Books for Canadian distribution.) The paperback version went out of print in 1977—well after Sam had retired—which is not a bad shelf life for a book that began its journey as a doctoral dissertation. Such numbers are nonetheless paltry when compared with the worldwide sales of *The Norton Anthology of English Literature* (1962). Now in its fifth edition, *The Norton Anthology* (as it is popularly known to an entire generation of students) keeps its vast sales figures a closely guarded trade secret.

It is not at all unnatural that scholars raised on *The Norton Anthology* should cite its introductions as a locus classicus for the received wisdom that must now be revised. The revisions are nonetheless far fewer than demanded for most books written over a quarter of a century ago. The general editor, M. H. Abrams, offers this estimate of Sam's contributions:

Sam Monk was superb, both as initiator and collaborator. He combined, in a rare way, the virtues of erudition and a sense of what a novice needs to be told, of firmness and tact, of respect for the traditional and openness to the innovative; and always, he recognized that to compose an anthology that represents the wealth and diversity of the English literary tradition is, like politics, an art of the possible. Most of what he initially proposed, both in the selections and in their editing, survive in the finished anthology; and a number of his introductions are, in their own right, small masterpieces of the critical art.

The editing and annotation of classic texts, of course, ranks among the major contributions that the humanist tradition quite deliberately undertook. It is to modern scholars in this tradition that we owe our brilliant collected editions of Pope, Dryden, Johnson, and the rest. Sam sometimes observed that *The Norton Anthology* drained him of creative energy. He gave it so much of his labor and thought that he felt he had nothing left to give.

There is no one better—or more delicately—placed to appreciate both the strengths and the weaknesses of Sam's contributions to *The Norton Anthology* than the scholar called upon, in the third edition, to supply revisions Sam no longer wished to provide. Lawrence Lipking notes that he needed to alter Sam's occasionally defensive language. (Lipking: "He often seems to write for students whose romantic preferences will blind them to the virtues of 'neoclassicism,' and he labors to set them straight. Like many of my generation, I'd rather take a more positive stance and assume students will like these writers if given a fair chance.") There are inevitably alterations responsive to recent changes in criticism: more selections by or about women, less *vers de société*, more works that will strike modern students as racy and lively. Lipking adds: "I also claim the credit (or blame) for Christopher Smart, whom Sam didn't much like; he had never wanted to put in 'My Cat Jeoffrey,' he explained, because he did not care for cats." Humor, often a self-deprecating irony, is among the human elements Sam never succeeded in weeding out. In any case, Sam always assumed that editors, like scholars, are fallible souls afflicted by what he once called "my dear old original sin." Humanism meant recognizing and accepting what it means to write under correction.

Lipking seems to me correct in his claim that "Sam's occasional defensiveness was also related to his identification with many values that he shared with the 18th century." For the humanist, empathy was not simply a technique of analysis but almost (like oppositional criticism in reverse) a condition of understanding. "Writing about *Pilgrim's Progress*," Lipking notes about Sam, "he drew on a vocabulary of belief (as well as praise) that isn't really available to me." What this example might help us to recognize is how far Sam's humanism embraced—rather than erased or denied—conflict. Samuel T. Lloyd III was among the young friends who shared Sam's life in Charlottesville after his retirement. (Sam joked that he required regular infusions of young blood. As it happened, the young seemed to require regular infusions of Sam.) The trouble with young friends, however, was that they kept leaving, and Sam Lloyd eventually left Charlottesville to enter the seminary for ordination within the Episcopal church. The loss was a sore one. Sam Lloyd continues:

He found my going to seminary puzzling. He treated the decision with respect and even something like awe, but he never quite knew what to make of it. He who had etched Herbert's "Love bade me welcome" into my heart, who had recited to me with tears in his eyes the opening paragraph of *The Pilgrim's Progress*, who dreamed in the last years of Bunyan's river of death and of being carried over to the other side, was also a stranger to the church. Like a true son of the eighteenth century he found himself more than a little leery of the institution of the church, and more than a little puzzled by the gospels.

When we discuss the virtues and defects of Christian humanism, we should try to understand the contribution of individual scholars who did not ignore conflict but who lived it—occasionally, as in the instance of Samuel Monk, with a reserve and grace that permit us to imagine a harmony that did not exist.

VII

Sam Lloyd delivered a eulogy for Samuel H. Monk on April 10, 1981, at the annual conference of the American Society for Eighteenth-Century Studies. The Christian humanist tradition placed a special importance on death: an importance our culture has forgotten or lost beneath the demands of hospital, funeral home, and cemetery. Addison on his deathbed called for his stepson so the young man might gaze on the spectacle of holy dying. Sam Lloyd's words describe a scene in which—as if planned by the scholar who refused to separate *Gulliver's Travels* from the House Un-American Activities Committee—death has not been artificially severed from life or life artificially severed from literature. (The text for Monk has no clear or absolute boundary separating outside from inside: it interpenetrates the social world where living and dying also prove hard to disentangle.) What follows is Sam Lloyd's account.

It all happened very quickly. Marguerite and I were with Sam the weekend he planned to go into the hospital for some tests; in the two weeks he was there his strength rapidly declined. Howard Anderson, a former student and in many ways Sam's chosen son, arrived from East Lansing to take him home from the hospital. Sam had been so weakened that it soon became clear he would not recover.

Then it began. People from all over the country converged on Charlottesville—from Seattle, from Iowa, from Bloomington, Princeton, Boston, and Washington. People whom I had heard Sam praise and agonize over for years now became enfleshed; the myths of the circle of Sam were coming to life. Sam had made it manifestly clear that he wanted no artificial means used to keep him alive; so through Thursday and Friday he grew increasingly weaker until Saturday he went into a coma.

Through all of Thursday, Friday, and Saturday this group of friends was with Sam in his apartment, getting to know each other, telling stories from our own histories with Sam, exchanging Monkisms of one sort or another. Sam was so weak that he couldn't talk then, but he could occasionally smile, or nod his head, or make simple gestures to acknowledge that he knew when another of his "beloveds" had arrived.

There were some exquisite moments. One afternoon we placed the speakers of his record player in his bedroom, and a group of us sat with him, as he lay barely conscious, and listened to Mozart's 21st Piano Concerto. As we sat with him there, light streaming in the window, he seemed to rise to a clearer awareness. And, as the slow movement ended, he raised his hand, making a circle with his thumb and forefinger.

During those days one of us would periodically read to Sam some of his favorite poems. And we read to each other such things as the end of The Pilgrim's Progress. We all remarked how Sam had the knack for making us feel larger than we were—that he created a myth about each of us, a bit sentimental, a bit naive, but when we were with him and lived inside that myth, we were actually ennobled and actually thought ourselves capable of finer things.

VIII

Samuel Holt Monk died two days short of his eightieth birthday, on March 23, 1981. The scholar who wrote the book on the sublime had lived on familiar terms with the ordinary. Perhaps the most ordinary act that regularly occupied him was the writing of letters. His correspondence was immense. And letters, it seemed, were where the ordinariness of life attained for Sam a special vitality. The rapid demise of correspondence—letters which communicate not just information but character, style, emotion, knowledge, and the nuances of social relationship—may be an infallible sign that the values of Christian humanism no longer count for much, since humanists from Petrarch and Erasmus to Pope and Horace Walpole viewed correspondence as a crucial activity. For Sam a letter provides the point where books and music and painting (the human spirit at its most inventive) meet the everyday world of common affairs. It was in that ordinary intersection—which now may begin to seem rather extraordinary—that literature for Sam came to play a role that it did not play in conferences or lectures or scholarly articles.

The letter that follows stood unfinished in his typewriter at the time of Sam's death. The addressee was impossible to determine. (He wrote on an antique portable so erratic and nonlinear that a friend once proclaimed him the only scholar able to type illegibly.) Maybe, more than a few years late, this final letter will one day reach its proper destination. For me its significance lies in its sheer everydayness: words summoning up a fabric of experience in which art proves inseparable from day-to-day material living. In this fabric Shakespeare and Mozart fit effortlessly into the same context that absorbs reflections on not smoking and memories of a distant wedding and a distant war. Here letter writing mirrors the power of art—at least as the humanist tradition would conceive it—to bring people into contact, to communicate insights about our various ways of life, to bridge the differences and distances that inevitably divide us, to give pleasure, to develop our capacity for feeling, to intensify our experience of life, to sharpen our thinking about the world we inhabit and the worlds we construct.

February 19, 1981

Dearest M:

At last I'm making a start! But first I want to thank you for the delightful music calendar, which came yesterday. It will be a delight for eleven and a half months. And will reside on my desk beside my typewriter, that I use so clumsily. Only the mug of thumpy old Brahms is there to remind me of the decay of music since my 18th century.

Now. I recently read (actually re-read) your two wonderful letters of late December. I thought I'd wait for a while before answering since I knew that the busy season was in full swing on Crockett Street. Well, I've waited longer than I intended, but not disgracefully long, in view of our long silences in past years. It is so very good to hear from you and to recognize that age cannot wither or custom stale your infinite variety. And paraphrasing that line reminds me that a post card would have identified "When to the sessions" as the first line of Sonnet 30.

Your life seems to be full and very enjoyable and so enjoyed. I'm very glad. The children have had problems, but seem to be holding their own, and I hope, indeed know, that they bring you happiness. Didn't I come to see Lin in hospital the fall or winter after Wanda's death? I know that we both attended your wedding and

continued to see you until the end. Then the war and my being transported far
away from Memphis and the Delta. I gather it is no longer true that the capital of
Mississippi is the lobby of the Peabody Hotel. I'm glad that the Met still comes to
Memphis and that you go up to hear them. Never miss hearing a Mozart opera, or
the curse of an ardent Mozartian will blight the rest of your life.

I am very proud of you for sticking to a non-smoking way of life. I promise
you that it is and will be worth the effort. How lucky I was to be able to stop so
easily and never to have felt a craving thereafter! My three stoutish rather heavy
drinks daily are just about the only vice I have left for my pleasure. My doctor
doesn't object to them, but if he knew their alcoholic content he might very well
take action.

I'm glad that you and Bobby frisk with your contemporaries. I much prefer the
company of the young, and thank goodness I have a lot of them to love and be
loved by. When I say "young" I mean 28 to 48. A great variety, mostly couples,
wedded or merely bedded, divorced and re-married, mostly academics, some brilliant, many beautiful. I know that I'm old and conduct myself with due dignity
(no pomposity) and they all seem to think I'm great. That suits me a lot. I have
no friends my age, though some in their sixties; and I refuse to speak of myself as
a "senior citizen." I hate all euphemisms—mortician, dentures, home for house,
funeral parlor or funeral home, etc. etc. Nothing is better for being dressed out in
a fancy Latin-French garb. A fact is a fact is a fact is a fact, whether beautiful or
ugly. I know and acknowledge that I'm an old man. I like it better that way.

IX

At war's end Sam commandeered a jeep and returned to visit Chartres.
As across the wide plain of Beauce he caught sight of the magnificent
thirteenth-century Gothic cathedral to which he felt so intimately connected, he suddenly stopped. The fabled windows with their radiant,
sacred, unearthly colors stood empty and blank. Sam later said he felt as if
he were gazing on the blinded eyes of the woman he loved. He soon discovered, however, that the artisans of Chartres had carefully removed all the
panels of stained glass and hidden them in fear of the very catastrophe he
had averted. I'm not sure how this happened, but it is said that when the
townspeople learned of his protective action they allowed Sam, in an ultimate sign of gratitude and honor, to ring the bells of Chartres cathedral—
an event he remembered with tears of pride.

Notes

This essay contains the words and thoughts of numerous people who knew Samuel Monk, and in some cases gave me access to their private correspondence. For extensive and indispensable help I wish to express deepest thanks to Gates Agnew, Howard Anderson, J. C. Levenson, and Samuel Lloyd. Others who assisted no less generously include M. H. Abrams, Lynne Blair, Elizabeth Brown, Joseph Butwin, Ralph Cohen, Gerald Elbers, Eleanor Falkenberry, Deborah Fort, Keith Fort, Lawrence Lipking, Earl Miner, Stanley Rowe, Pamela Schwandt, G. Robert Stange, Elizabeth Swedenberg, Willard Thorp, Leonard Unger, and Adrienne Marie Ward.

Works Cited

Bruns, Gerald L. "Midrash and Allegory: The Beginnings of Scriptural Interpretation." In *The Literary Guide to the Bible*, ed. Robert Alter and Frank Kermode. Cambridge: Harvard University Press, 1987. 625–46.

Cooper, Waller Raymond. *Southwestern at Memphis: 1848–1948*. Richmond, VA: John Knox Press, 1949.

Crane, R. S. Review of *The Sublime: A Study of Critical Theories in XVIII-Century England*, by Samuel H. Monk. *Philological Quarterly*, 15 (1936), 165–67.

Housman, A. E. *A Shropshire Lad* (1896). *The Collected Poems of A. E. Housman*. New York: Henry Holt and Company, 1940.

James, William. "Pragmatism and Humanism." *Pragmatism* (1907). *The Works of William James*, ed. Frederick H. Burkhardt et al. Cambridge: Harvard University Press, 1975–.

James, William. "The Essence of Humanism." *Essays in Radical Empiricism* (1912). *The Works of William James*, ed. Frederick H. Burkhardt et al. Cambridge: Harvard University Press, 1975–.

Johnson, Samuel. *The Yale Edition of the Works of Samuel Johnson*. Ed. Allen T. Hazen et al. New Haven: Yale University Press, 1954–.

Monk, Samuel H. "A Grace Beyond the Reach of Art." *Journal of the History of Ideas*, 5 (1944), 131–50.

Monk, Samuel H. "Colleges and Freedom of Opinion in a Revolutionary Era." *Southwestern Bulletin*, 34, no. 3, extra (1947), 3–16.

Monk, Samuel H. "The Pride of Lemuel Gulliver." *Sewanee Review*, 63 (1955), 48–71.

Monk, Samuel H. *The Sublime: A Study of Critical Theories in XVIII-Century England*. New York: Modern Language Association, 1935.

Monk, Samuel H. Unpublished correspondence. Willard Thorp papers. Princeton University Library.

Studies in Criticism and Aesthetics, 1660–1800: Essays in Honor of Samuel Holt Monk. Ed. Howard Anderson and John S. Shea. Minneapolis: University of Minnesota Press, 1967.

Tate, Allen. *The Fathers* (1938). Rpt. Denver: Alan Swallow, 1960.

Whitman, Walt. *Leaves of Grass* (1860–61). *Leaves of Grass: A Textual Variorum of the Printed Poems*, ed. Sculley Bradley, Harold W. Blodgett, Arthur Golden, and William White. 3 vols. New York: New York University Press, 1980.

11 *Leo Damrosch*

Reaching Mid-Career in "the Eighteenth Century": Some Personal Reflections

J. G. A. Pocock, a historian whose work has become increasingly influential in literary studies, remarked fifteen years ago, "It is part of normal experience to find our thought conditioned by assumptions and paradigms so deep-seated that we did not know they were there until something brought them to the surface; we suspect, if we are historians, that there are others present and operative of which we shall never be aware because they will only be visible from the vantage-points provided by historical moments in the future."[1] Literary scholars have shared the historians' interest in hidden assumptions, but even while they have professed the importance of acknowledging what they believe, they have tended to do so as team members of highly organized *équipes* whose theoretical debates are more concerned with adjusting internal disagreements than with persuading nonbelievers to share their fundamental premises. It is often difficult, therefore, to tell why (or even whether) a scholar finds a particular set of questions interesting, and critics who insist on the historically conditioned basis of all discourse tend nonetheless to be reticent about their own.

One ought not to forget that academic work proceeds unpredictably even in so subdivided an area as eighteenth-century studies. Attention may often turn to particular authors or problems for prudential gap-filling reasons—the *PMLA Bibliography* abhors a vacuum—but the work that gets done reflects the development of individual imaginations. Some people's careers may indeed revolve around crucial conversion experiences: they were halfhearted New Critics until one day they found Marx, or Foucault, or Lacan, and knew at last what to do with their lives. But even in such cases, a career need not necessarily be predictable and smooth; like the economists' fiction of "rational man," the Deconstructionist and the Cultural Materialist are abstract types. So far as I am able to judge, the majority of scholar-teachers have proceeded in an essentially ad hoc way, tackling projects that change shape disconcertingly, and responding to competing intellectual and institutional influences that do not resolve into any single program.

In these pages I offer a brief retrospective view of the eighteenth-century wing of "the profession" as I myself have experienced it, believing that my experience has been, if not typical, at least not untypical. At times I have flattered myself that I was a rebel against prevailing orthodoxies, but of course Pocock's law holds true: the establishment was more tolerant and capacious than I cared to admit, and I have been more securely inside it than I knew. At the same time, my tendency to draw eclectically on a variety of methods (or approaches, as they are now known) has entailed limitations that have generalizable implications for a profession that has been groping to redefine itself. My aim, then, is to offer neither an autobiography nor an apologia, but to reflect on some of the ways in which—as Marshall Brown observes in his "Commentary" in this volume—the profession is made up of individual people, with idiosyncratic interests and blind spots.

The English department at Yale, where I was an undergraduate in the early 1960s, was the acknowledged headquarters of a still regnant New Criticism, and "explication" was the accepted model for reading and writing all the way from freshman English to graduate seminars. Formalism, that dread term of reproach nowadays, would be too grand a name for what we were taught, since not much was really said about form. Whatever the party line may have been on the heresy of paraphrase, thematic interpretation was the customary procedure, with due attention to imagery and to the union of sound with sense. In those years I had very little notion of the eighteenth century (I knew Maynard Mack only as a compelling lecturer on Shakespeare), but by chance I got interested in Samuel Johnson and read through Bronson's Riverside selections.

Cambridge came next. If Yale was at the end of an era, Cambridge was between eras. Basil Willey had retired, C. S. Lewis and E. M. W. Tillyard were dead, and the turbulent F. R. Leavis was effectively exiled (though he still gave private tutorials to a select few). My tutor was R. T. H. Redpath of Trinity College, the Donne scholar whose wide sympathies and polymathic learning allowed me to read very widely, with an orientation toward the history of genres and ideas. If Cambridge stood for anything in particular, it was the version of explication known as "practical criticism," in homage to I. A. Richards' book of that name. In addition, "tragedy" was the traditional centerpiece of the Cambridge exams (I'm not sure why), and consequently we read a lot of tragedies. Along the way I happened to write an essay on Johnson's conception of tragedy, and from this nearly random event many consequences flowed.

In the graduate program at Princeton, where I completed my academic novitiate, no particular school of thought prevailed. The example and encouragement of Lawrence Lipking, then a junior professor, impelled me to go on with the eighteenth century and therefore with Johnson. My Cambridge essay cried out for expansion, or so I tried to believe, and before long a dissertation emerged with the noncommittal title *Samuel Johnson and Tragedy*. (The connective *and* formed the basis of many a literary study in those days, as a fulcrum on which two disparate, or even unrelated, ideas could be temporarily balanced.)

What was the "field" into which I found myself dragging my plow? Not an altogether inviting one, it seemed. The New Critics had insisted on the importance of literature "as literature," and at Cambridge a good deal of Leavisite influence survived, so that ranking and "placing" literary works seemed a normal thing to do. But other areas than the eighteenth century furnished most of the grist for those mills: Renaissance drama, the metaphysical lyric, the symbolist poem, and so on. Most specialists in the eighteenth century saw as a primary mission the rehabilitation of their period from unfair prejudices, generally blamed on "the Romantics." While there was a certain amount of rivalry between "scholars" and "critics," rather analogous to the seventeenth-century quarrel between ancients and moderns, the most distinguished figures—for instance, Mack, R. S. Crane, and Earl Wasserman—belonged to both camps. W. K. Wimsatt and his opponents might argue about the intentional fallacy, but whether one held that a writer's intentions were relevant to interpretation, or alternatively that the only intentions that counted were those somehow embodied in the work "itself," both sides took it for granted that the object of study was a unified text that could be counted on to speak coherently. ("Irony" was a reliable tool for smoothing out any difficulties in texts that seemed disunified, though occasionally, as with Defoe's novels, the disjunctions remained embarrassingly apparent.)

Criticism, however, had its limits, and much of eighteenth-century scholarship represented the last refuge of 1930s positivism. Study of the period was dominated by "background," always generalized and usually inert. Apart from routine information about the parliamentary career of Sir Robert Walpole, this background tended to be highly abstract; Ian Watt's

superb *Rise of the Novel* was regarded as unsound by conservative scholars—that is to say, by most scholars—because it made serious use of
sociological contexts. A series of hypostatized "isms" controlled interpretation: deism, latitudinarianism, benevolism, sentimentalism, empiricism,
and, of course, neoclassicism. One often saw references to "the neoclassical
creed," as if Pope and Johnson had taken an oath to uphold it.

In those days one could "keep up," as the saying went, with most of the
articles on eighteenth-century literature and with nearly all of the books.
And in those days much of the job of preparing for the Ph.D. was a matter
of knowing what had been said and by whom. Criticism of what they said
was not exactly encouraged; the young aspirant was expected to adopt a
filial posture toward "Bill" Wimsatt or "Fred" Pottle, as they were referred
to in the gossipy *Johnsonian News Letter* edited at Columbia by "Jim"
Clifford. This was a (men's) club into which one might someday be invited
if all went well.

As a neophyte in the late sixties, I saw myself as opposed to the positivist backgrounding and reflexive boosterism of my elders. The book on
Johnson that developed from my dissertation addressed the paradox that
a critic widely praised for his "tragic sense of life" (still a highly honor-
ific term at that time) should have had such negative views about most
literary tragedies.[2] That paradox now looks like a function of sixties critical attitudes rather than of Johnson's: it was still possible to believe that
the term "tragedy" was susceptible of a comprehensive generic definition,
and that Johnson ought somehow to have anticipated truths that Hegel or
Nietzsche or A. C. Bradley later formulated.

Such a critique now appears painfully ahistorical, and its weaknesses
occasioned a rather disagreeable debate with Howard Weinbrot and
Donald Greene. In my defense I proclaimed, with an orotundity that is
now embarrassing,

King Lear is a great play because it moves us in profound ways, not because it
once moved the Elizabethans. Most readers in the eighteenth century thought *Cato*
a masterpiece, but even their saving hypothesis, that it was a great poem if not a
great play, no longer looks adequate to salvage it. The criticism of the past should
be treated in the same way: we should pay it the compliment of bringing our own
best ideas to bear on it.[3]

The *we* and *us* that now look so dubious were intended as an appeal,
against Greene and Weinbrot, to the larger community of intelligent readers. But of course it was too late: "our own best ideas" no longer bore
much resemblance to those of Bradley or Unamuno, and critics increasingly thought it pointless to claim that *Cato* (or for that matter *King Lear*)
was or was not "great."

By this time I was teaching at the University of Virginia, whose department of English was widely considered to be "strong in the eighteenth
century." In the decade and a half between 1968 and 1983 there were never
fewer than five of us specializing in it. The three patriarchs were Martin
Battestin, Ralph Cohen, and the late Irvin Ehrenpreis. All were generous
with advice and encouragement for their younger colleagues (who included
David Morris, Stephen Land, and James Turner). But it was hard to discern
much common ground between Battestin's Augustan harmonies, Cohen's
paradigms of literary change, and Ehrenpreis' ironies of aggressive common sense. By contrast with the intensely collaborative Renaissance studies
at Berkeley in the same era, or with the theoretical revolution at Yale,
one got the impression of individual scholars pursuing discrete projects
in an environment of genial laissez-faire. Indeed, my deepest intellectual
debts (I imagine this is a common experience) were not to colleagues at
all, but to the undergraduate and graduate students with whom I studied
eighteenth-century literature.

Continuing to read and teach Johnson, I returned to the theme of my first
book, and conceived a sequel that would show how Johnson continued to
live as a critical intelligence. Such an aspiration was by now seriously out
of phase with the times. To be sure, *The Uses of Johnson's Criticism* made
better sense of Johnson's own assumptions than the previous book had, exploring attitudes that he shared with such contemporaries as Lessing and
Diderot.[4] But I continued to assume that "we" understood certain secure
truths about literature and would like to be assured that Johnson did too. In
effect, I believed I was refuting New Critics like Wimsatt and René Wellek,
who had claimed that Johnson couldn't tell the difference between art and
life, but I still accepted their premises and argued as if Johnson's criticism
was valuable in proportion as it approached Coleridge's. In hindsight I
would say that my real argument was that Johnson's criticism continues
to live (as John Dennis', say, does not) because people have absorbed so
much of his way of thinking, even when they disagree with his particular judgments. As Eliot replied to the objection that the old writers were
no longer relevant because we know so much more than they did, "Precisely, and they are that which we know."[5] But in claiming that Johnson
could still speak to readers, I was translating his thoughts into "modern"
language that was already dated and would soon become totally obsolete.
And in any case, it is hard enough to understand what Johnson thought
he was doing without showing that it was, or was not, what Wimsatt or
Wellek thought he should have thought. In a later essay, when I did try
to place Johnson in explicit dialogue with a fashionable modern mode of
criticism, I came to see much more clearly that the underlying differences
were at least as significant as the apparent affinities.[6]

Considered more largely, my experience is instructive of the vulnerability of any scholar who tries to occupy a middle ground, or to put it another way, who does not join any of the organized *équipes* whose members can count on mutual solidarity on points of doctrine. I knew that my right flank was open to attack from "background" scholars who would find it anachronistic to confront an eighteenth-century English writer with ideas generated in any other time or place. But I failed to perceive that my left flank was even more vulnerable to up-to-date critics for whom my implicit categories would be indistinguishable from those of the New Critics I intended to argue with—above all, in the assumptions about literary value that both of my books so freely made.

Looking back on the time at Virginia, I find it particularly interesting to reflect on the vehemence with which Ehrenpreis asserted his dogmatically commonsense position. His *Literary Meaning and Augustan Values* was published in 1974, just as the theoretical revolution was getting under way, and it managed to be passionately defiant of both the old academic order and the new. Attacking the establishment's favored criteria of irony and allusion, Ehrenpreis complained, "It is remarkable how often they give minute attention to poems or parts of poems that hardly deserve to be read, but which they apparently believe they are endowing with excellence."[7] He was facing resolutely in one direction while the attack came from another: all canons of value, not just those of Maynard Mack and Reuben Brower, were even then falling into disrepute. At the same time, Ehrenpreis insisted that texts by competent writers mean what they say (his affinity with his colleague E. D. Hirsch is apparent here) and that any mode of interpretation that went beyond their self-evident meaning was pernicious. Or rather, there might be other kinds of meaning, but they should be strictly quarantined:

The world does not want for critics who dissolve the line between conscious and unconscious. In my view this dissolution sinks poetry to the level of growls and grunts. It is only through the habit of attributing deliberate intention to a speaker that we can handle unconscious meanings. . . . The interpreter treats the unconscious aspect of the author as a separate creature with intentions of its own. (15)

It seems to me no accident that Ehrenpreis devoted his career to understanding Swift; his position is highly reminiscent of the paradoxical conservatism that Swift himself espoused.

In Michael McKeon's analysis, Swiftian skepticism represents a third term in a progression whose first is an aristocratic ethos with values that are accepted as self-evidently right, and whose second is a progressive individualism that debunks aristocratic assumptions. Swift's mode of conservatism uses skepticism to defeat itself, turning back to the old beliefs with a weary and disillusioned sense that they are better than nothing, since they are all there is.[8] This account could easily be adapted to describe Ehrenpreis' position in the 1970s, too skeptical to adopt the complacencies of his teachers in the 1940s, too conservative to accept the decentering methodologies that were already engaged in saturation bombing of the New Criticism from a great height. Like Swift, Ehrenpreis had a complex and subtle intelligence that was attracted to every kind of paradox, but that ended by asserting that things remain what they seem. To put it another way, for someone of Ehrenpreis' generation, it was important that "the eighteenth century" stand as a stable and dependable icon; in a world of disorder and change, it offered a field in which skepticism could play freely because one could always rely on a secure harbor at the end of the journey.

When "theory" burst into everyone's consciousness in the mid-1970s, however, most of us in the next generation began to see that other disciplines offered more exciting ideas than traditional literary studies did. I had always found Blake compelling (I had studied the *Songs* with Hirsch at Yale, and the later works with Lipking and Charles Ryskamp at Princeton), and I now began to teach Blake in some depth. One could hardly walk off that precipice unscathed. It was not just a question of encountering Romantics criticism, which was certainly more alive than eighteenth-century criticism, but also of confronting the immense range of psychological, philosophical, and aesthetic dilemmas that underlie Blake's work. A Virginia colleague, the medievalist James Earl, introduced me to Paul Ricoeur's profoundly suggestive *Symbolism of Evil*. Another colleague, the Miltonist William Kerrigan, led me not only into Milton but into Cassirer and psychoanalytic theory as well. In addition, the three of us joined a discussion group in the anthropology department, presided over by the late Victor Turner, that explored problems of symbolic meaning from a cultural perspective.

A move of some kind toward "theory" was probably inevitable, but these chance connections turned me in certain directions rather than in others, and my inquiry was so remote from the interests of most professional Blakeans that the resulting book has had more acceptance from Romanticists in general than from Blake specialists.[9] Some reviewers, indeed, emphasized that it was written by an eighteenth-century scholar whose training led him to misapprehend as philosophical dilemmas what were actually inspired paradoxes. My own view was that Blake had not been well served by admirers who thought that he sprang fully armed from his own brain. I tried to draw upon intellectual history to show that Blake learned as much from Berkeley as from Boehme, that the thought of contemporaries like Hegel had much in common with his vision of the world, and that his attempt to rebuild Western thought from the ground up, though magnificent, was bound to fall short of its goal. That critique still seems accurate to me, but it has suffered, in institutional terms, from not hewing to the line of some particular methodology. For instance, I would have won much easier assent in some quarters (though of course not in others) if I had argued that Blake promoted a deconstructive philosophy of language. Instead, I argued that he used deconstructive methods to break through to a visionary truth that would have been anathema to disciples of Nietzsche, and that he himself was never able to articulate in terms that noninitiates could grasp.

I next resumed work on representations of "reality" in the eighteenth century, a project from which the Blake book had quite unexpectedly sprung, and for which the Blake work turned out to provide a decisive shift in direction. There had been a number of studies of "Puritanism" as a factor in "the rise of the novel" (one abstraction cooperating with another), but these did not, in my opinion, sufficiently address the way Augustinian ideas worked from the inside—the cultural and psychological needs they satisfied, and the pictures of reality that were developed by the persons who were drawn to them. As with Blake, my models were psychological and philosophical. I wanted to understand, for example, how convictions of guilt and determinism underlie *The Pilgrim's Progress* and *The Holy War*, and how *Clarissa* exposes implications in Augustinian symbolics that the more doctrinal seventeenth century had repressed.[10]

But if the theoretical purview was both wider and more explicit than it had been in the Johnson books, the new models too were rapidly losing authority. I well remember my surprise when an eminent questioner at the English Institute in 1980, where I presented a preliminary version of my account of Bunyan and Defoe, wanted to know why I thought psychoanalysis had any relevance to Bunyan. *Grace Abounding to the Chief of Sinners* is virtually a Freudian case study, and although I am no committed Freudian, I have found Freud's myth (together with his ethical sympathy) a valuable means of illuminating it. But for anyone who thinks that Freud's myth is a systematic mystification and that the very notion of the "subject" needs to be exposed as false consciousness, the wrong questions were certainly being asked. Similarly, several reviewers complained that I presented a misleading view of Puritanism, and pointed out as well that Richardson was an Anglican, not a Puritan. But I had tried to emphasize that I was using the term "Puritan" to denote a complex of imaginative attitudes, not a sociopolitical movement, and that these attitudes survived in Richardson's fiction even though Richardson himself was a conventional Anglican.

It has become increasingly apparent that to eschew the language of a well-defined critical "approach" is to invite misunderstanding, or rather misprision: as Sidney Smith said of the women quarreling over the back-yard fence, "They will never agree, they are arguing from different prem-ises." A New Critic, if he or she thought *Clarissa* worth studying at all, would have aspired to win through to the "right" interpretation. Critics today are increasingly aware that what one finds is a function of what one looks for, and that one's presuppositions, whether overtly theorized or not, rule out the possibility of an all-embracing and universally acceptable conclusion. If William Warner, Terry Castle, and Terry Eagleton are indeed describing the same thing, they do it from such different angles as to make one question the very notion of sameness.[11]

In short, my Johnson books were written for a community that was ceasing to exist even as the pages were set in type; my Blake and fiction books, only a few years later, were addressed to a fragmented community where every approach must defend itself in open debate, and where some-one who does not belong to a definable camp cannot expect the benefit of the doubt where presuppositions are at issue. Perhaps as a consequence of these experiences, I have become increasingly interested in the ways in which eighteenth-century culture prefigured the breakdown of consensus that is endemic today, with reverberations that are both unsettling and stimulating. My recent study of Pope stresses—in contradiction to the Mack-Brower-Wasserman image of Pope as the last Renaissance poet—Pope's reluctant discovery of new ambiguities and occlusions when he gave up on Renaissance poetics and "stooped to truth." And my book on the nonfiction writers of the later eighteenth century explores the ways in which Humean skepticism and Johnsonian and Burkean conservatism respond very consciously to the dilemmas that arise when a society loses confidence in consensus.[12] Here as always the zeitgeist is at work; we hear a good deal nowadays about the new pragmatism, and predictably enough I find pragmatism relevant to the experience of the eighteenth century. Other symptoms of immersion in the present will doubtless become apparent when the present recedes into the past.

Peering toward the future, I regard the intervention of theory as a crucial and irreversible change in literary studies, but I find myself as unwilling to speak the language of *Representations* or *Diacritics* as I used to be to speak the language of *Philological Quarterly* and the *Johnsonian News Letter*. Meanwhile, I have the impression that many scholars have experienced some version of my journey: a love of certain authors (for me, Johnson and Blake above all) that has led to the slow and never-completed growth of a miscellaneous body of work, like a coral island that rises toward the ocean surface but never quite reaches it, and participates in certain elements of the zeitgeist that are neither freely chosen nor fully grasped. A few critics are nimble enough to leap from one bandwagon to another whenever the "cutting edge" veers in a new direction, but most people, I think, find that personal preoccupations make that kind of maneuverability impossible, even if it were desirable. If eclecticism means not knowing what you think, or choosing at random from an array of incompatible theoretical models, then no one would want to be an eclectic. But I still believe it is possible to try to know the past by assimilating a range of disparate approaches rather than by espousing any one of them exclusively. And there is something oddly parasitic in the sedulous application, to literary texts, of systematic ideas generated by a few canonical theorists in other fields, though such a procedure has the advantage of defining in advance what is relevant, what is interesting, and what is brilliant.

At any event, the old interests persist in my teaching and writing, altered by new perspectives but never entirely transformed. Johnson has turned up again in *Fictions of Reality*, in a context of cultural consensus that I never would have conceived in the 1960s or 1970s, and in surprising but (I believe) fruitful alignment with Hume. Yet he is still the wise and eloquent Johnson who first drew me into the "field," and—to name two scholars whose work I admire—he more closely resembles the Johnson of Walter Jackson Bate than the Johnson of John Barrell. Similarly, Blake, though not officially one of the book's subjects, makes himself heard often, particularly in a sort of imagined dialogue with Godwin and Burke. And sure enough, he turns out to be much more like the Blake of Northrop Frye (though *Symbol and Truth* was at bottom an attack on Frye's system) than like the Blake of Nelson Hilton or Morris Eaves. I am to some extent responsive, as anyone must be, to the current preoccupation with political and social contexts, but for me the individual imagination and its texts remain central, and although the canon has widened to embrace nonfiction (it always seemed bizarre that Collins and Mackenzie enjoyed a "literary" priority over Gibbon and Burke), it remains a canon after all.

In *Symbol and Truth* I wrote, "We read Blake's myth to know what it would be like to believe in man's spiritual power while fully recognizing the self-deluding tendencies of the imagination and its symbols." That remains my fundamental conviction: that powerful works of imagination, including Johnson's *Lives of the Poets*, Gibbon's *Decline and Fall of the Roman Empire*, and Hume's *Dialogues concerning Natural Religion*, not only enlarged the experience of their original readers but can continue to do so today. As Robert Darnton has eloquently said,

The reconstruction of worlds is one of the historian's most important tasks. He undertakes it, not from some strange urge to dig up archives and sift through old paper, but because he wants to talk with the dead. . . . If we lost all contact with the worlds we have lost, we would be condemned to live in a two-dimensional, time-bound present, and our own world would turn flat.[13]

So I still teach and write about texts in a way that Brooks and Warren would have recognized as intelligible, however much they would have disliked my reliance on "extrinsic" information—which to cultural critics nowadays must seem all too intrinsic. One person's fad is another person's paradigm shift, and the human mind, as Johnson always said, hungers for novelty. The study of literature is immensely more interesting now than it was when benevolism and neoclassicism reigned, and I hope to keep on contributing to the coral atoll for a long while to come, unsure though I may be that I am working in harmony with my fellow polyps.

Notes

1 J. G. A. Pocock, *Politics, Language and Time* (New York: Atheneum, 1973), 32.
2 Leo Damrosch, *Samuel Johnson and the Tragic Sense* (Princeton: Princeton University Press, 1972).
3 Leo Damrosch, "On Misreading Eighteenth-Century Literature: A Defense," *Eighteenth-Century Studies*, 8 (1974/75), 203–4.
4 Leo Damrosch, *The Uses of Johnson's Criticism* (Charlottesville: University Press of Virginia, 1976).
5 T. S. Eliot, "Tradition and the Individual Talent," *Selected Essays* (London: Faber & Faber, 1951), 16.
6 Leo Damrosch, "Samuel Johnson and Reader Response Criticism," *The Eighteenth Century*, 21 (1980), 91–108.
7 Irvin Ehrenpreis, "Explicitness in Augustan Literature," in *Literary Meaning and Augustan Values* (Charlottesville: University Press of Virginia, 1974), 37.
8 Michael McKeon, *The Origins of the English Novel, 1600–1740* (Baltimore: Johns Hopkins University Press, 1987).
9 Leo Damrosch, *Symbol and Truth in Blake's Myth* (Princeton: Princeton University Press, 1980).
10 Leo Damrosch, *God's Plot and Man's Stories: Studies in the Fictional Imagination from Milton to Fielding* (Chicago: University of Chicago Press, 1985).
11 William Beatty Warner, *Reading Clarissa: The Struggles of Interpretation* (New Haven: Yale University Press, 1979); Terry Castle, *Clarissa's Ciphers: Meaning and Disruption in Richardson's Clarissa* (Ithaca: Cornell University Press, 1982); Terry Eagleton, *The Rape of Clarissa: Writing, Sexuality and Class Struggle in Samuel Richardson* (Minneapolis: University of Minnesota Press, 1982).
12 Leo Damrosch, *The Imaginative World of Alexander Pope* (Berkeley: University of California Press, 1987); *Fictions of Reality in the Age of Hume and Johnson* (Madison: University of Wisconsin Press, 1989).
13 Robert Darnton, *The Literary Underground of the Old Regime* (Cambridge: Harvard University Press, 1982), v.

Marshall Brown

Commentary

Le privilège traditionnellement conféré à la conscience et à la
connaissance réflexives est dépourvu de fondement et . . . rien
n'autorise à établir une différence de nature entre la connaissance
de soi et la connaissance d'autrui.
—Pierre Bourdieu, *Esquisse d'une théorie de la pratique*

The heterogeneity of the present volume honors the British eighteenth century for its freedom of opportunity in both thought and action. The period
offers exemplary stimulation to critics who would draw on the resources
of the past, of theory, of methods, schools, and ideologies, without being
bound to any. I shall gratefully use Leo Damrosch's permission to comment critically on the essays in this volume, for they often show best the
strength of their empirical learning and associative insight in moments of
systematic weakness. Testimonials, briefs, and syntheses, all witness that
the world of scholarship is an open elite, and must remain so.[1]

Critic, know thyself. In its multiple mirrorings a commentary on a collection of reflections about criticism past and present makes a mockery
of the earnest injunction to look inward. Yet the urge toward sincerity
and authenticity is hard to resist. Why, when so many of the histories in
this volume show us that self-knowledge is unattainable, do we persist
in wanting it? Whence the impulse to relate hard-won and fragile objec-
tivities to mere opinion? This volume is predicated on the assumption,
which I endorse, that critics are people, and best regarded as such. Yet so
variously do the contributors draw the consequences that a summing up
becomes foolhardy. Our Scylla is Landry's commodification, our Charyb-
dis Braudy's affective turbulence. Between those perils, these essays and
eighteenth-century common sense can help us to negotiate a course.

211

Start with the soft core of eighteenth-century studies. The "human-ism" that Richetti advocates has never seemed to me a focused ideal, and Morris' "Christian humanism" has a forbidding ring to one not born to the club. Nor have I yet learned to love the authors in connection with whom these values are invoked: Watt and Monk. Lacking the self-consciousness that the essays in the present volume promote, their books yield to the temptations to judge without rationale and to relate without discrimina-tion. They encourage the indefinite "some imponderable that deserves to be called genius," the undemonstrable "full access" and "full achievements" (Richetti 103), and the mystical aura that "somehow communicated an understanding" that "literature was where the values of humanistic learn-ing might be said to live most intensely" (Morris 180, 187). We continue to digest their insights at least in part, I think, because they accumulated so much incompletely digested material.

All the more welcome, then, are the reminders of the engaged labor required to accumulate knowledge. I suggest linking Richetti's particular-ism and objectivism, Braudy's individualism, and Lipking's antiquarian-ism into a complex of values that aim to save persons from the fatalism of the persona. McKeon and (in more detail) Epstein demonstrate how spon-taneity risks lapsing unnervingly into system—even if only a system of disorder. Critical reserve congeals into a spectral self-image; even the most seemingly innocent or self-effacing of hermeneutic gestures can betray complicity with a disciplinary network. Yet I wonder whether Epstein's indictment of Gray scholars applies so convincingly to poets less skeptical about the paths of glory. Morris' parable reminds us that heroism is messy and that the cult of a personality or an idea can at least rescue us from the obsessive cult of ourselves.

This reading of the volume's exercises in panegyric aligns heroism with Landry's version of feminism. I too attended the MLA session that she re-calls and observed the competitive, more-feminist-than-thou tone of many of its speakers. There was a struggle to forge a unified following among the sex which is not one. Yet surely the urgency of feminism at the present mo-ment bears some relation to the evasiveness of its categories. Landry con-joins anti-essentialism and materialism because women's labors shape their lives and ours in ways that more closely resemble the workings of genius than the diligence of ordinary men. Tristram Shandy, a son of leisure, may "hold together" the "individual bits and pieces" of experience, as Braudy suggests (34), but his mother and the novel's other mute inglorious women had first to produce them for his delight, as I have argued elsewhere. All the critics in this volume, it seems to me, put production, discovery, and individuality before impersonal order.

The volume's diverse accounts of heroism and accusations of apostasy illuminate how many different ways there are to slip into reification. Lipking warns us of the arbitrariness of periodization, yet McKeon presupposes the oft-questioned existence of an "Augustan period." Would his subtle dialectics be possible without such an entity to be deconstructed? How often these essays exhort us to liberate our thinking from rigid oppositions, yet, as Bender says, how naturally binarism comes to Enlightenment thinkers and to those who study them. And how many of our claims could be staked without the aggrandizement that turns "I" into "we"? Braudy and I are the most overt instances in the volume of this rhetorical ploy. But it infects all those who stake claims for the contemporaneity of the eighteenth century: we have met the Enlightenment, and it are us. Our heroes—well, my heroes—are those who recognize the individual, the particular, and the objective even as they resist conflating my values with those of my team, of the past, or of the universe.

It is a fitting tribute to the democratic character we like to see in the eighteenth century that this volume opens with a critique of an earlier one, *The New Eighteenth Century*, to which five of the present authors contributed. For the moment, *The New Eighteenth Century* seems like a watershed in the field; it has fixed the Enlightenment for a contemporary critical sensibility. The present collection, responsively, might be called "The Eighteenth Century New and Old." It aims to restore the long view to our sense of contemporaneity. It evokes ways that the eighteenth century has changed in response to changes in us. Following McKeon and Bender, we can learn to value it as a time of crisis, a model of never-ending transformations, a regulatory ideal, a horizon of our expectations and our comprehension.

By returning us to the manifold histories of our discipline, this collection thus returns us to the historicity of the period that invented historicism. I have always found it hard to understand why so many critics want the past to be "modern." Why study sameness when so much more can be learned from difference? But as we see ourselves through reflection on our forebears—both exemplars and warning examples—we can recognize a different kind of contemporaneity: though the world of two hundred or three hundred years ago was not really like the present, its changes can still help to model our changes. The critic cannot *know herself* in the mirror either of the past or of the present. (I use the feminine pronoun here in order to ally myself with the aspirations of the two female essayists in the volume, as I interpret them.) But she can learn to know better her direction in the unpredictable trajectories of personal and collective history.

History is Dowling's subject, above all. His Jamesonian story tells of an all-embracing myth that, when exploded by a successor myth, sublimates itself as esthetics. Needless to say, the art-for-art's-sake legend has as many versions as it has tellers: McKeon would place the point of origin in Dryden, I in Goldsmith, others in Kant, or Huysmans, or Shakespeare, or Boccaccio. To tell it, you have to posit a preexisting unified field that is built on the shards into which it splinters. In the esthetic, in other words, linearity and recursion feed off one another: at the end a "state of alienation and fragmentation . . . must occur when the bonds of traditional society are dissolved" (150), yet at the start "the logic of a single embracing proto-narrative [had given] unexpected coherence to the scattered fragments of story and myth and ideology" (141). Dowling's majestic sentences would almost persuade us that the pieces can all be encompassed by a single period, nay, a single "this." But where, to throw out one example, do we place Dyer's *Ruins of Rome?* Can we so easily separate line from circle, loss from persistence, dissociation from recuperation? The passage Dowling quotes in his note 1 continues with more mingling of distancing and appropriation than you might anticipate.[2] The systematizing gestures of a "genuine understanding" (136), "*a* logic" (141), "*the* meaning," "the ultimate significance" (147) represent the critic's inescapable romance with history. Yet the rich and compelling detail that Dowling's strong critical personality newly sifts and arranges persists in confronting him with the complexities and multiplicities of clashing and interacting *histories.*

Dowling's enterprise thus allies itself with the essays in this volume that it would seem to oppose. Althusser (whom Dowling invokes) is not the appropriate patron saint for the contending force-fields Dowling describes, nor is Foucault in the role (which, indeed, he often shunned) of the prophet of Paris. But Foucault, the student of microstructures and disciplinary dispersion, is. And so, curiously, is the always misrecognized master whom Dowling silently invokes, the great positivist historian Leopold von Ranke. Alternately viewing reality as "projected by literary texts," as "created or projected by the work," or "as an already-constituted field," Dowling wants "to grasp 'history' in the way it really did and does exist" (136). That phrase deforms a famous slogan in which objectivism, particularism, and individualism fall together. With more colloquial modesty than popular renown accords him, Ranke "just wants to show how things actually were" ("will blos zeigen, wie es eigentlich gewesen").[3] A personalist ("Die Absicht eines Historikers hängt von seiner Ansicht ab" [v]) and a pluralist (his history "umfaßt . . . nur Geschichten, nicht die Geschichte" [vi]) who refrains from imposing contemporary standards and judgments, the positivist anxiously drives beyond the canonical Popes to the "truer" documents of the obscure Browns (Dowling 143). Yet he is also an idealist. "Human decisions proceed from the possibilities offered by the general situation. Meaningful successes occur only in collaboration with homogeneous world-elements. . . . Events develop in an interaction of individual forces with the objective world situation. Success is the measure of these forces."[4] Shorn of Ranke's religious and monarchist teleologies, Dowling's neopositivism becomes an admirable ideal, spanning the empirical and the theoretical as it learns to regulate contemporary debates and dialectics from the example of eighteenth-century ones.

It is from Epstein's essay that I have just misappropriated the term misrecognition. That is Pierre Bourdieu's word for the temporizing tactics people use to relax the rigidities of their social structures. Epstein reflects himself (unknowingly, I think) in his brilliant narrative of New Criticism's gestures of self-consolidation. His dichotomized dialectic of profession and discipline, practice and institution, resumption and replacement, biography and criticism, speech and silence, reveals him as an arch-structuralist, or a New Critic of New Criticism. The larger story that he has told elsewhere is of the implication of New Criticism in the developing spy networks of OSS and the CIA. And that story he discovered by good honest detection: intricate inference, in-depth interviews of some of the suspects, and unraveling networks of association and complicity. Epstein, in short, misrecognizes himself in his targets, for whom his affection is evident. And in so doing, he misrecognizes the character of misrecognition and, by implication, that of the eighteenth century, though, as with Dowling, in ways that are more fruitful than many sterile truths.

Misrecognition, as Bourdieu uses the term, is indeed lying, but only in the eighteenth-century sense that associates lying with social graces. A writer in the pragmatist vein of the sociologist Erving Goffman and the linguist Harald Weinrich,[5] Bourdieu opens the English version of the *Outline of a Theory of Practice* with a stringent critique of Lévi-Straussian structuralism. Writing about an Algerian group as an ethnographic near-insider, he opposes the structuralist's stance of perpetual outside observer: he is an intimate, not a spy. Misrecognition is preparing a face to meet the faces that you meet: by bringing into play the structures of the savage mind, it converts forms into life. Bourdieu's aim is not to categorize, and hence not to engage in the practice of theory, but to recover the particularity and contingency of society as it actually is and of history as it actually was.

Epstein's sinuous syntax could evoke labyrinthine entanglement. But I prefer to regard it, Bourdieu-style, as felicitously evasive. Here is the model:

Une analyse plus précise de la position sociale des intellectuels ferait en outre voir que ces membres d'une fraction dominée de la classe dominante sont prédisposés à entrer dans le rôle de *middlebrows,* comme dit Virginia Woolf, c'est-à-dire d'intermédiaires entre les groupes ou les classes: députés ou délégués, qui parlent *pour* les autres c'est-à-dire en leur faveur mais aussi à *leur place,* ils sont portés à tromper, le plus souvent de bonne foi, aussi bien ceux dont ils parlent que ceux à qui ils parlent; quant à ceux d'entre eux qui sont issus des classes dominées, transfuges ou parvenus, ils ne peuvent parler que parce qu'ils ont abandonné la place sans parole de ceux dont ils portent la parole en se mettant à leur place en parole, et ils sont enclins à livrer, en échange de la reconnaissance (au double sens du terme), le capital d'information qu'ils ont emporté avec eux.[6]

Bourdieu's twists and turns and puns record the traces left on a writer's analysis by past history and present situation, by conscious and unconscious intentions, by articulated or unspoken affiliation, proximity, or rejection. His genius lies in objectively characterizing the particular and personal determinants of social forms, as when, rather than accepting prima facie the genealogies provided by informants, he substitutes a Ranke-like critique of the motivations underlying them. It is no accident if this sounds more like the passionate Max Weber—who is most famous today as a student of the religion and social history of our period—than, say, like the bloodless group dynamics of a Talcott Parsons. For Bourdieu makes of the intellectual what has been called, apropos of Weber, a "vanishing mediator,"[7] producing "an implicit theory of practice that is correlative to the forgetting of the social conditions of possibility of theory" (*Esquisse* 158). That role could hardly be further from the masterminding at which surveillance operations aim. Taken together, the essays in the present volume— memoirs, personal histories, self-critiques, genealogies, confrontations, revolts, and reactions—illustrate how powerfully our situation as critics is determined, in multiple and often conflicting ways, by our history, the history of our discipline, and the history that we study. They remind us that our theories are produced in our times and do not rise above them.

It may well be that any period of study could teach that lesson. Still, and though I have at most only one scholarly foot in the eighteenth-century camp, I want at last to make my special plea for the period covered in this collection as a portal to improved self-awareness. Who, I began by asking, can truly know himself? And yet, too, who can know something other without first knowing himself? There is a frequent consensus that the modern world is heir to the age of Romanticism and of the great revolutions. There is, then, a case to be made (and Braudy's essay is most explicit here) that the bridge to self-awareness is the period on the threshold of the modern world, neither wholly within, nor wholly without. Its sense of historical pageant and historical contingency can liberate us from the all-too-neat patterns of Romantic and post-Romantic historicism. Call it postmodern if you must, but recognize that the eighteenth century serves as a worthy inspiration for a galaxy of worthies threading their eccentric courses through a universe of data. The essays in this volume, convex mirrors all, are a collective portrait of ourselves in our multifarious becomings.

May our understanding, as Damrosch urges, grow by accretion like the coral, rather than with the overly self-limiting, mammallocentric model of organicism imposed by the nineteenth century.

It is no accident that Swift appears as the role model for so many of the essayists. For Swift was the ultimate insider's outsider. I accepted Fabricant's challenge to read and ponder Swift's lifelong and unsuccessful encounter with history. *The History of the Four Last Years of the Queen*, as a composition, is unlovable. It has been rightly maligned as biased, evasive, and tumid.[8] Rightly, that is, if you try to read it as a Romantic, mammalian organism. Yet how exhilarating are so many of its sentences! Court intrigue may not be everyone's cup of tea, but, as Fabricant says, Swift wrings remarkable life from its bones, even in moments of negative triumph like the famous fall of Marlborough at the end of book I, and all the more so when his irrepressible optimism springs up anew, out of apparent defeat. Consider the trajectory of the following sentence, reporting a verbal response concerning peace proposals to the French, given by the Dutch Pensionary to the English Ambassador:

That, they (the States) looked upon these Propositions as very dark and general; and they observed, how the Enemy would create Jealousies between the Queen, their Republick, and the other Allies: But, they were satisfyed it would have no Effect; and relyed entirely on the Justice and Prudence of Her Majesty; who they doubted not, would make the *French* explain themselves more particularly in the several Points of their Proposals; and send a Plan of the particular Conditions whereupon they would make a Peace; after which the States would be ready either to join with Her Majesty, or to make their Objections, and were prepared to bring with them all the Facility imaginable towards promoting so good a Work.[9]

Even without irony, Swift's ear for nuance and innuendo is unexcelled. Explicitly and implicitly, every maneuver that Swift reports by these very manipulative politicians is designed at once to stake a position and also to provide room for further maneuver by suspected allies and admired enemies. With responsibility referred to the shadowy Queen in the background, Swift's characters remain vanishing mediators, middlebrows all. Closure does not come so easily in this world as it does to Romantic structuralists, and it did not come to Swift's abortive enterprise. But if we read him in parts, not as a totality, we can see the facility with which the human spirit comes to light even amid propositions dark and general. As it juggles past conditions, present situations, and future interests, Swift's account of the intricate negotiations leading to the Peace of Utrecht models a kaleidoscopic understanding. The optimism that Fabricant celebrates springs from a flexible hermeneutic not bound to impersonal, uniformitarian reconciliations.

Jonathan Culler has recently written that "formerly the history of criticism was part of the history of literature, [but] now the history of literature is part of the history of criticism."[10] This volume's encounters with the traditions of eighteenth-century studies corroborate that judgment: what we see grows out of what has been seen by ourselves and others, and it fluctuates according to our cumulative experiences. Yet an eighteenth-century perspective will not support the definiteness—or limitedness—of Culler's claim. For he (like many others) inherits a Romantic perspective that would find the past encapsulated in the singularity of the present moment. Here is the continuation of the sentence just quoted: "the history of literature is part of the history of criticism, dependent upon what is canonised, what is explicated, what is articulated as a major problem for literature in the critical communities in universities." History, whether of literature or of criticism, is contained not in "what is," but in what was, and often in what is no more, what has gone astray, escaped the net, fled to the margin, sunk out of sight. In the spirit of its age, this collection foregrounds the tugs and pulls of past scholarship. It will serve its function if it reminds us that the symbolic and abstract, enduring forces of history are propelled by agents personal and peculiar. In their quirks, Swift and Pope, Johnson and Sterne, along with the historians and poets of their day, will not let us forget either the *Eigentlichkeit* or the *Eigentümlichkeit* of history, "wie es eigentlich gewesen."

Notes

1 Having poached their title phrase, I mention as a case in point Lawrence and Jeanne C. Fawtier Stone's book, *An Open Elite? England, 1540–1880* (Oxford: Clarendon, 1984). Their contention that British society was a closed network results from posing a yes-or-no question about structures. Yet they document that the British perceived their society as open (16–29), that mobility was considerably greater near London than in the remote north, and that the quality of permeability persisted, with "no great obstacles to . . . social acceptance" of newcomers (290). The picture might look very different if the investigation were reconfigured—with a hermeneutic rather than a structural emphasis—to inquire what justified or explains the impression of openness.

2 From the page that follows Dowling's quote I cite lines and italicize words that suggest the conscious seeker of the past, rather than Dowling's melancholy dreamer. The point is not that Dyer was the one or the other, but that the two stances can't be clearly disentangled. "Away, my Muse," says the poet—is it away from, or away to?—

> Though *yet* the prospect please, ever new
> In vast variety, and *yet* delight

The many-figur'd sculptures of the path
Half beauteous, half effac'd; the traveller
Such antique marbles *to his native land*
Oft hence conveys; and ev'ry realm and state
With Rome's august remains, heroes and gods,
Deck their long galleries and winding groves;
Yet *miss we not* th'innumerable thefts,
Yet *still* profuse of graces teems the waste.
    Suffice it *now* th'Esquilian mount to reach
With weary wing, *and seek the sacred rests*
Of Maro's humble tenement.

John Dyer, *Poems* (London: Dodsley, 1761), 36–37.

3 Leopold von Ranke, *Sämmtliche Werke* (Leipzig: Duncker und Humblot) 33 (1874): vii. An earlier state of Dowling's essay invoked Ranke by name.

4 Leopold von Ranke, *The Secret of World History: Selected Writings on the Art and Science of History*, ed. and trans. Roger Wines (New York: Fordham University Press, 1981), 245, trans. slightly modified.

5 See in particular Weinrich's booklet, *Lügt man im Deutschen, wenn man höflich ist?* Duden-Beiträge zu Fragen der Rechtschreibung, der Grammatik und des Stils 48. Mannheim, Vienna, Zurich: Bibliographisches Institut, 1986.

6 Pierre Bourdieu, *Esquisse d'une théorie de la pratique, précédé de trois études d'ethnologie kabyle* (Geneva: Droz, 1972), 158 (Bourdieu's italics). I do not find this particularly wonderful sentence in the completely recomposed English version, though its characteristics are in evidence there as well. I translate as follows, preserving Bourdieu's sometimes eccentric punctuation: "A more precise analysis of the social position of intellectuals would show in addition that these members of a dominated segment of the dominant class are predisposed to enter into the role of middlebrows, as Virginia Woolf says, i.e. of intermediaries between groups or classes: deputies or delegates, speaking *for* others i.e. in their favor but also in *their place*, they are led to deceive, most often in good faith, both those of whom they speak and those to whom they speak; as for those among them who have issued from the dominated classes, refugees or parvenus, they can only speak because they have abandoned the wordless place of those whose words they bear as they put themselves into words in their place, and they are inclined to deliver, in exchange for *reconnaissance* in the double sense of the term [gratitude and gratuity], the information capital they have taken with them."

7 Fredric Jameson, "The Vanishing Mediator; or Max Weber as Storyteller," *The Ideology of Theory: Essays, 1971–1986* (Minneapolis: University of Minnesota Press, 1988), 2:3–34. See also Fredric Jameson, *The Political Unconscious: Narrative as a Socially Symbolic Act* (Ithaca, NY: Cornell University Press, 1981), 172, 249, 279.

8 See, however, the nice stylistic appreciation in Peter Steele, *Jonathan Swift: Preacher and Jester* (Oxford: Clarendon, 1978), 84–87.

9 Jonathan Swift. *The History of the Four Last Years of the Queen, The Prose*

Works of Jonathan Swift, ed. Herbert Davis (Oxford: Blackwell, 1951), 7:39.

10 Jonathan Culler, "Criticism and Institutions: The American University," in *Post-Structuralism and the Question of History*, ed. Derek Attridge, Geoff Bennington, and Robert Young (Cambridge: Cambridge University Press, 1987), 97.

Notes on Contributors

JOHN BENDER, Professor of English and Comparative Literature at Stanford University, is the author most recently of *Imagining the Penitentiary: Fiction and the Architecture of Mind in Eighteenth-Century England*, which was awarded the Gottschalk Prize by the American Society for Eighteenth-Century Studies in 1987. He is co-editor of *The Ends of Rhetoric: History, Theory, Practice* and *Chronotypes: The Construction of Time*.

LEO BRAUDY, Leo S. Bing Professor of English at the University of Southern California, is the author of *Narrative Form in History and Fiction: Hume, Fielding, and Gibbon*; *Jean Renoir: The World of His Films*; *The World in a Frame: What We See in Films*; *The Frenzy of Renown: Fame and Its History*; and, most recently, *Native Informant: Essays on Film, Fiction, and Popular Culture*, which includes several articles on eighteenth-century literature. He is currently writing a book on politics and literature in the Restoration.

MARSHALL BROWN is Professor of English and Comparative Literature at the University of Washington. He has written *The Shape of German Romanticism* and *Preromanticism*, as well as articles on eighteenth- and nineteenth-century literature, the theory of literary history, and music and literature.

LEO DAMROSCH is Professor of English at Harvard University and author of several books on eighteenth-century subjects, most recently *God's Plot and Man's Stories: Studies in the Fictional Imagination from Milton to Fielding, The Imaginative World of Alexander Pope*, and *Fictions of Reality in the Age of Hume and Johnson*.

WILLIAM C. DOWLING is Professor of English at Rutgers University, where he is a Fellow of Douglass College. He is the author, most recently, of *Jameson, Althusser, Marx: An Introduction to "The Political Unconscious," Poetry and Ideology in Revolutionary Connecticut*, and *The Epistolary Moment: The Poetics of the Eighteenth-Century Verse Epistle*.

WILLIAM H. EPSTEIN, Professor of English at the University of Arizona, is the author of *John Cleland: Images of a Life* and *Recognizing Biography*. He is completing a book, *Professing the Eighteenth Century*, on the professional practice of eighteenth-century studies in America from 1925 to 1975.

CAROLE FABRICANT, who teaches at the University of California, Riverside, is the author of *Swift's Landscape* and has published a wide variety of essays on eighteenth-century subjects, including "Binding and Dressing Nature's Loose Tresses: The Ideology of Augustan Landscape Design," which was awarded the James L. Clifford Prize in 1980.

DONNA LANDRY teaches at Wayne State University in Detroit, and is the author of *The Muses of Resistance: Laboring-Class Women's Poetry in Britain, 1739–1796*.

LAWRENCE LIPKING, Chester D. Tripp Professor of Humanities at Northwestern University, is the author of *The Ordering of the Arts in Eighteenth-Century England, The Life of the Poet* (which received the Christian Gauss Award in 1982), and *Abandoned Women and Poetic Tradition*. He is currently writing a book on Samuel Johnson.

MICHAEL MCKEON is Professor of English at Rutgers University and author of *Politics and Poetry in Restoration England* and *The Origins of the English Novel*, which was awarded the MLA Lowell Prize for 1987.

DAVID B. MORRIS is a writer and lives in Kalamazoo, Michigan. His books include *The Religious Sublime*, awarded the SAMLA Prize (1972); *Alexander Pope: The Genius of Sense*, awarded the Gottschalk Prize by the American Society for Eighteenth-Century Studies (1984); and *The Culture of Pain* (1991).

JOHN RICHETTI is Leonard Sugarman Professor of English at the University of Pennsylvania, and author of *Popular Fiction before Richardson, Defoe's Narratives: Situations and Structures*, and *Philosophical Writing: Locke, Berkeley, Hume*. He is completing a book on the British eighteenth-century novel.

Index